Encountering China

Encountering China

Michael Sandel and Chinese Philosophy

Edited by
MICHAEL J. SANDEL and PAUL J. D'AMBROSIO

Harvard University Press

Cambridge, Massachusetts

London, England

2018

Library of Congress Cataloging-in-Publication Data

Names: Sandel, Michael J., editor. | D'Ambrosio, Paul J., editor.

Title: Encountering China : Michael Sandel and Chinese philosophy / edited by
  Michael J. Sandel and Paul J. D'Ambrosio.

Description: Cambridge, Massachusetts : Harvard University Press, 2018. |
  Includes bibliographical references and index.

Identifiers: LCCN 2017024155 | ISBN 9780674976146 (alk. paper)

Subjects: LCSH: Sandel, Michael J. | Capitalism—Moral and ethical aspects—China. |
  Confucian ethics—China. | Taoist ethics—China. | Mixed economy—China. |
  Communitarianism—China.

Classification: LCC BJ1289.3 .E53 2018 | DDC 170.951—dc23

LC record available at https://lccn.loc.gov/2017024155

Contents

IV. Conceptions of the Person: Sandel and the Confucian Tradition

V. Reply by Michael Sandel

Foreword

China's Encounter with Michael Sandel

EVAN OSNOS

One night in December 2012, I was on the campus of Xiamen University, on China's southeastern coast, when students massed outside the auditorium—far more of them than the building could handle. I stood inside the doors and watched a growing throng of young, flushed faces on the other side of the glass. Security guards appealed to the crowd to keep calm. The president of the university had phoned the organizers of that evening's event and cautioned them not to lose control.

The object of such fervent anticipation—a figure who had acquired a level of popularity in China "usually reserved for Hollywood movie stars and NBA players," as the *China Daily* put it—was a soft-spoken Minnesota native named Michael J. Sandel. At Harvard, where Sandel is a professor of political philosophy, he taught a popular course called "Justice," which introduced students to the pillars of Western thought: Aristotle, Kant, Rawls, and others. He framed their theories of moral decisionmaking in real-world dilemmas. Is torture ever justified? Would you steal a drug that your child needs to survive? The classes had been filmed for an American public television series and put online. As they began to circulate in China, Chinese volunteers came forward to provide subtitles, and within two years Sandel had acquired an astonishing level of celebrity. *China Newsweek* magazine named him the "most influential foreign figure" of 2010.

Yingyi Qian, the dean of the School of Economics and Management at Tsinghua University, told me, "Sandel's approach to moral issues is not only innovative to Chinese readers, but also relevant to daily discussions of some important social issues." By the time I visited the campus to gain a first-person sense of Sandel's encounter with China, his subtitled lectures on Western political philosophy had been watched at least twenty million times. The Chinese edition of *Esquire* put him on the cover, above the headline "Masters of Our Time."

To live in China in the early years of the twenty-first century, as I did from 2005 to 2013, was to witness a philosophical and spiritual revival that could be compared to America's Great Awakening in the nineteenth century. In the 1960s and 1970s, Chairman Mao's Cultural Revolution had largely dismantled China's traditional belief systems. In the 1980s and 1990s, Deng Xiaoping's economic revolution could not rebuild them. The pursuit of prosperity had relieved the deprivation of China's past, but it had failed to define the ultimate purpose of the nation and the individual. Chinese citizens often described a sensation that, in sprinting ahead, they had bounded past whatever barriers once held back the forces of corruption and moral disregard. There was a hole in Chinese life that people named the *jingshen kongxu*— "the spiritual void"—and something was going to fill it.

The more people satisfied their basic needs, the more they challenged the old dispensation. For new sources of meaning, they looked not only to religion but also to philosophy, psychology, and literature for new ways of orienting themselves in a world of ideological incoherence and unrelenting change. What obligation did an individual have to a stranger in a hypercompetitive, market-driven society? How much responsibility did a citizen have to speak the truth when speaking the truth was dangerous? How shall a society define fairness and opportunity? The search for answers awakened and galvanized people in a way that the pursuit of prosperity once had.

Sandel, who was accustomed to a relatively quiet life in Brookline, Massachusetts, with his wife and two sons, was learning to expect extraordinary reactions abroad, especially in East Asia. In Seoul he lectured to 14,000 people in an outdoor stadium; in Tokyo the scalpers' price for tickets to his talks was $500. But in China, he had inspired near-religious devotion, and his visits plunged him into an alternative dimension of celebrity. Once, at the airport in Shanghai, the passport-control officer stopped him to gush that he was a fan.

Outside the auditorium in Xiamen, the crowd kept growing, until the organizers finally decided that they had a better chance of keeping the peace if they threw open the doors. So, fire codes notwithstanding, they let the crowd pour into the aisles, until young men and women covered every inch of floor space.

Sandel climbed the stage. Behind him, an enormous plastic banner carried the Chinese title of his latest book, *What Money Can't Buy*, in which he asked whether too many features of modern life were becoming what he called "instruments of profit." In China, the pendulum had swung fast and far from the heyday of socialism, and now everything in society seemed to have a price tag: a military commission, a seat in kindergarten, a judge's consideration. Sandel's message was urgently relevant, and his audience was rapt. "I am not arguing against markets as such," he told the crowd. "What I am suggesting is that in recent decades we have drifted, almost without realizing it, from having a market economy to becoming a market society."

Sandel mentioned a story from the headlines: Wang Shangkun was a seventeen-year-old high school student from a poor patch of Anhui Province who was illegally recruited in a chat room to sell his kidney for $3,500, a transaction his mother discovered when he returned home with an iPad and an iPhone and then went into renal failure. The surgeon and eight others—who had resold the kidney for ten times what they paid—were arrested. "There are 1.5 million people in China who need an organ transplant," Sandel told the crowd, "but there are only ten thousand available organs in any year." How many here, he asked, would support a legal free market in kidneys?

A young Chinese man named Peter, in a white sweatshirt and chunky glasses, raised his hand and made a libertarian argument that legalizing the kidney trade would squeeze out the black market. Others disagreed, and Sandel upped the stakes. Say a Chinese father sold a kidney and then, "a few years later, he needs to send a second child to school, and a person comes and asks if he would sell his other kidney—or his heart, if he is willing to give up his life. Is there anything wrong with that?" Peter thought it over, and said, "As long as it's free and transparent and open, rich people can buy life, and it's not immoral." A ripple of agitation passed over the crowd; a middle-aged man behind me shouted, "No!"

Sandel settled the room. "The question of markets," he said, "is really a question about how we want to live together. Do we want a society where everything is up for sale?"

"Of the various countries I've visited," Sandel told me the next day, "China is the place where free-market assumptions and moral intuitions run deepest, with the possible exception of the United States." What interested him most, however, was the countervailing force—the ripple through the crowd at the idea of selling the second kidney. "But if you probe and test those intuitions through discussion, you can glimpse a moral hesitation about extending market logic to everything," he said. "For example, Chinese audiences are generally accepting of ticket-scalping—reselling tickets at high prices for concerts or even doctor appointments at public hospitals. But when I ask about the scalping of train tickets during the Chinese New Year, when everyone goes home to be with their family, most people are opposed."

In China, foreign ideas have a history of inspiring waves of public attention and scholarly debate. After World War I, China remained closed in many respects, but it attracted several influential visitors. Wang Hui, a professor of literature and history at Tsinghua University, told me, "In the 1920s, very few famous Western philosophers visited China, with the exception of John Dewey and Bertrand Russell—as well as Indian poet Rabindranath Tagore. They were introduced by famous Chinese intellectuals such as Liang Qichao and Hu Shi, who was Dewey's student." With those prominent introductions, Dewey and others attracted legions of followers. Later, that path was followed by Freud and Habermas.

When Sandel visited for the first time, in 2007, Chinese audiences were no longer charmed by the novelty of a visiting Western scholar; the engagement would need to run deeper than curiosity. Wang Hui said, "When Michael came to China, there were a lot of Western scholars who had visited China. Some philosophers, such as John Rawls, and his theory of justice, and Friedrich Hayek and his theory of 'spontaneous order,' were very influential among Chinese intellectuals. So, the acceptance of Michael's work among intellectuals has been a process of debate and negotiation, which, from my point of view, is very positive." The timing was ripe for a set of probing conversations. Introducing Sandel at Tsinghua University in Beijing, Professor Junren Wan said China had a "crying heart."

Sandel had spent much of his career considering what he called "the moral responsibility we have to one another as fellow citizens." After living for his first thirteen years in Hopkins, Minnesota, a suburb of Minneapolis, he moved with his family to Los Angeles, where classmates cut school to go surfing. It grated against his midwestern reserve. "The formative effect of Southern California," he told me, "was seeing the unencumbered self in practice." He took an early interest in liberal politics, went to Brandeis, then Oxford on a Rhodes Scholarship, and over a winter break he and a classmate planned to collaborate on an economics paper. "My friend had very strange sleeping habits," Sandel said. "I would go to bed, maybe around midnight, and he would stay up until all hours. That gave me the mornings to read philosophy books." By the time school resumed, he had read Kant, Rawls, Robert Nozick, and Hannah Arendt, and he set aside economics for philosophy.

In the years that followed, he argued for a more direct conversation about morality in public life. He said, "Martin Luther King drew explicitly on spiritual and religious sources. Robert Kennedy, when he ran for president in 1968, also articulated a liberalism with moral and spiritual resonance." But by 1980, American liberals had put aside the language of morality and virtue because it came to be seen as "what the religious right does," he said. "I began to feel that something was missing in this kind of value-neutral politics. I worried that the moral emptiness of mainstream public discourse was creating a vacuum that religious fundamentalism and strident nationalism would fill. American liberalism became increasingly technocratic and lost its capacity to inspire."

In China, in 2010, a group of volunteers calling itself Everyone's Television had come together to subtitle foreign programs. When it ran out of sitcoms and police procedurals, it turned to American college courses, which were becoming available online. Sandel had visited China once before, to speak to small groups of philosophy students, but when he returned, after his course was online, he found that something had happened. "They told me that, for a seven P.M. lecture, kids were starting to stake out seats at one-thirty in the afternoon," he said. "They had overflow rooms, and I waded into this spirited mass of people." Sandel had seen his work ignite in other countries, but never as abruptly as it had in China. As we talked, we tried to make sense of this phenomenon. The Harvard brand didn't hurt, and the professional polish of the public television production made it more fun to watch than other courses. But for Chinese students, his style of teaching was also a revelation: he called upon students to make their own individual moral arguments, to engage in vigorous debate in which there was no single right answer, to think creatively and independently about complex, open-ended issues in a way that was largely unheard of in Chinese classrooms. Yingyi Qian observed that students were devouring the Chinese translation of Sandel's book *Justice*. "This is partly due to the fact that very little Western philosophy is taught in China," Yingyi Qian explained. "In addition, *Justice* is very accessible to Chinese college students, with interesting examples to illustrate alternative schools of thought."

Beyond style, Sandel sensed a deeper explanation for the intense Chinese interest in moral philosophy. "In the societies where it has caught fire, there has not been the occasion—for whatever reason—for serious public discussion of big ethical questions," he said. Young people especially "sense a kind of emptiness in terms of public discourse, and they want something better." China, in a sense, was the land of the unencumbered self, a place where individuals could unfetter themselves from social bonds and history and make their decisions based on self-interest in a way that was previously impossible. It was ruled by technocrats who publicly espoused a socialist ideology while, in practice, they placed their faith in economics and engineering with pitiless efficiency. Deng Xiaoping, the leader who launched China on its economic transformation, had argued that prosperity was paramount. "Development is the only hard truth," he said in 1992, and China adopted a path toward abundance on a scale it had never known, but also at a heavy cost. In the decades that followed, China confronted the risks of a market society awash in counterfeit medicines, shoddy construction, and rampant corruption.

By the time Sandel arrived, the Communist Party was not allowing the growth of faith as much as it was trying to keep up with it. Sandel offered Chinese young people a vocabulary that they found useful and challenging but not subversive, a framework in which to talk about inequality, corruption, and fairness without sounding political. It was a way to talk about morality without posing direct questions about political legitimacy and authority. Sandel never explicitly challenged the taboos of Chinese politics: the separation of powers, the Party's superiority over law. But occasionally the Chinese authorities brushed him back. Once, a salon of Chinese scholars and writers in Shanghai arranged for him to give a public talk to a crowd of 800, but on the eve of the lecture the local government canceled it. Sandel asked the organizers, "Did they give a reason?" "No," they said. "They never give a reason."

At times Sandel encountered skepticism from Chinese critics. For some, his argument against markets was fine in theory, but gauzy notions of equity triggered Chinese flashbacks of ration coupons and empty store shelves. Others argued that, in China, having money was the only way to defend oneself against abuses of power, so limiting markets would only fortify the hand of the state. "Some neoliberal intellectuals criticized his views angrily, but most of his audience likes his ideas," said Wang Hui of Tsinghua. "Michael's topics, such as justice, equality, the role of morality in human life, are all relevant to our society."

After the Xiamen lecture, I watched Sandel speak to several more college groups in Beijing, and it was clear that when Sandel described the "skyboxification" of life—the division of America into a world for the affluent and a world for everyone else—Chinese listeners heard much in common. After thirty years of marching toward a future in which everything was for sale, many people in China were reconsidering.

On his last night in Beijing, Sandel gave a lecture at the University of Business and Economics, and then met with a group of student volunteers who were working on perfecting the translations of his "Justice" lectures. One young woman gushed, "Your class saved my soul." Before Sandel could ask her what she meant, the crowd swept him away for photos and autographs. I hung back and introduced myself. Her name was Shi Ye and she was twenty-four years old. She was getting a master's degree in human resources, and when she came upon Sandel's work, it was "a key to open my mind and doubt everything," she told me. "After a month, I began to feel different. That was one year ago. And today, I often ask myself, what is the moral dilemma here?"

Her parents had been farmers, until her father went into the seafood trade. "I accompanied my mom to visit the Buddha to pray and to put some food on the table as an offering. In the past, I didn't think anything was wrong with that. But a year later, when I accompanied my mom, I asked her, 'Why do you do this?'" Her mother was not pleased by all the questions. "She thinks I am posing a very stupid question. I began to question everything. I didn't say it's wrong or right; I'm just questioning."

Shi Ye had stopped buying train tickets from a scalper because, she said, "when he sells them at a price he chooses, it limits my choices. If he wasn't setting the price, I could decide to buy economy or first class, but now he is taking away my choice. It's unfair." She had begun lobbying her friends to do the same. "I'm still young and I don't have much power to change much, but I can influence their thinking," she said.

Shi Ye was getting ready to graduate, but her discovery of political philosophy had made things more complicated. "Before I encountered these lectures, I was sure I was going to be become an HR specialist and an HR manager and serve the employees in a big company. But now I'm confused; I doubt my original dreams. I hope to do something more meaningful." She didn't dare tell her parents, but secretly she was hoping she wouldn't get a job in human resources. "I might take a gap year and go abroad and travel and take a part-time job to see the world. I want to see what I can do to contribute to society."

For Shi Ye and others who came of age with growing control over their economic and personal lives, the limits on what they could ask seemed antique. Embracing a vast feast of new ideas, including those proposed by Michael Sandel, was about more than curiosity. It represented nothing less than the search for a new moral foundation, as men and women of China's middle class set out in search of what to believe.

Encountering China

I
Justice, Harmony, and Community

Community without Harmony?

A Confucian Critique of Michael Sandel

CHENYANG LI

Michael Sandel has been one of the most powerful critics of liberalism in the past decades. His work, especially in *Liberalism and the Limits of Justice*, exposes some of the fundamental flaws of Rawlsian liberalism and shows the need for a community-based framework in order for us to adequately understand and appreciate the concept of the individual and that of a just society. Confucians can endorse many of Sandel's critiques of liberalism. From a Confucian perspective, however, Sandel's version of communitarianism is too thin for a robust communitarian society. Confucians maintain a thick notion of community and take it to be vital to human flourishing. I will first discuss a key point where Confucians converge with Sandel as an example of the common ground between the two philosophies, and then I will turn to one important difference between them. The key point of convergence regards the circumstances of justice; the difference regards harmony. Harmony lies in the very center of the Confucian notion of community, but Sandel has given it no place in his conception of community.[1] This essay offers a Confucian critique as well as an endorsement of Sandel's communitarian philosophy.[2] It also extends a friendly invitation to Sandel to incorporate harmony into his conception of community.

Sandel's powerful argument on the circumstances of justice affects how we determine what value or values are primary for a good society.

John Rawls (1971) based his own theory of justice on his conviction in the primacy of justice in society: "Justice is the first virtue of social institutions, as truth is of systems of thought. A theory however elegant and economical must be rejected or revised if it is untrue; likewise laws and institutions no matter how efficient and well-arranged must be reformed or abolished if they are unjust" (3). For Rawls, justice is not merely one virtue among many or merely one value among other values for a good society. It is the primary value against which all other values are to be gauged. As Sandel (1998) puts it, for Rawls, "justice is the standard by which conflicting values are reconciled and competing conceptions of the good accommodated if not always resolved" (16). On such a conception, the first question to ask when evaluating a society is whether the society is just, regardless of what type of society it is. This understanding of justice, Sandel points out, fails to adequately consider the importance of the circumstances of justice—that is, a society's background conditions that necessitate certain mechanisms in order for the society to function. Following Hume, Rawls divides these circumstances into two types: objective circumstances, such as the relative scarcity of resources, and subjective circumstances, such as the fact that individual persons have different interests and ends in their lives. Rawls holds, at least implicitly, these conditions are universal and thereby make justice the primary virtue of any society. Sandel argues, instead, that justice is a first virtue of social institutions only conditionally and not absolutely—analogous to physical courage in a war zone (Sandel 1998, 31). A decrease in the need for justice may indicate an improved society: "If the virtue of justice is measured by the morally diminished conditions that are its prerequisite, then the *absence* of these conditions—however this state of affairs might be described—must embody a rival virtue of at least commensurate priority, the one that is engaged in so far as justice is not engaged" (32).

Sandel's analysis reveals the remedial aspect of justice as a virtue. Justice is called on to "fix" things when they are broken, so to speak, or at least to prevent social institutions from falling apart. However, Sandel maintains that the circumstances of justice do not obtain universally, at least not in certain spheres in society. For instance, in a more or less ideal family situation, in which relations are governed largely by spontaneous affection, the circumstances of justice obtain only minimally. Justice does not play a central role in the more or less ideal family, not because injustice prevails but because family members interact with sufficient mutual affection and care. In such a situation, it would not be appropriate to see justice as a primary virtue (33). We can just as easily imagine similar circumstances in a traditional tribal society when the situation is more or less ideal.

Sandel's argument in this regard is largely aligned with Confucian social and political philosophy. Classical Confucian thinkers made their case in terms somewhat similar to Sandel's. They saw two main apparatuses regulating and facilitating the operation of society. One is called "*fa* 法", literally meaning "law"; this word has been closely associated with *xing* 刑, "criminal laws." The other is "*li* 礼", usually translated as "ritual" or "ritual propriety." It encompasses a host of social norms, etiquettes, and ceremonies that aim to cultivate people's sense of appropriateness and affection toward one another. Cultivation though *li* leads people toward *ren* 仁, namely "human-heartedness" or benevolence—a characteristic disposition of kindness toward others.[3] To use a simple example, if you say "Good morning" and smile at someone you pass by every morning on your way to work, and that person does the same back, you two will gradually develop a positive attitude toward each other and will be more inclined to care about each other. Moreover, you will be more disposed to be kind toward people in similar circumstances and in general. The Confucian ideal is to practice *li* in order to cultivate people's sense of care and benevolence toward fellow human beings and to establish and maintain positive relationships in society. Though the Confucian notion of *fa* does not amount to justice in the Rawlsian sense, it is congruent with the general sensibilities of justice in that it sets rules against behaviors that damage the social fabric. Classical Confucian thinkers did not regard *fa* as lacking value, but they held that a good society should not rely on *fa* (or *xing*) as the primary measure to govern its operation. Confucius maintained that if we rely on criminal laws to manage a society, people might stay out of trouble but they will not develop a moral sense of "shame" (*chi*), and only by way of practicing *li* can people not only stay out of trouble but also develop a moral sense of shame. A moral sense of shame will guide people to steer clear of bad behavior (*Analects* 2.3). For Confucians, a society's heavy reliance on *fa* or *xing* is an indication that the social fabric has deteriorated.[4] The Confucian classic *Kongzi Jiayu* (Confucius's Family Teachings) records that when Confucius served as the minister of justice in the state of Lu, he was able to help the king create a social order in which the penal code was never applied because there were no wicked people.[5] Regardless of the historical accuracy of this record, it makes the point abundantly clear: Confucians strive for a society where justice does not have to be the primary virtue. As important as justice is, it might not be the primary measure for a society when *li* and the virtue of *ren* prevail. Indeed, promoting *li* and *ren* has been the primary concern for Confucian thinkers. Their goal has been to create a social environment where the circumstances of justice are such that justice does not have to be the primary virtue.

In the Confucian view, practicing the virtues of *li* and *ren* establishes positive human relationships. These virtues enable people to develop a strong sense of community. In such communities, the highest virtue is harmonious relationship rather than justice. It is in this regard that Confucians see a major lack in Sandel's notions of self and community: Sandel's notion of community does not include harmony as a defining characteristic.

To be sure, Sandel's conception of community is profoundly different from that of Rawls. Rawls attaches a positive value to community, but it is subordinate to the value of right. To use Sandel's characterization, on Rawls's view, "community must find its virtue as one contender among others within the framework defined by justice, not as a rival account of the framework itself" (Sandel 1998, 64). In other words, for Rawls, communitarian aims can be pursued after the establishment of the principles of justice and the concept of right, not prior to or in parallel with them. Coupled with the principle that the right is prior to the good is the view that self is prior to community. Sandel argues that Rawls's thin conception of the self falls far short in providing a foundation for a coherent account of justice in society. A well-founded conception of justice requires a conception of community that penetrates the self profoundly and defines the bounds of the self beyond what is drawn by Rawls. Sandel maintains that community is far more than an instrumental good that provides conditions for the self in pursuit of its own aims or an object of benevolent feelings that some members of society may develop and use as motivations for certain common pursuits. Rather, community is inescapably part of people's identity: "Community describes not just what they *have* as fellow citizens but also what they *are,* not a relationship they choose (as in a voluntary association) but an attachment they discover, not merely an attribute but a constituent of their identity" (150). In this sense, citizens of the same community not only share communitarian sentiments and pursue communitarian aims but also conceive their identity as constituted by the community of which they are a part. Without a strong notion of an identity-constituting community, Rawls cannot bridge the gap between his conception of the individual in the original position, on the one hand, and the principles of justice, on the other. To do this, a constitutive conception of community is needed. Therefore, Sandel argues, community cannot be understood as merely an attachment to be added to the self after the original-position stage when individuals begin to pursue their pluralist aims. A conception of the self as grounded in community must be antecedent to any reasonable conception of justice.[6]

Confucians would unhesitatingly endorse Sandel's conception of community as a primary value. In the Confucian view, personal identity is partly constituted by social relationships and is integral to the very fabric of the community—and so the importance of community in Sandel's philosophy makes it not less, but even more, conspicuous that Sandel does not include harmony as a primary virtue. To illustrate this point, I will now turn to the Confucian conception of harmony and its close connection to community; and then I will look at Sandel's argument against Dworkin's justification of affirmative action. I aim to show that, without a concept of harmony, not only do Dworkin and Rawls fail, but even Sandel is unable to make a strong case in support of affirmative action.

There are widespread misconceptions of harmony. Classical Confucian thinkers refused to take harmony as merely the absence of strife or as indiscriminate conformity to social norms. They developed a conception of harmony on an analogy to soup-making and orchestral music. In harmony, each component (ingredient of a soup, or instrument in an ensemble) contributes to the overall condition in which each can realize its potential, and yet together with others they form a whole that brings out the best of each. Understood this way, harmony or harmonization ("*he*" 和) is best understood as a verb rather than a noun, indicating a productive ongoing process rather than a finished state of affairs (cf. Li 2014, 34). Instead of mere agreement or conformity, Confucian harmony is a dynamic, developmental, generative process, which seeks to balance and reconcile differences and conflicts through creativity and mutual transformation.[7] This Confucian philosophy of harmony was initially developed against a background of disharmony. Much of the pre-Qin Chinese philosophy during the "Spring–Autumn" and Warring States periods can be understood as various responses and proposed solutions to the problem of disharmony of those periods.

Disharmony is characterized by disorder and conflict. Seeking alternatives to disharmony, people found either domination or harmony. Domination exists when one party (or more) controls the other (or others) by direct force or explicit and implicit threat of undesirable consequences. The essence of domination is power. Domination may coexist with peace and may thus present the appearance of harmony, but such peaceful states are not examples of harmony. Domination usually produces order, but it is a forced order based on the use or threat of violence, a kind of order with a high human cost. Ancient Confucian thinkers did not take domination as harmony because it does not involve a mutual engagement that is constructive to all parties, nor is there an adequate measure of equity in mutual recognition and compensation, which is crucial to harmony.

Harmony is the other alternative to disharmony. Ancient Confucians promoted a form of harmony that is characterized by constructive, active engagement of involved parties, with equity between them as a crucial condition. When Confucius famously claimed that the *junzi* (君子, morally cultivated persons) seek harmony without going along with the flow in an unprincipled way (*he er bu liu; Zhongyong*, chap. 10) and that the *junzi* harmonize without becoming the same with others (*he er bu tong; Analects* 13:23), he identified one of the most important characteristics of harmony. It is worth noting that the Confucian idea of harmony was initially developed as an alternative to domination that is disguised as harmony. In the classic text *Chunqiu Zuozhuan*, chapter Zhaogong Year 20, the philosopher Yanzi distinguishes harmony from conformity (*tong* 同). In a conversation with the duke of Qi, the duke bragged about his relationship with his minister Ju, who was always in agreement with the duke. Yanzi pointed out that the kind of relationship between the duke and Ju is mere "being the same" (conformity) rather than harmony. Yanzi used the examples of making a soup by mixing various ingredients and making music by orchestrating various instruments, in contrast to the duke's case. For Yanzi, the relationship between the duke and the minister should be a harmonious one, not one of conformity. Just like making a tasty soup calls for integrating various ingredients, some of which even carry opposite flavors, a harmonious relationship presupposes that people engage one another with different perspectives and different views on various issues. This is evidently not the case with the duke and his minister. The minister was without his own independent voice and was merely in conformity with the duke. In light of the above discussion of domination, we can say that it is no coincidence that the minister always held the same opinions as the duke. The duke had power over the minister. Out of fear or a desire to please the duke or both, the minister always had to agree with the duke, creating the appearance of the two always seeing eye to eye on everything. This is a classic example of domination disguised as harmony. In history, this kind of misconception of harmony has given Confucian harmony a bad name. But that is not what classic Confucian thinkers have advocated when they explicated their philosophy of harmony.

While the difference between harmony and disharmony is usually obvious, the difference between harmony and domination is not always clear and sometimes can be blurred deliberately. Dominating forces tend to disguise domination as harmony. The confusion of domination with harmony is the greatest challenge to the ideal of harmony today as it was more than 2,000 years ago. In his influential book *The Open Society and Its Enemies*, Karl Popper targeted his main criticism at Plato's idea of justice as harmony. Popper held that Plato's idea of conflict-free harmony leads to totalitarianism and is contrary to freedom (Popper 1971). However, Plato's conception of the harmony of the three parts of the soul and of the three classes of people in society is characterized by one element dominating others. It is a model for domination, not for harmony in the sense explicated in the Confucian tradition. Largely because of this tendency to take harmony as conformity and domination, the pursuit of harmony in a diverse world is often regarded in contemporary West as naive at best and harmful at worst. The Confucian conception of harmony, however, should be distinguished not only from disharmony but also from domination. Confucian harmony is based on a strong conception of community and on constructing dynamic and equitable human relationships. In harmonious communities, each individual not only forms and discovers his or her identity, but also contributes to the identity and the good of other members; in harmonizing with others, each person benefits from the contributions of fellow community members. In the Confucian conception, the community is not merely a collection of individuals with disparate aims of pursuit, as Rawls would have it. Nor is the community an identity-constituting social body without an overall defining character, as seems to be Sandel's view. Members of Sandel's community can be equipped with such personal characteristics of affection, benevolence, and responsibility, but these are not overall characteristics of the community as a whole. The Confucian conception of community is a social harmony that is to be realized by its members through mutual transformation for the common good.

Now we turn to the issue of affirmative action as a test case. Affirmative action has been a troubling issue for some liberals because it exposes a deep contradiction between their philosophy and their moral intuition. On the one hand, their liberal philosophy is based on the "trump card" of individual rights, which supposedly allow their holders to act in certain ways even if certain social aims would be served by doing otherwise (Dworkin 1984). On the other hand, an understandably strong moral intuition compels these people to think that certain social aims, including affirmative action, must be served, even if they result in restricting individual rights, which otherwise would have to be upheld. Accommodating such a moral intuition, some liberals have taken rather creative approaches to reconciling the contradiction. Ronald Dworkin tried to justify affirmative action on the basis of its social utility, presenting an awkward position that does not sit well with his rights-based anti-utilitarian philosophy. Rawls (1971) would justify affirmative action on the ground that people's natural talents do not belong to individuals but are a "common asset" (101). Rawls's approach may be defensible on the ground of certain metaphysics of personhood, but it is nevertheless not commonsensical to people on the street. Few people would accept that their natural talents are not really theirs but a common asset. Moreover, as Sandel (1998) has argued, "a wider subject of possession" is needed in order for Dworkin and Rawls to make their case; without an adequate conception of community-based and community-constituted self, they cannot justify their support for affirmative action (Sandel 1998, 149): "Where this sense of participation in the achievements and endeavors of (certain) others engages the reflective self-understandings of the participants, we may come to regard ourselves, over the range of our various activities, less as individuated subjects with certain things in common, and more as members of a wider (but still determinate) subjectivity, less as "others" and more as participants in a common identity, be it a family or community or class or people or nation" (143).

Sandel's solution is subjective in that he relies on the individual's exercise of "reflection" to discover her community-based identity. In the case of admissions to law school or medical school, when a candidate of a racial majority with slightly higher academic score is passed over for a candidate of an underrepresented racial minority, the former's "sacrifice" is in the service of a common endeavor with the latter. Instead of feeling that one has been used for the benefit of others, proper reflection on one's identity will enable the rejected candidate to feel that he or she is making a contribution to the community of which he or she is part. That person's "sacrifice" is justified on the ground that it contributes to the realization of a way of life to which his or her identity is bound (143).

Confucians would support Sandel's point but nevertheless consider it inadequate. Confucians would agree that, in the above affirmative action case, the candidate of a racial majority should, upon proper reflection, realize that he or she is making a contribution to a common endeavor and that by making a contribution to strengthening the community, his or her own identity is also enriched. However, in Confucian philosophy this kind of community-minded understanding is not to be achieved merely through reflection, no matter how deep and thorough such reflection is. Instead it is to be achieved through a long-term project of self-cultivation, through which one develops a proper sense of self and sees one's own success and flourishing as more aligned with those of the community, not opposed to it. But Confucians do not stop there. In the Confucian view, Sandel's solution is focused on the individual person and on reflection, which is more a theoretical than a practical virtue, to borrow a distinction from Aristotle, whereas Confucians would focus on social harmony, extending their solution beyond the individual and beyond theoretical and subjective reflection.

In the Confucian view, social harmony is essential to the good life; or, put more strongly, it *is* the good life. In harmonizing with fellow citizens of our community (or different levels and overlapping varieties of communities), we realize our own potentials and flourish. In harmonizing with others, we develop relationships with others, and become good persons, good family members, and good citizens in our community. If the candidate of a racial majority with slightly higher academic scores has actively engaged in community-building by constructing harmonious relationships with others, including members of underrepresented racial minorities, he or she will be more likely to feel the need for racial equality and to share a strong sense of common cause with the society—and will be more likely to see the admissions outcome as a worthy contribution to social harmony. This is not to deny that sometimes people may need to endure sacrifice in order to promote the common good in the community, which would in turn enrich the person's own life. A flourishing community is like a beautiful garden. One kind of plant, no matter how impressive it is individually, does not make a good garden. One kind of flower, no matter how beautiful each is separately, does not make an astonishing bouquet. In the Confucian view, a single type of thing, no matter how good it is, cannot make harmony. Yanzi emphasized that "mixing water with water" does not make a soup (not to mention a good soup).[8] Shi Bo, another ancient philosopher, made a similar point: "One note does not make music, one thing does not generate a colorful pattern, one fruit does not make much flavor, and one item presents no comparison."[9] Diversity is a necessary condition for harmony. In the case of affirmative action, social harmony requires racial diversity and a balanced racial representation in stations that are highly prized in society. Persistently disadvantaging a racial minority in a society is contrary to achieving a harmonious society. Even though one person loses an opportunity to attend a particular medical school or law school, his community is strengthened; he and his children will be better off because the community is strengthened and more harmonized. A more harmonious society is beneficial not only to fellow citizens but also to oneself in the long term. From the Confucian perspective, social harmony provides a strong justification for affirmative action and similar social policies. The Confucian approach goes farther than Sandel's in that it not only connects personal identity to social relationships but also provides an account of what kind social relationships and what kind of community should be promoted.

A more recent example illustrating the Confucian understanding of harmony: Singapore has begun a serious national discussion about making the nation's presidency more racially representative and balanced. Singapore's multiracial population consists of approximately 74 percent ethnic Chinese, 13 percent Malays, and the rest being Indians, Eurasians, and others. Singapore has long made social harmony a central goal of its nation-building aspiration. It is no secret that such a theme has a historical and cultural connection to Confucian philosophy, as does much of its political vocabulary.[10] For the majority of Singaporeans, social harmony is of vital importance to their nation as well as to their individual lives. The nation has a parliamentary system, with the president primarily serving as the ceremonial head of state. Constituencies of its parliamentary election are classified as either single-member constituencies or group-representation constituencies. Group-representation constituencies are contested by teams of candidates from different political parties. In each group-representation constituency, at least one candidate of each team of a party must be from a minority (non-Chinese) race.[11]

This system guarantees that minorities are represented in the Parliament no matter which party's candidates are elected. It also encourages (or even compels) political parties to actively recruit and cultivate minority members. Thus, the system directs political parties to be racially diverse and inclusive.[12] Since 1993, Singapore has selected its presidents by popular vote through direct election. Since then, Singapore has elected three presidents, two of whom have been ethnic Chinese and one Indian. A recent survey shows that although Singaporeans generally believe their president can come from any race, the majority of every racial group prefers a president of their own race.[13] This has caused concerns that, as the nation-state becomes more democratic and relies increasingly on its citizenry to pick political leaders of their own preferences, with less and less paternalistic influence from political leaders, the chance of electing a minority president will diminish.

Recently a constitutional commission proposed a constitutional amendment that would guarantee the representation of all racial groups in the office of the president. One proposed solution is that when a member of any racial group has not occupied the president's office for five continuous terms, the next presidential election will be reserved for candidates from that particular racial group.[14] If such a plan materializes, proponents maintain, it will ensure that the office of president represents all three of the largest racial groups over a period of time and will promote social, religious, and cultural harmony in Singapore. Liberals may lament that such a move would violate individual citizens' political and civil rights. If the past five presidents have all been Chinese or Indian, the next president will be a Malay. A Chinese (or Indian) person would no longer be eligible to run for president until after there is a Malay president. Furthermore, by then that person might no longer meet other qualifications, such as experience of holding a major position not too long before the time of election, and would lose the opportunity to run for president for good. Ethnicity would make a huge difference.

So far, however, there has not been much concern about such a move.[15] From a Confucian perspective, a mechanism to ensure that all major racial groups are represented in the office of president can be justified on the ground of harmony. One of the main roles of the president is to represent the nation. When all racial groups are well represented in the nation's highest office and no racial group feels alienated, racial equality is enhanced; individuals are more likely to develop a strong sense of ownership of the country, a strong sense of citizenship, and a strong identity deeply rooted in the community of the nation-state. Hence, adopting the new mechanism of electing the president is conducive to social harmony and to building a strong national identity in Singapore. Such a move would be justified on the ground of the Confucian philosophy of harmony.

The Confucian philosophy of harmony not only provides an important vantage point for assessing such delicate social issues as affirmative action and racially inclusive presidency, but also gives us a vigorous account of the community and of community-rooted personal identity in general. In such a view, harmonizing with others in the community is to actively engage one another in building human relationships and to form and renew our identities as community members. The process of constructing personal identities and building communities are meant to achieve social harmony and the good life. Neither can be attained without the other. A communitarian philosophy without a concept of harmony leaves a big hole in its framework and is inadequate to produce a robust account of the individual and society. Sandel's communitarian philosophy will be greatly strengthened if he takes harmony seriously into account.

Notes

I thank Paul J. D'Ambrosio, coeditor of this volume, for his comments on an earlier version of this essay. Thanks also to my students in a graduate seminar at Nanyang Technological University in the fall of 2016, especially Jacob Bender, for their comments on an early draft.

1. The word "harmonious" occurs once in the book: "Now imagine that one day the harmonious family comes to be wrought with dissension" (Sandel 1998, 33). Here the word is used evidently in a positive sense but without conceptual significance. Sandel does not elaborate on how a family is harmonious or why harmony is an important characteristic of a family.

2. Sandel cautions that he is not communitarian in the majoritarian sense, whereby the majority is always right, or in the sense that "rights should rest on the values that predominate in any given community at any given time" (x).

3. *Ren* is a key concept of Confucian ethics. The term has been used by classical thinkers to describe the primary quality of a person of ideal virtuosity. Broadly speaking, it can be understood as a caring disposition toward fellow human beings and beyond. See Li (2007).

4. Confucius reportedly commented that in "ancient times," criminal laws were rarely used because people's behavior was mostly led by ritual propriety, but that in his times they had to use criminal laws abundantly because ritual propriety had deteriorated. See *Kong Cong Zi: On Xing*, section 1, at http://ctext.org/kongcongzi/xing-lun/zhs.

5. http://ctext.org/kongzi-jiayu/xiang-lu/zhs.

6. For a discussion of Sandel's notion of self, see Paul J. D'Ambrosio's discussion in this volume, Chapter 10.

7. See Li 2014, chap. 1.

8. "以水济水, 谁能食之." http://ctext.org/chun-qiu-zuo-zhuan/zhao-gong-er-shi-nian/zhs.

9. "声一无听, 物一无文, 味一无果, 物一不讲." http://ctext.org/guo-yu/zheng-yu/zhs. "味一无果" (*wei yi wu guo*) literally means "one flavor does not make a fruit." It may have been a typesetting error. I render it as "one fruit does not make much flavor."

10. In a 1987 interview with the *New York Times*, Lee Kuan Yew said, "Looking back over the last 30 years, one of the driving forces that made Singapore succeed was that the majority of the people placed the importance of the welfare of society above the individual, which is a basic Confucianist concept" (http://www.nytimes.com/1987/01/04/world/western-influence-worries-singapore-chief.html). To this day, Singapore's Ministry of Culture, Community and Youth still hosts a National Steering Committee on Racial and Religious Harmony, and periodically organizes a "Filial Piety Campaign," without associating it explicitly with Confucianism.

11. The opposition party (the Workers Party) won its first ever GRC in 2011. A recent study shows that an increase in group-representation constituencies also increases women's political participation (Tan 2014).

12. Singapore's system contrasts with that of its neighbor Malaysia, where some major political parties are exclusively race-based and explicitly exclude minorities from membership.

13. http://www.straitstimes.com/singapore/singaporeans-respect-people-from-all-races-but-quite-a-number-find-racism-still-an-issue.

14. http://www.straitstimes.com/singapore/constitutional-commission-report-released-key-changes-proposed-to-elected-presidency.

15. As this essay goes to print, the measure has been adopted by the Singapore Parliament and the 2017 Presidential Election is reserved for the Malay ethnicity.

References

Dworkin, Ronald. 1984. "Rights as Trumps." In *Theories of Rights,* edited by Jeremy Waldron, 153–167. Oxford: Oxford University Press.

Li, Chenyang. 2014. *The Confucian Philosophy of Harmony.* London: Routledge.

———. 2007. "Li as Cultural Grammar: On the Relation between *Li* and *Ren* in Confucius' *Analects.*" *Philosophy East and West* 57 (3): 311–329.

Popper, Karl. 1971. *The Open Society and Its Enemies.* Princeton, NJ: Princeton University Press.

Rawls, John. 1971. *A Theory of Justice.* Cambridge, MA: Harvard University Press.

Sandel, Michael J. 1998. *Liberalism and the Limits of Justice.* 2nd ed. Cambridge: Cambridge University Press.

Tan, Netina. 2014. "Ethnic Quotas and Unintended Effects on Women's Political Representation in Singapore." *International Political Science Review* 35 (1): 27–40.

Individual, Family, Community, and Beyond

Some Confucian Reflections on Themes in Sandel's Justice

TONGDONG BAI

As a political philosopher, Michael Sandel is well known for his communitarian challenge to John Rawls's classic work *A Theory of Justice.* As a teacher and public intellectual, he has brought philosophy down to the "city," making apparently opaque and difficult philosophical texts and ideas intelligible to the college educated and even the general public, in China and around the world, by showing their relevance to everyday political and moral decisions. In this paper I introduce some Confucian ideas into the debates, both over some liberal and communitarian ideas and over some public issues, so as to enrich the projects Sandel started.

A central topic in chapter 9 of Sandel's *Justice: What's the Right Thing to Do?* (2009) is whether an individual is atomic and autonomous, or fundamentally social. This apparently abstract distinction has many practical implications, suggesting distinct answers to questions such as whether an individual is somewhat responsible for the wrongs his or her country or ancestors did to others—for instance, whether an American, an Australian, a German, or a Japanese who lives today has a duty to apologize, or encourage his or her present government to apologize, for slavery before its abolishment under President Lincoln, for the mistreatment of the Australian Aboriginal people in the past, for the Holocaust, or for sex slavery in World War II, respectively. If we take an individualist understanding of a person, then the answer to the above questions seems to be that one should not be held responsible for an act someone else has chosen to do. But if an individual is profoundly associated with this "someone else," then it seems that the individual should take up the responsibility.

In arguing for the latter understanding of the individual, Sandel has drawn on Alasdair MacIntyre's narrative conception of the person: "We all approach our own circumstances as bearers of a particular social identity. I am someone's son or daughter, someone's cousin or uncle; I am a citizen of this or that city, a member of this or that guild or profession; I belong to this clan, that tribe, this nation. Hence what is good for me has to be the good for one who inhabits these roles. As such, I inherit from the past of my family, my city, my tribe, my nation, a variety of debts, inheritances, rightful expectations and obligations. These constitute the given of my life, my moral starting point. This is in part what gives my own life its moral particularity" (MacIntyre 1981).[1]

But a problem with this type of argument is that it only argues that we human beings *are* originally social, but doesn't say that we *ought to* be social. After all, it is in our human nature (or so many believe) that we can choose to deviate from our nature, if by "nature" we mean things human beings originally have, or have biological tendencies toward. Otherwise put, human beings are by nature not natural. Therefore, the question is really why human beings should follow their social nature, if we are indeed naturally social beings. One way to answer this is to argue that it is good, in the sense of being desirable, to stay social.

Now, let us take a look at how some early Confucian thinkers answered the above question. According to Mencius (372–289 BCE), what distinguishes humans from animals is that we humans have *proper* human relations with our family members, friends, and superiors / inferiors in a political setting. Without these relations, we are not really different from beasts, and are human look-alikes at best.[2]

What Mencius offered is what many would consider a metaphysical account of human nature. A problem with such an account is that if I don't hold this metaphysical understanding of human beings, it will not have any force over me. One could also say that Mencius tried to shame people into believing his account by calling those who don't follow his proposed human norm "beasts," but shaming won't work for the "shameless," or for those who reject this shaming strategy.

Xun Zi (313–238 BCE), another early Confucian thinker, offered a different account. He, too, believed that proper social relations are what distinguish humans from animals. Xun Zi further argued that these relations are good for us and that therefore we should try to keep them the way they are.[3] For we human beings are not self-sufficient, and there has to be a division of labor among us, meaning that we need others to survive. In particular, we need to be united to defend ourselves against other animals. Apparently, in order to form a unit, proper relations need to be maintained. Moreover, we all desire certain goods. But their supply is limited, whereas our desires are not. If our desires are not ordered by proper social relations, we will end up killing one another and eventually killing off the human species.

Therefore, what Xun Zi offered is a more "naturalistic" account that appeals to human desire for a good life. This conception of good life (security and the satisfaction of basic desires) seems to be widespread. But it is by no means universal. For example, a Nietzschean might believe that a life of chaos with a possibility of domination is much more desirable than a life of security that is nonetheless dull. We shouldn't deny this possibility, but maybe it is a fool's errand to search for a philosophical answer to Nietzscheans and the like (because maybe there is none).

Putting aside the Nietzschean challenge, let us suppose not only that human beings are social but also that we should maintain proper social relations. The next question is how to develop proper social re-lations. Confucius's answer is "to take as analogy what is near at hand" (*Analects* 6.30) (Lau 1979, 15).[4] A very important institution that is near at hand is one's own family. This is perhaps why Confucian thinkers pay so much attention to family values. For them, the family is a commonly available stepping stone for us to transcend our mere self, and is a training ground for us to become moral agents, persons who can appreciate and maintain proper social relations. Through family, we can learn to care not merely for ourselves but for family members as well. If we push this care outward, we will eventually em-brace all of humanity, even the whole world. In this social network of care or compassion, to take responsibility for the wrongs of our fore-fathers is just natural.

But this expanding network of care gives rise to complexities. What if my care for one party in this network is in conflict with my care for another party? In chapter 9 of *Justice*, Sandel discusses two cases in which a brother is faced with a difficult choice: whether to protect his brother (who happens to be a criminal) or to betray him for the public good. This kind of conflict is also a focus for Confucian thinkers. There are some famous cases in the *Analects* and the *Mencius* (for example, *Analects* 13.18 and *Mencius* 5A3 and 7A35), and there are still con-temporary debates over how to understand the morals of these passages.[5] To get a sense of the discussion going on in these passages, consider *Mencius* 7A35: A pupil asks, If the father of legendary ruler Shun had killed someone, what would Shun have done? Mencius rejects the suggestion that Shun should interfere with the police chief's attempt to capture the father, saying that Shun should allow the police chief to do his job.[6] Then the question becomes how Shun should perform his filial duty to his father. Mencius suggests that Shun should give up his throne, carry his father away, and run to a deserted place to hide with his father as a fugitive (without any complaints!). We could question the adequacy of the solution Mencius offered, but we have to admit that he did realize the conflicts of duties and tried to solve them.

We shouldn't take this case as offering a clearly set criterion when dealing with this kind of conflict. Life is complicated, and there is hardly any ready-made, universally applicable, unproblematic field manual that can guide us through life. Various accounts and stories in the *Mencius* and *Analects* may have been intended to serve only as context-dependent examples that offer hints and inspirations for us to handle our own problems. There may be cases for which not even a compromised solution can be found. After all, life (sometimes) sucks.

Another example of the conflict of duties in this network of care is between patriotism and care for humanity in general, which Sandel also discusses in chapter 9 of *Justice*. In the case of the conflict between Shun's care for his father and his duty to his people, from a Confucian point of view we can say that these two duties cannot be ordered because they are equally important. We can at best find a compromise solution. But the case of the conflict between patriotism and care for humanity is different, from a Confucian perspective.

Although the Confucian ideal is universal care that develops from caring for those who are near, another important feature of this Confucian universal care is that it is hierarchical. Confucian thinkers have argued that it is natural and justifiable that we care more for those closer to us than those for farther away from us. In the case of patriotism versus care for the humanity in general, the two duties are not equal. Our care for our own people has priority over care for foreigners. At the same time, we also have (weaker) compassion for the latter. Thus, for a Confucian, it is justifiable that we take care of our people first. But this priority is not supreme, and we can't satisfy our own people's needs by totally disregarding and even harming the interest of foreigners. For example, in the recent refugee crisis in Europe, a Confucian would be against unconditionally opening up the borders, as the German chancellor Angela Merkel did at one point during the crisis, but also against closing down the borders, as some right-wing European politicians and people advocate. Rather, refugees should be allowed in when the security and the living standards of the people of the host country are not severely harmed by the influx of refugees. Of course, an extremely difficult issue in practice is how to define "severely," but at least Confucians can offer a reasonable theoretical model in dealing with this kind of issue.

Another implication of the Confucian expanding network of care is that there shouldn't be a sheer divide between the private and the public. How we behave in the public has its root in the private. What we do in our bedrooms has a ripple effect on what we do in the public arena. If that is the case, then the typical liberal stance that the government should be value-neutral and should stay out of people's bedrooms begins to appear problematic. The government justifiably plays a role in promoting certain family values or morals in general. This issue is also discussed in chapter 9 of *Justice*. To be clear, this doesn't mean that the government should be involved in the promotion of all kinds of morals. What are considered morals by one group of people may not be so considered by another group. What the government should promote is what can become an overlapping consensus, to borrow John Rawls's terminology. Otherwise put, the governmental involvement in promoting morals should be "thin" and should, as liberals would argue, be limited to the political. The problem is that, according to the Confucian conception, the political is not sharply separated from the moral, and thus the thin morality the government can be allowed to promote is thicker than what liberal thinkers tend to allow. Moreover, this promotion doesn't have to be coercive. It could be tax policies, public reward, or denunciation of those who fail to perform family duties (such as an extremely irresponsible son or daughter). There should be mechanisms of checks and balances, accountability, and so forth. Nonetheless, for a Confucian, what is going on in one's bedroom is not categorically outside of the public concern.

So far, we have seen that many issues discussed by Sandel are also concerns for the Confucian. Although sometimes drawing on different resources and making different arguments, there are many overlapping ideas between Sandel and Confucians. To be clear, "Confucianism" is a philosophical tradition that has lasted for more than 2,000 years, and different Confucian thinkers may have sharply different views. My discussion here follows mostly from the *Analects* and the *Mencius*. As I understand these texts, however, there is a crucial idea that may reveal a fundamental difference between Confucianism and Sandel's philosophy (or communitarianism, a label Sandel often rejects).

In *Beyond Liberal Democracy*, Daniel Bell (2006) puts this difference well: "The Western communitarians [writers like David Miller and Sandel] tend to be republicans, meaning that they favor active, public-spirited participation by the many. The [East] Asian communitarians tend to be more family oriented and more accepting of the idea that active political participation should be reserved for the educated few" (335). By Asian communitarians, Bell means the Confucians. Confucians such as Mencius believe, on the one hand, that all human beings have the same potential to become morally superior, a spirit of equality that is shared by the communitarians. But on the other hand, they believe that, in reality, only the few can make it. The latter point is where Confucians differ from communitarians, Sandel included.

Therefore, although Confucians and communitarians can agree on the idea that we start from the family and community, and develop our virtues outward, Confucians believe that only the few can go really far and thus can participate fully in politics. If this is the case, the average voter's lack of knowledge and relevant morals cannot be compensated by promoting politically relevant virtues through communal efforts, as communitarians would suggest, but can be rectified only by introducing meritocratic elements into politics. Otherwise put, Confucians would reject the strong republicanism in communitarianism. They would fully support the communitarian effort to promote communities, and would also consider the state responsible for providing basic goods, including education, as well as opportunities for political participation, to all. But Confucians would also insist that this effort has a limit, and that in a large society of strangers, which is the default condition for most contemporary nations, the masses can never be lifted up to a level of competence that can make their political participation meaningful, even in terms of selecting their own representatives. This doesn't mean that Confucians would reject democratic procedure completely, and one person one vote can be considered an effective tool for people to express their satisfaction with governmental leaders and policies, which is what Confucians believe the people are competent to do. But they are not competent to make sound political decisions, either directly or through selecting their representatives. Regarding a bicameral legislature, a Confucian would support a structure in which members of the lower house are elected by the people to express their opinions of the government, whereas members of the upper house are selected based on their merits, especially their moral capacity to care for the people and their intellectual capacity to actualize this care.[7]

A hidden premise of this Confucian idea of a hybrid regime is that there is a fundamental gap between a small community of acquaintances and a large society of strangers. In fact, it was the so-called Legalist philosopher Han Fei Zi (280–233 BCE), an early critic of Confucianism, who made an explicit and powerful argument for this point.[8] According to him, moral values are doomed to be pluralistic in a large society of strangers, and thus what can be developed from one community may not be applicable to those from other geographical or intellectual communities. Thus, he rejected the Confucian idea of developing virtues from the family outward. In defense of Confucians, we can argue that although many, even most, values are doomed to be cherished only by people of a certain community, there may be certain values that are cross-communal. Then the issue is how to discover these cross-communal values. Following this idea, we can defend liberal thinkers such as John Rawls against Sandel's criticisms.

One target of Sandel's criticisms is the liberal understanding of the state of nature, in which we are all taken to be asocial individuals. But from Jean-Jacques Rousseau to Rawls, many thinkers take the state of nature not as a description of reality, but as a hypothetical tool. That is, for example, the reason Rawls puts individuals behind the veil of ignorance and makes them asocial—it is not because of some individualist metaphysical standpoint, but because he wanted to use this mechanism to discover the cross-communal values. To find the cross-communal values he was looking for, he needed to take away the particularistic communal features of the individual. In Rawls's ideal state, the government is allowed to promote certain values, but this must be done under the premise of pluralism.

A Confucian can criticize Rawls for taking too much away in the veil of ignorance. For example, we can add some abstract social features to the individuals behind the veil of ignorance, such as the desire for social stability and the knowledge that a stable family is important to maintain such stability. Put in this way, the difference between liberal thinkers such as Rawls, on the one hand, and Confucians ("East Asian communitarians") and thinkers like Sandel ("Western communitarians"), on the other, is not really between an individualism-based, value-neutral philosophy and a community-based philosophy that recognizes the role of the government in promoting certain values. Instead, the difference lies in how many values a government should be allowed to promote. This is a difference in degree, not in kind.

Notes

1. Quoted in Sandel 2009 at 222.
2. Many passages in the *Mencius* imply this understanding of human beings. See 3A4 for an example. For all references to passages in the *Mencius*, see Lau 2003 for an English translation. See Bai 2012, 32–33, for a more detailed discussion.
3. For a more detailed account with references to the related passages in the *Xun Zi*, see Fung 1966, 145–147.
4. For a complete and superb English translation of the *Analects*, see Lau 1979.
5. See, for example, Bai 2008a.
6. He is not literally the police chief, as we understand that role today. But not to complicate the story with details, I will use this term to describe the office this person held. There are also some other simplifications in my recapitulation here.

7. For more detailed discussions, see Bai 2008b, 2012 (chap. 3), and 2013.

8. See Bai 2011 for a detailed discussion.

References

Bai, Tongdong. 2008a. "Back to Confucius: A Comment on the Debate on the Confucian Idea of Consanguineous Affection." *Dao: A Journal of Comparative Philosophy* 7 (March): 27–33.

———. 2008b. "A Mencian Version of Limited Democracy." *Res Publica* 14 (March): 19–34.

———. 2011. "Preliminary Remarks: Han Fei Zi—First Modern Political Philosopher?" *Journal of Chinese Philosophy* 38 (March): 4–13.

———. 2012. *China: The Political Philosophy of the Middle Kingdom*. London: Zed Books.

———. 2013. "A Confucian Version of Hybrid Regime: How Does It Work, and Why Is It Superior?" In *The East Asian Challenge to Democracy: Meritocracy in Comparative Perspective*, edited by Daniel A. Bell and Chenyang Li, 55–87. Cambridge: Cambridge University Press, 2013.

Bell, Daniel. 2006. *Beyond Liberal Democracy*. Princeton, NJ: Princeton University Press.

Fung, Yu-lan. 1966. *A Short History of Chinese Philosophy*. New York: The Free Press.

Lau, D. C. (刘殿爵), trans. 1979. *Confucius: The Analects*. New York: Penguin.

———. 2003. *Mencius*, rev. bilingual ed. Hong Kong: Chinese University Press.

MacIntyre, Alasdair. 1981. *After Virtue*. Notre Dame, IN: University of Notre Dame Press.

Sandel, Michael. 2009. *Justice: What's the Right Thing to Do?* New York: Farrar, Straus and Giroux.

Justice as a Virtue, Justice according to Virtues, and / or Justice of Virtues

A Confucian Amendment to Michael Sandel's Idea of Justice

YONG HUANG

In *Justice: What's the Right Thing to Do?* Michael J. Sandel examines three approaches to justice: the utilitarian idea of justice as maximizing welfare or happiness, the freedom-based idea of justice as respecting freedom and human dignity, and the Aristotelian idea of justice as recognizing, honoring, and rewarding virtues. Sandel is not neutral with respect to these approaches. In his view, the first two, which dominate contemporary political philosophy, are inadequate, and he himself aims to develop a version of the third approach (Sandel 2011, 1303). Two central features of this approach can be summarized as justice as a virtue and justice according to virtues.

On the one hand, in this conception, justice is not something that merely facilitates a group's activities and distributes the fruits thereof—otherwise a band of thieves may also be regarded as just. It is in this sense that Sandel, in one of his early works, claims that "if an increase in justice does not necessarily imply an unqualified moral improvement, it can also be shown that in some cases, justice is not a virtue but a vice" (1982, 34). To ensure that justice is a virtue rather than a vice, he argues, we must adopt the Aristotelian teleological view, regarding justice as a character trait—the appropriate excellence in accordance to which the unique human function is performed, aiming at the uniquely human good. It is in this sense that Sandel claims that "arguments about justice and rights unavoidably draw on particular conceptions of the good life, whether we admit it or not" (2005, 28); and it is also in this sense that he argues against the liberal view, best represented by John Rawls, that our conception of justice should be neutral with respect to religious and metaphysical conceptions of the good.

On the other hand, Sandel stresses two related ideas that he claims are central to Aristotle's political philosophy: "1. Justice is teleological. Defining rights requires us to figure out the *telos* (the purpose, end, or essential nature) of the social practice in question. 2. Justice is honorific. To reason about the telos of a practice—or to argue about it—is, at least in part, to reason about what virtues it should honor and reward" (2009, 186). Before I explain what Sandel means, it is important to point out that the teleology he talks about here is different from the teleology related to the idea of justice as a virtue. In the latter, the teleology is concerned about the telos of human life itself, according to which a character trait can be defined as either virtuous or vicious. In the former, however, the teleology is concerned with the telos of the particular social practice. For example, if university teaching positions are being distributed, we need to inquire into the telos of the university. This is what Sandel considers to be the first central idea of Aristotle's political philosophy, to which the second idea is closely related, because it is the telos of the social practice that can tell us what kind of virtues a person ought to have in order for them to have the things being distributed.[1] In the case of a university, a person must excel in relevant knowledge and teaching skills in order to receive a teaching position. Justice in this sense is to distribute things according to (relevant) virtues, as a way to recognize, honor, celebrate, and reward people with virtues, and, correspondingly, to punish those with vices.[2] Sandel uses numerous examples to illustrate his point, and we can summarize two of them, one positive and one negative. As a positive example, Sandel mentions the distribution of the Purple Heart: "In addition to the honor, the medal entitles recipients to special privileges in veterans' hospitals . . . [T]he real issue is about the meaning of the medal and the virtues it honors. What, then, are the relevant virtues? Unlike other military medals, the Purple Heart honors sacrifice, not bravery" (2009, 10). As a negative example, Sandel uses the U.S. government bailout of certain failed companies in 2008–2009. There was public outrage over this bailout, particularly when some of the money was used to pay bonuses to the managers of the failed companies. As Sandel points out, "The public found this morally unpalatable. Not only the bonuses but the bailout as a whole seemed, perversely, to reward greedy behavior rather than punish it" (14).[3] In short, justice in this sense requires us to reward the virtuous and punish the vicious.

In the following, I shall briefly discuss Sandel's idea of justice as a virtue and then focus the rest of my discussion on his conception of justice according to virtues. In both cases I shall draw on Confucian resources. In discussing justice as a virtue, my main concern is the relationship between justice as a virtue of individual person and justice as a virtue of social institution and the Confucian contribution on this issue.

Justice as a Virtue

To say that justice is a virtue does not seem problematic, and I think Confucianism generally agrees on it. However, there is an issue that must be brought to light. When we say that justice is a virtue, we of course are saying that it is not a vice. However, whether it is a virtue or a vice, justice originally is a human character trait. Other senses of justice are derivative. For example, when we say an action is just, we mean that this is an action proceeding from a person with a character trait of justice; when we say that a state of affair is just, we mean that it is brought about by a person (or persons) with the character trait of justice.[4] This is similar to health, the original meaning of which is related to a person's body. When we say, in a derivative sense, that one's food is healthy, the environment is healthy, or someone made a healthy decision, we mean that they are all related to one's being healthy.

In this sense, justice is a personal virtue. However, contemporary discussions of justice, which to a great extent are inspired by the work of John Rawls, are primarily, if not exclusively, concerned with social justice. The main question asked is not whether, in what sense, to what degree, and how a person can be just or act justly in his or her interactions with others or in his or her handling of interactions among others; instead those discussions focus on whether, in what sense, to what degree, and how a society is just in its regulating interactions among its members. It is in this sense that John Rawls (1999) famously said, "Justice is the first virtue of social institutions" (3). This is to see justice as a virtue, not of individuals, but of a social institution. The question thus arises: How these two notions of justice as a virtue— justice as a virtue of the individual and justice as a virtue of social institutions—be related, if at all?

Mark Lebar (2014) distinguishes two ways to connect the two: "The first way . . . takes the individual virtue as logically prior, and sees the justice of political institutions as composed of the just relations of individuals. On this conception we begin with the relations the virtuous person seeks to maintain with others . . . and we ask what kinds of institutions and public rules will allow for and maintain those relations"; in contrast, "the second way . . . gives logical priority to the justice of the structure of institutions, practices, and so forth that constitute the state (the political body that is the primary bearer of the attribute of social, institutional or political justice). The crucial idea here is that we have some idea of what a just society . . . should look like . . . The duties of the just individual then are derived from this structure, in virtue of the obligations and reasons they have as members of that society" (270–271). The representative of the first way is

Aristotle.[5] John Rawls represents the second. However, in my view, neither view is without problems.

The Aristotelian model, which derives the justice of social institutions from the justice of individuals, rightly emphasizes the important function of government to make people virtuous and, in this particular case, just. I shall return to this important point later. However, such a model assumes that social justice can be realized only if everyone in the society acts justly, and this further assumes that everything just, whether in terms of distribution or in terms of rectification, is done by individuals and not by the government. The first assumption is clearly unrealistic, and so as long as there is one unjust person, the society cannot be just. If the second assumption did have some plausibility in an ancient small city-state, it is certainly implausible in a contemporary large-scale nation-state. For example, a farmer in Maine cannot know whether and how much a homeless person in San Francisco deserves to have what he produces. In such a large-scale society, distribution of resources has to be done by the state. It is not enough that individual members are just; the distribution and rectification done by the state should also be just.

This seems precisely to be the strength of the second model, represented by Rawls, who emphasizes justice as a virtue of social institutions. The question is how it is related to justice as an individual character trait. Because Rawls's principles of justice are chosen by people in the original position, it might be said that they reflect or express their virtuous or just character, and in this sense it might be said that his justice of social institutions is also derived from the justice of individuals. Obviously, however, this is an implausible interpretation, because parties in Rawls's original position, as he describes them, are primarily self-interested, or indifferent to the interest of others, and thus cannot be claimed to be virtuous in general or just in particular.[6] The proper way to see it is that Rawls uses the original position as an independent procedure to determine principles of justice for social institutions. In Rawls's view, although we know that *principles* of justice thus independently determined for social institutions must be principles of *justice,* if individuals in the society do not accept such principles, the society is not stable, and so it is important to cultivate a sense of justice among individuals starting in early childhood. Thus, Rawls (1999) argues that "when institutions are just . . . those taking part in these arrangements acquire the corresponding sense of justice and desire to do their part in maintaining them" (398). However, even if Rawls's *principles* of justice are indeed principles of *justice* for social institutions, it is inherently problematic to use such principles of justice, which are derived without any consideration of human nature (what makes humans human), to determine the virtue of justice as an individual character trait. Whatever virtues individual human beings ought to have are character traits that make them good human beings, but one cannot understand what makes human beings good unless one has a concept of human nature, any conception of which, however, is explicitly excluded from the parties in the original position in charge of choosing principles of justice. It is perhaps in this sense that Lebar (2014) complains that conceptions of political justice like Rawls's "may constrain the possibilities for individual justice in ways that have yet to be thought through" (274).

Given that neither of the two ways to connect justice as a virtue of individuals and justice as a virtue of social institutions is promising, Lebar laments, "We may yet not be in sight of a conception of justice as a virtue of individuals that can be congruent with institutional justice" (272). However, I think we have reason to be more optimistic on this issue. I have in mind here Michael Slote's approach. Slote is a virtue ethicist, but unlike most contemporary virtue ethicists who are Aristotelians, he is a sentimentalist, even though, it seems to me, one does not have to be a sentimentalist to agree with Slote on the issue we are concerned with here. In the most updated version of his virtue ethics, a virtuous person is an empathic person, where empathy is regarded as a virtue. To explain the connection, Slote (2009) states that "the laws, institutions, and customs of a given society are like the actions of that society"; just as individual actions reflect or express an agent's character, they reflect or express the character of the social group who create them: "So a sentimentalist ethics of empathic caring can say that institutions and laws, as well as social customs and practices, are just if they reflect empathically caring motivation on the part of (enough of) those responsible for originating and maintaining them" (125). Slote's approach to the issue is similar to the Aristotelian one in the sense that in both approaches justice as a virtue of social institutions is derivative from justice as a virtue of individuals. But on the Aristotelian model, justice as a virtue of social institutions aims to cultivate just persons. On Slote's model, justice as a virtue of social institutions ensures just interactions or transactions among individuals.

Confucians will generally accept Slote's view that the justice of a social institution reflects the virtuous characters of its leaders. Their idea of inner sageliness and external kingliness expresses precisely the same idea: external kingliness, that is, political institution, is merely a manifestation of inner sageliness, moral virtues. Mencius, for example, claims that "the root of [governing] the world lies in [governing] the state, the root of [governing] the state lies in [governing] the family, and the root of [governing] the family lies in [governing] oneself" (*Mencius* 4a5). *The Great Learning,* one of Confucianism's Four Books, goes further: "To cultivate oneself, there is a need to rectify one's heart-mind; to rectify one's heart-mind, there is a need to make one's intention sincere; to make one's intention sincere, there is a need to extend one's knowledge; and to extend one's knowledge, there is a need to investigate things" (*Liji* 42.1). This makes it clear that a government is good in general and just in particular only because persons who govern it are good. Elsewhere, Mencius states, "Only because former kings have a heart that cannot bear to see people suffer can they have a government that cannot bear to see its people suffer. As they are running a government that cannot bear to see people suffer with a heart that cannot bear to see people suffer, it was as easy for them to run the empire as rolling it on their palms" (*Mencius* 2a.6). Here, Mencius emphasizes that a government is virtuous because it is governed by a virtuous leader.

However, in one respect Confucians are more demanding than Slote. Although Slote claims that a law is just when it reflects or expresses the empathic motives of the lawmakers, he also allows that "a law is just even if it merely fails to reflect or exhibit a lack of appropriate empathic concern on the part of those who promulgate it" (2009, 126). He illustrates it thus: "Morally unsavory national legislators who are largely indifferent to the welfare of their compatriots, to the good of their country, might pass a law that in no way displayed or reflected their greediness or selfishness: for example, a law allowing right turns at red stoplights throughout the nation. That law would be just or at least not unjust" (126). We can see the problem with this concession of Slote's if we return to the analogy between a just law of the society and just action of an individual, an analogy that Slote himself makes use of. What Slote has in mind is a law made by nonvirtuous or even vicious lawmakers that nevertheless does not reflect their vices and is consistent with a law made by virtuous lawmakers that does reflect and express their virtues. This parallels an act by a vicious person that nevertheless is no different from an act done by a virtuous person. We know that such an act by the vicious person cannot be regarded as virtuous; it simply accords with virtue. However, Aristotle points out that "if the acts that are in accordance with the virtues have themselves a certain character, it does not follow that they are done justly or temperately. The agent also must be in a certain condition when he does them; in the first place he must have knowledge. Secondly he must choose the acts, and choose them for their own sakes, and thirdly his action must proceed from a firm and unchangeable character" (Aristotle 1963, 1105a28–35); and he further points out that "actions, then, are called just and temperate when they are such as the just or the temperate man would do; but it is not the man who does these that is just and temperate, but the man who also does them as just and temperate men do them" (115b5–8). It is for this reason that Confucians always emphasize that one ought not only to do the right things; one also needs to do them from the right heart-mind. Thus, Mencius praises sage king Shun, saying that "he is not just doing humane and just things; he is doing them from his humane and just heart-mind" (*Mencius* 4b19).

A question might be raised regarding what practical difference there is between a law that is made by a just person and an identical law made by an unjust person. One way to answer this question, from a Confucian perspective, is that laws can never be perfect, and there are always loopholes around them. To regard a law as merely a law, we tend to treat it literally, and thus may be led to do things that are clearly unjust and yet not unlawful. But when we regard the law as an expression and reflection of the lawmakers' virtue, we tend to emphasize its spirit, and thus will not be led to do certain clearly unjust things even if the law allows or even requires us to do them. Let's use Slote's own example of the law that allows drivers to make a right turn on red. If we treat it merely as a law, then drivers can always try to make a right turn on red, even when traffic is jammed and turning right on red simply blocks the intersection, or when seeing a car from the opposite direction turning left (illegally). However, if we see the law as proceeding from the lawmakers' virtuous characters, we will not do either of these, as we can understand that such actions cannot be what virtuous persons intend us to do. We can also use Rawls's difference principle as another example. Assume that this principle is just, that is, it is in accordance with the virtues of lawmakers (or political philosophers), but it is not legislated by a virtuous lawmaker (or political philosopher). If I am a person of exceptional talent, what this principle means to me is that I will not make full use of my talent and thus best benefit the worse-off unless I am paid more than others; if I am a worse-off person, it means that I will not allow a talented person to earn more unless he makes full use of his talents, which benefits me.[7] However, if we regard this principle as being not merely in accordance with the just characters of lawmakers but also actually just—that is, as reflecting and expressing the virtue of justice of lawmakers—then if I am a person with exceptional talents, I understand that the intention of this principle is that I should make full use of my talents to benefit worse-off people in the most efficient way. Thus, even if I am not paid more, I will still make full use of my talents (although something parallel may not be easily said on behalf of worse-off people).[8]

Justice according to Virtues or Justice of Virtues?

We can now turn to the second feature of Sandel's neo-Aristotelian conception of justice, which I characterize as justice according to virtues: Things are distributed to people according to the relevant merits, excellences, or virtues these things are meant to recognize, honor, and reward. This conception of justice is most plausible in distributing offices, particularly political offices and honors, but not so plausible, if at all, in distributing economic benefits. For example, today economic benefits are distributed mostly in the form of money. Unlike flutes or other particular entities that may have a telos that can help us determine what relevant virtues we should consider when distributing them, it is at least odd to ask what the telos of money is (to buy things?) and what virtues (skills in investment or expertise at bargaining?) it is meant to recognize, honor, or reward. This is also true of many types of services provided by social institutions. For example, we may plausibly say that the telos of a hospital is to provide health care, and so those who can serve this purpose better than others should be offered positions as physicians. However, it is odd to ask how we should distribute the health care that a hospital provides and what virtues patients should have in order to merit such care. Even if we say that wealth and health (care) should be distributed to people according to their contributions to society, which seems to be Aristotle's view on such matters, this has been made very implausible by John Rawls's idea of the natural and social accidents that affect the amount of contributions people can make to society and yet should not determine how much they should be distributed to.

Sandel also seems to suggest that his justice according to virtues is a general principle of distribution, applicable to anything to be distributed.[9] But sometimes he seems to limit it to the distribution of honors and political offices, the areas where his justice according to virtues can be most plausibly applied. There are at least two hints that Sandel holds this more restricted and thus more plausible view. We find the first hint when he contrasts Aristotle and contemporary political philosophers: "When we discuss distributive justice these days, we are concerned mainly with the distribution of income, wealth, and opportunities. For Aristotle, distributive justice was not mainly about money but about offices and honors" (Sandel 2009, 192).[10] It is plausible to think that Sandel also mainly has offices and honors in mind with his distributive justice according to virtues. We find the second hint in his defense of the idea of desert as at least the partial basis of justice in distribution. As is well known, John Rawls has made powerful arguments against distributive justice based on desert, as he essentially claims that no one deserves anything due to, again, his or her natural and social accidents. Sandel discusses this part of Rawls's theory of justice in a most approving way (153–166). Even when he tries to defend the idea of desert, at least partially, he still claims that Rawls's argument is morally attractive, as "it undermines the smug assumption, familiar in meritocratic societies, that success is the crown of virtue, that the rich are rich because they are more deserving than the poor" (178). He does also claim that Rawls's argument is "disquieting" because "it may not be possible, politically or philosophically, to detach arguments about justice from debates about desert" (179). When he makes such claims, though, the examples he uses include "jobs and opportunities" (178) and positions in such social institutions as "schools, universities, occupations, professions, public offices" (179). Indeed the whole discussion ends with university admissions policies.[11]

I will focus on what seems to me the most plausible part of Sandel's conception of justice: distributing offices, particularly political offices, according to the virtues such offices, given their telos, recognize, reward, and honor. Confucianism will have a serious reservation even regarding this most plausible part. The best way to explain this Confucian reservation is to highlight an aspect of the Confucian idea of justice, which should be not only consistent with but could indeed also be a constituent part of the Aristotelian conception of justice, including the version Sandel develops. I call it "justice of virtues."[12] Put most bluntly, if the Sandelian justice according to virtues is justice about distributing certain things according to virtues, the Confucian justice of virtues is justice about the distribution of virtues themselves. In other words, if the Sandelian justice according to virtues regards political offices as things to be distributed, the Confucian justice of virtues regards them as tools that can be used to distribute virtues. It may sound odd to talk about distribution of virtues, as virtues are not commonly considered to be things at anyone's disposal, things that can be distributed, justly or unjustly. Let me explain.

In any given society, it is most likely that there are people who have virtues and people who lack virtues or positively possess vices. In other words, people do not possess virtues equally. Before we discuss what justice requires us to do with such a state of affairs, we first need to understand the nature of virtue and, for that matter, vice. Confucians adopt a health model in their view of virtue, which I believe Aristotle or at least some contemporary Aristotelians would find congenial. According to this model, a virtuous person is analogous to a healthy person and a vicious person is analogous to a person who suffers some physical pain. For example, Mencius compares all humans' possession of the four moral sprouts (the heart of commiseration, shame, modesty, and right and wrong) to their possession of the four limbs (*Mencius* 2a6). Wang Yangming, one of the most influential neo-Confucians in the Ming Dynasty, says that a person who lacks virtues or is positively vicious is like a person in danger of falling off a cliff. Just as the latter is going to suffer great physical harm, if not death, the former suffers internal harm (Wang 1992, 2:80). If there is any difference, Confucians think that the health of one's internal well-being, virtues, is more important than one's external well-being, physical health. Thus, when the two come into conflict, one ought to take care of the internal rather than the external. It is in this sense that Mencius makes the famous distinction between the small body (our physical body) and the great body (our moral heart-mind), and ridicules people who care about their small body that has minor issues and yet are negligent of their great body that has major problems: "Different parts of one's person (*ti* 體) differ in value and importance. One should never harm the part of greater value and importance for the sake of the part of less value and importance. The person who nurtures the part of great value and importance is a great person, while the person who nurtures the part of less value and importance is a small person . . . A person who takes care of his or her finger to the detriment of his or her shoulder and back without realizing the mistake is a deluded person" (*Mencius* 6a14).

Such a view, as I said, is not alien to Aristotle, who frequently compares the health of the body and the health of the soul. For example, he argues that, just as merely listening to a doctor will not make patients healthy in body, merely listening to a philosopher will not make people healthy in soul.[13] At the very beginning of his discussion of justice in *Nicomachean Ethics*, Aristotle makes an analogy between a just person acting justly with a healthy person walking healthily (1129a). When he contrasts vulgar self-lovers, who love their external well-being, and genuine self-lovers, who love their virtues (1169a), he also agrees with Confucians that one's internal health is more important than one's external health.

Understood this way, it becomes clear that when there are virtuous people and vicious people, what justice requires us to do is not to reward people with virtues and punish people with vices but to help the latter get rid of their vices and become virtuous, just as when we find both healthy people and sick people, what justice requires us to do is not to reward the former and punish the latter but to relieve the latter of their sickness. It might be said that the analogy between the health of one's body and the virtue of one's character is not appropriate, given that one's health is not within one's control but one's character is. This, however, is not entirely correct. To a great extent one's health is within one's control—one can exercise regularly, refrain from smoking, eat healthy food, and get enough sleep—but one's character is not entirely within one's control.

Confucians, particularly neo-Confucians, have a very good explanation for why our character is not entirely within our control. Take Wang as an example again. In Wang's view, there are at least two factors involved in one's lacking virtues or possessing vices that are beyond one's control. First, one is born with physical / psychic stuff, the so-called *qi* or *qizhi*. In his view, "one's innate moral knowledge by itself is originally bright. In those whose material stuff is not good, there is a great deal of dredge, causing a thick layer of blockage, which makes it difficult for the original bright innate moral knowledge to shine. In those whose material stuff is good, there is little dredge, hardly causing any blockage; thus, with a little effort to reach one's innate moral knowledge, it becomes thoroughly bright. How can the little dredge, which is like the floating snow in hot soup, cause any blockage?" (Wang 1992, 2:68). Today's philosophers, especially those trained in the Western philosophical tradition, may well find Wang's metaphysical talk of *qi* unintelligible, but many of us may still agree on the main point he tries to make: just as there is a natural inequality in terms of people's inborn natural talents, there may also be a natural inequality in terms of people's inborn moral qualities. At least Aristotle holds a similar view in his contrast between people with characters gently born and people who by nature do not obey the sense of shame (Aristotle 1963, 1179b5–15); when he responds to the view that we are made good by nature by saying that "nature's part evidently does not depend on us, but as a result of some divine causes is present in those who are truly fortunate" (1179b21–23); and when he says that punishments and penalties should be imposed on those who "are of inferior nature" (1180a8).

Second, Wang emphasizes the importance of the environmental influence upon a person's moral character by citing an ancient saying: "The bitter fleabane will naturally be upright when growing among hemps, and white sands become black, with no need of dyeing, when put into mud"; then he states that the custom's being good or bad is the result of the long accumulation of the habit, which affects the moral quality of people living in it: "Those people in the past who abandoned their families and betrayed their neighbors, going out to do violent things everywhere, are so not because of their nature being different from others and so to be blamed for on themselves. It is rather caused by the lack of proper political governance and moral cultivation" (1992, 17:599). This includes the lack of early moral education within a family, the absence of inducement of good behaviors, and being driven further into evil by others' angry curses. Therefore, Wang claims that the government, parents, and neighbors should all share the blame for those people gradually falling into evil. If Wang's view about the natural inequality of people's inborn moral qualities still sounds controversial to some, his views on the impact of environment on people's moral development is obviously not. John Rawls, for example, argues that not only are people's natural abilities and talents subject to natural and social accidents, but their moral virtues cannot be claimed to be entirely their own: "That we deserve the superior character that enables us to make the effort to cultivate our abilities is also problematic; for such character depends in good part upon fortunate family and social circumstance in early life for which we can claim no credit" (1999, 89).

However, the analogy between physical health and virtue of character does fail at certain points. One the one hand, if one's physical body has a terminal illness, current medical knowledge will not be of much help. Similarly, even if justice requires us to distribute physical health equally among people, we may be unable to achieve it. In contrast, Confucians believe that however vicious a person becomes through whatever reasons, this person can still become virtuous. In other words, equal distribution of virtues is always possible, and that is why for Confucians everyone can become a sage. On the other hand, it is true that physical health and virtues are similar to each other and dissimilar to material things such as flutes and money. To have a better flute or more money than one had previously means another's having a worse flute and less money, because such things, however much abundant, are limited in supply. In contrast, to become healthier and more virtuous does not mean that anyone else must become less healthy or virtuous, because their supply is virtually infinite. If anything, one person's becoming healthier and more virtuous is conducive to another person's becoming healthier and more virtuous, or so I shall argue. Still, there may be a disanalogy between health and virtue. If there is a widespread disease for which medicine is in short supply, then one person's receiving the medicine and thus becoming healthy can certainly mean another person's not receiving the medicine and thus not becoming healthy. However, no analogue to such a shortage of medicine can be easily found in the case of making nonvirtuous or vicious people virtuous.

Can Virtues Be Distributed?

So the idea of justly or equally distributing virtues among people is not as absurd as it may first appear. The question is how to do it. Confucianism provides two avenues. First is the need for self-cultivation. Confucians believe that, although becoming vicious is not entirely a person's own fault, individuals are at least partially responsible for their becoming vicious; moreover, they can also become virtuous as long as they are willing to make the effort (it is true that those who endure more adverse or less favorable natural and social conditions need to make far stronger effort than those who experience less adverse or more favorable ones). Second, justice requires us, whether as individual agents or as political leaders, instead of rewarding the virtuous and punishing the vicious, to help vicious people overcome their vices so that they may cease to be vicious and may become virtuous, so that virtues can be distributed equally or justly among all. The first avenue is moral self-cultivation, and the second is moral education.[14] I shall focus on the second aspect, as our concern here is what justice requires us to do when there is injustice—that is, inequality, in the distribution of virtues.

As I have argued elsewhere (see Huang 2010), one unique feature of Confucianism is that being virtuous does not consist simply in helping others who are hungry, cold, sick, or otherwise physically suffering; it also involves aiming to make others virtuous. Consider the so-called Confucian Golden Rule. To follow the Golden Rule, as commonly understood in the Western tradition, a person is supposed to do (or not do) unto others as he or she would (or would not) like to be done unto. However, a person who desires to follow the Golden Rule is not required by the Golden Rule to make others also follow it. For example, the Golden Rule requires a person, who desires to be helped by others when in need, to help others in need, but it does not require that the person, for the sake of following the Golden Rule, make others help (their) others in need; it requires that a person who does not like to be treated unfairly not treat others unfairly, but it does not require that the person, for the sake of following the Golden Rule, make others not treat (their) others unfairly. However, the Confucian version of the Golden Rule goes beyond that. Instead of merely asking us to do unto others as we would like to be done unto, Confucius states: "One who wants to get established (*li* 立) ought to help others get established; and one who wants to prosper (*da* 達) ought to help others prosper" (*Analects* 6.30). The meaning of *li* is clear enough, to establish or realize oneself, which according to Confucius is more about one's internal character than one's external well-being. When

Confucius lists several important landmarks in his life, he mentions that at the age of thirty he established (*li*) himself (*Analects* 2.4). There is no doubt that he is talking about the formation of his character. With regard to the term *da*, Confucius himself provides a definition: "A person of *da* is one who is upright (*zhi* 直) in character, fond of rightness, sensitive to what other people say, observant of other people's facial expressions, and mindful of being modest" (*Analects* 12.20). All these clearly show that *da* is primarily related to one's inner well-being, one's moral qualities. So, the Confucian version of the Golden Rule essentially says that if I want to be a virtuous person, I ought to help others be virtuous persons, and, by implication, if I do not want to be a vicious person, I ought to help others not be vicious persons.

Most interestingly, Confucius uses the term, *zhi* (uprightness), to explain the meaning of *da* here. A person of *da* would help others to also become *da*, and one essential feature of a person of *da* is being upright (*zhi*). Such an understanding of *zhi* can help us understand two difficult but relevant passages in the *Analects* where the term *zhi* appears. The first passage is *Analects* 14.34. When asked what he thought about repaying injury with a good turn, an idea promoted by the Daoist Laozi (*Daodejing* 49, 63), Confucius responded: "If so what do you repay a good turn with? You repay an injury with uprightness, but you repay a good turn with a good turn" (*Analects* 14.34). The exact meaning of Confucius's "repaying injury with uprightness" is subject to scholarly disagreement, although it is clear that Confucius does not agree with the attitude that Laozi, and, for that matter, Jesus, recommends us to have toward wrongdoers: to repay an injury with a good turn. Some read *zhi* 直 as *zhi* 值, meaning "value," and thus claim that what Confucius says is that you ought to repay injury by the wrongdoer with an injury of equal value, not more or less than the injury you received.[15] Most scholars, however, interpret Confucius's teaching as occupying a middle position, in terms of moral demandingness, between repaying injury with injury, which is regarded as too permissive, and repaying injury with a good turn, which is seen as too demanding. The middle position is to repay injury with what one sincerely feels at the moment.[16]

I have argued against both interpretations elsewhere (Huang 2013: 38–39). In my view, what Confucius means by repaying injury with uprightness is to do things that can help the person who unfairly injures me, the non-upright person, become an upright person. One way to see it is to see how Confucius contrasts uprightness with crookedness (*wang* 枉). He says that "promoting the upright person above the crooked person can make the crooked person upright" (*Analects* 12.22). In this same *Analects* passage, his student Zixia illustrates what Confucius means by saying that when sage Kings Shun and Tang promoted upright persons Gaoyao and Yin Yi, respectively, there were hardly people lacking in humanity, as people originally lacking in humanity were made upright by Gaoyao and Yin Yi. In the same spirit, Confucius praised Shi Yu, an upright minister in the state of Wei. Shi Yu, about to die, told his son that he had not been able to persuade his ruler, King Ling of Wei, to promote the worthy Ju Boyu and demote the unworthy Mi Zixia. Therefore, his funeral should not be held in the main hall but only in a side room. Soon he died and his son did as instructed. Coming to the funeral, King Ling of Wei asked why, and the son told him what his father had said. Hearing this, the king finally felt embarrassed and accepted the advice, promoting Ju Boyu and demoting Mi Zixia. In Chinese history this is known as the famous story of "remonstration with a corpse" (*shijian* 屍諫)," and Shi Yu was regarded as a person who not only made himself upright (*zhi ji* 直己) but also made other people (King Ling of Wei, in this case) upright (*zhi ren* 直人). Clearly with this double sense of uprightness in mind, Confucius exclaimed, "How upright Shi Yu was indeed!" (*Analects* 15.7).[17] Here we see the unique feature of uprightness: a person with the virtue of uprightness is not only upright himself or herself but one who makes others upright. In his commentary on *Analects* 17.8, where Confucius states that a person fond of uprightness (*zhi*) and yet not of learning tends to be acrimonious to people, Xing Bing 邢昺 in the Song Dynasty points out that "to straighten the crookedness is called uprightness." This is a feature of uprightness that is also highlighted by Confucius's follower Mencius. When saying that "a person who is not upright himself or herself cannot make others upright" (*Mencius* 3a1), Mencius emphasizes that an upright person makes non-upright persons upright (*Mencius* 3a4). A statement connecting straightness (*zheng* 正) and uprightness (*zhi*) also appears in *Zuo's Commentary on the Spring and Autumn Annals:* "To straighten the crooked is called uprightness" (*Zuozhuang:* Duke Xiang, Year 7).

This meaning of uprightness also helps us better understand another controversial passage in the *Analects*, where the character *zhi* also appears. The passage records a conversation between the governor of She and Confucius. The governor told Confucius, clearly with some pride, "In our village there is an upright person, Zhigong. He bears witness against his father stealing a sheep." Instead of praising him, Confucius responded, "In my village, an upright person is different: father does not disclose son's wrongdoing, and son does not disclose father's wrongdoing, and the uprightness is in it" (*Analects* 13.18). This passage has posed difficulties for interpreters throughout the commentary history of the *Analects* and has indeed become the focus of a heated and prolonged debate among Chinese scholars in the last dozen years or so. Both sides see the passage as presenting us with a dilemma of filial piety and social justice, with one side defending Confucius for putting filial piety before social justice, and the other side criticizing Confucians for failing to put social justice before filial piety. I have argued elsewhere that both sides are wrong.[18] The key to understanding this passage is also the character *zhi*, which, as we have argued, means to straighten the crooked. In this passage, the fact that one's father steals a neighbor's sheep indicates that he is not upright. An upright son ought to make his non-upright father upright. The question is in what sense the son's nondisclosing his father's stealing is conducive to making his father upright, even though Confucius says only that uprightness lies in the son's nondisclosure and not that his nondisclosure itself is uprightness.

Confucius provides us with a clue when he says that "in serving one's parents, one ought to remonstrate gently," with low tone, appropriate facial expressions, and soft voice, when they do immoral things (*Analects* 4.18). This passage is significant in several aspects. First, when parents do something immoral, children are not supposed to just stand by it or even follow their actions. Instead they are supposed to remonstrate with their parents, or if it is too late, to urge their parents to rectify the situation. So if the father steals a sheep, an upright son should remonstrate with him to rectify it. This shows that Confucius in this passage does not advocate filial piety at the price of social justice. Second, to remonstrate with one's parents against wrongdoing here is seen as a way of "serving" them. In other words, remonstration is one important thing a filial child is supposed to do. To be filial does not simply mean to be obedient to parents. For example, when Zigong, one of Confucius's students, wants to confirm with Confucius that one's obedience to parents is filial piety, just like a minister's obedience to the king is loyalty. However, Confucius replies, "How shallow you are! You do not understand. In the ancient, when a good king of a big state has seven ministers who dare to remonstrate, the king will not make mistakes; if a middle sized state has five remonstrating ministers, the state will have no danger; if a small state has three remonstrating ministers, the official salaries and positions can last. If a father has a remonstrating child, he will not fall into doing things without propriety; and if a scholar has a remonstrating friend, he will not do immoral things. So how can a son who merely obeys the parents be regarded as being filial, and a minister who merely obeys the ruler be regarded as being loyal? To be filial and loyal is to examine what to follow" (*Kongzi Jiayu* 9; 57; the same passage with slight variance also appears in *Xunzi* 29.3). This shows that Confucius does not promote social justice at the price of filial piety. These two points above, combined, indicate that for Confucius, there is no dilemma between filial piety and social justice. Third, in order for the remonstration to be successful, it has to be done gently. The very reason that one's parent is going to do or has done something immoral shows that the parent is not virtuous, and so scolding them certainly does not help to make them realize their wrongdoing and thus overcome their vices. If your father steals a sheep, and you report him to the public authority, your father will certainly be mad at you, and it is impossible for him to listen to your remonstration. So, in the passage we have been discussing, the reason Confucius says a filial son ought to not disclose his father's stealing a sheep (which does not mean to cover it up or obstruct public authority in investigating it) is to create a favorable environment in which rectification of his father's vices can be more effectively done, which is precisely what ƶhi, uprightness, means: to make the non-upright upright.

I have been arguing that Confucian justice of virtues—justice in distributing virtues equally—requires that, instead of rewarding the virtuous and punishing the vicious, we ought to help the vicious overcome their vices and thus become virtuous, just as justice requires that, instead of rewarding healthy people and punishing the sick, we ought to help those who are sick overcome their sickness and become healthy. It should become clear now that this does not mean that we should be lenient with the wrongdoers or forgive their wrongdoings.[19] Confucians do think that, if there are vicious people, and if these vicious people remain vicious despite our effort to help them overcome their vices, instead of blaming them for failing to become virtuous, we should reflect upon ourselves, trying to see whether we have not done things properly in our effort to help them and how we can improve ourselves in our attempt to help them.[20] However, Confucians insist that we cannot allow those vicious people to continue to be vicious, as it is simply unfair, that is, unjust, for them to lack virtues while others have them, just as it is unfair to leave sick people unattended while others are healthy.

How Confucians Are Different from Aristotelians

What I have been saying in the name of justice of virtue is that a moral agent with the virtue of justice, whether an individual or a government, should have the goal of cultivating people's virtues. This, however, does not sound much different from Sandel's Aristotelian justice according to virtues: "For Aristotle, the purpose of politics is not to set up a framework of rights that is neutral among ends. It is to form good citizens and to cultivate good character"; and in his support Sandel quotes Aristotle: "Any polis which is truly so called, and is not merely one in name, must devote itself to the end of encouraging goodness. Otherwise, a political association sinks into a mere alliance . . . instead of being, as it should be, a rule of life such as will make the members of a polis good and just" (Sandel 2009, 193).[21] In this sense, I trust Sandel will also accept this Confucian justice of virtues. Still, I think there are some subtle but also important differences between this Confucian conception of justice of virtues and Sandel's Aristotelian conception of justice according to virtues, which would give Confucians serious reservations about the Sandel's theory.

First, even though Confucians and Aristotelians think that we should let virtuous people hold political offices, their reasons for doing so are not entirely the same. Sandel emphasizes that these offices exist to recognize, reward, and honor virtuous people. This is made most clear in his use of Aristotle's analogy of distributing the best flutes. We may agree with Aristotle that the best flutes should be given to the best flute players. "But why?" Sandel asks, and then answers: "Well, you might say because the best musicians will play the flutes well, and create music that everyone enjoys. *That would be a utilitarian reason. But it's not Aristotle's reason.* He believes the best flutes should go to the best flute players because that's what flutes are for—to be played well. The purpose of flutes is to produce excellent music, and so those who can realize this purpose most fully ought to have the best ones"

(2009, 188; emphasis added).[22] In the sense that Sandel means to distinguish between the utilitarian reason and the Aristotelian in giving the best flutes to the best players and thus, by implication, in giving the most influential offices to the most virtuous people, I think Confucians will adopt the utilitarian reason.[23] The reason to let virtuous people hold political offices is not to reward, honor, or recognize them but simply because holding such offices can enable them to better perform their function of making other people virtuous. In any case, virtuous people are virtuous not because they seek recognition, reward, or honor. Even for Aristotle such things are external, sought only by vulgar self-lovers; true self-lovers are willing to sacrifice such external things if necessary, as what they are concerned with is their virtues, which belong to their internal well-being.

Second, Confucians may also disagree with Aristotelians, including Sandel, in terms of the way those who hold political offices do things to make people virtuous. Aristotle claims that arguments will not work. Most people "do not by nature obey the sense of shame, but only fear, and do not abstain from bad acts because of their baseness but through fear of punishment" (1963, 1179b5–10). Thus, political leaders accomplish their job of making people virtuous by making laws. He points out that "it is difficult to get from youth up a right training for virtue if one has not been brought up under right laws; for to live temperately and hardily is not pleasant to most people . . . For this reason, their nurture and occupations should be fixed by laws . . . For most people obey necessity rather than argument, and punishment rather than the sense of what is noble" (1179b31–1180a4). Sandel seems to agree with Aristotle when he complains that "the idea of legislating morality is anathema to many citizens of liberal societies, as it risks lapsing into intolerance and coercion," and then immediately claims, "But the notion that a just society affirms certain virtues and conceptions of the good life has inspired political movements across the ideological spectrum" (2009, 20). In another place, Sandel asks,

"Does a just society seek to promote the virtue of its citizens? Or should law be neutral toward competing conceptions of virtue?" (9), implying that the virtue of citizens can be (if not can only be) promoted by law.

As we have seen, Confucians agree with Aristotelians that an important function of the government is to make its people virtuous; and they will also agree with Aristotelians that such a job cannot be done purely by arguments. However, the whole idea that people can be made virtuous by legislating and applying punitive laws is totally alien to Confucians. There is a famous saying of Confucius recorded in the *Analects:* "If you lead common people with political measures and keep them in order with punitive laws, they will stay out of trouble but will have no sense of shame; if you lead them with virtue and keep them in order with propriety, they will have a sense of shame and not make trouble" (*Analects* 2.3). The first half of this passage is directly opposite to what Aristotle says, and I think Confucius is clearly right. Punitive laws, however harsh they are, may indeed deter people from doing immoral things but cannot make vicious people virtuous, because, as Aristotle acknowledges, they thus "do not abstain from bad acts because of their baseness but through fear of punishment" (1963, 1179b10). So not only will they not abstain from bad acts when they are reasonably sure that their acts can escape detection and thus punishment, but they will have to always go through an inner struggle even when try to abstain from the acts they would very much like to do or try to do things that they would very much not like to do, which is certainly not conducive to becoming virtuous. The second half of the passage is Confucius's alternative proposals to make people virtuous, rules of propriety and virtues. Rules of propriety are different from punitive laws. When violated, people will not be punished but will be looked down upon and feel ashamed. By virtue, Confucius means the exemplary virtuous actions of political leaders.[24]

This leads to the third difference between Confucianism and Aristotelianism. Although both maintain that government has the function to make people virtuous, and that those who hold political office should possess virtues, the relevant virtues they think these political office-holders should have are different. As we have seen, Aristotle stresses the importance of legislators in making punitive laws, which can deter people from bad acts. Let's assume that such laws can not only deter people from bad acts but also make people virtuous. The question is what kind of people are qualified to be legislators—what kind of virtues ought people possess in order to be recognized, rewarded, and honored by such political offices? Interestingly, Aristotle makes the use of the analogy to a medical doctor. Suppose your child is sick. You, as the parent, know many particular details about your child. The medical doctor has never seen your child before. Will you try to cure your child by yourself or go to the doctor? Of course, the doctor. But why? Because the doctor "has the general knowledge of what is good for everyone or people of a certain kind" (1180b13–15). One can become a doctor and cure disease not because the doctor himself or herself is healthy or at least does not have the disease the patient has, but because he or she has the relevant knowledge and skills to cure the disease. Similarly, Aristotle argues that making a child virtuous is the job of legislators and not the parent. Legislators can perform such a function because, in addition to the authority they have due to the simple fact that they are legislators, they have the knowledge and expertise in making laws that can effectively reach their goals, not merely because they possess the virtues that they aim to make people have, as there are many other people possessing such virtues. To push Aristotle's analogy a little further, whether the legislators should have the virtues that the laws they make aim to train people to have really does not matter. A doctor can cure a patient's disease not because he or she does not have the disease, but because he or she has the knowledge and skill. Without such knowledge and skill, however healthy the doctor is, he or she is not able to cure the patient of the disease; with such knowledge and skill, one can still cure the patient even if he or she has the disease himself or herself. Similarly, even if a person does not have the virtues that government wants its people to have, as long as the person has good knowledge and skills about what laws can make people virtuous, this person is still qualified to be a legislator.

For Confucius it is not the laws made by government but the exemplary virtues that people who hold political offices display in their acts that can make people virtuous. So political leaders must have precisely the same virtues that they aim to make their people have. In this respect, we can find numerous sayings of Confucius in the *Analects*. In his advice to political rulers, he repeatedly emphasizes the importance of being virtuous. For example, he says, "If the ruler makes oneself correct, what difficulty will the ruler have to govern people? If the ruler cannot make oneself correct, how can the ruler make others correct?" (*Analects* 13.13). In this passage, the term for "govern" is *zheng* 政, which is a cognate of the word for "correct," *zheng* 正. In another passage, when Ji Kangzi asks about government, Confucius says that "to govern (*zheng* 政) is to be correct (*zheng* 正). If you [a ruler] are correct, who dares be not correct?" (12.17). Ji Kangzi is worried about burglary, and Confucius advises him: "If you yourself were not one with desire [to steal things from your people], no one would steal even if you reward them for stealing" (12.18). Ji Kangzi further asks whether it is permissible to kill people who do not follow *Dao*, Confucius replies: "Why do you need to kill in governing? If you want to be good, then your people will be good. The nature of the superior person is like wind, while the nature of inferior person is like grass. When the wind blows, the grass will bend" (12.19). For Confucius, if a ruler "is correct, then no commands are issued and yet people all follow, while if the ruler is not correct, then even if commands are issued, people will not obey" (13.6); "a ruler who governs by being virtuous himself can be compared to the Polar Star which commands homage of the multitude without leaving its place " (2.1). *Confucius's Family Sayings* records a long passage that makes the point most clearly:

> The more those in higher positions revere their parents, the more those in lower positions will practice filial piety; the more those in higher positions respect their older brothers, the more those in lower positions will practice brotherly love; the more charitable those in higher positions are, the more generous those in lower positions will become; the more those in higher positions maintain a close relationship with worthy people, the more those in lower positions will choose good people as friends; the more those in higher positions love morality, the less likely those in lower positions will hide their moral deficiency; the more those in higher positions dislike greed, the more those in lower positions will feel it shameful to compete for benefit; the more deferential those in higher position are, the more shame those in low positions will feel for being impolite. These seven teachings are the foundations of governing people . . . Those in higher position are exemplars of those in lower positions. When the exemplars are rectified, who else will not be rectified? (*Kongzi Jiayu* 3:20)

In sum, the virtues that Confucius thinks political leaders should have are precisely the virtues that they want their people to have. If they want their people to be honest, these political leaders must first have the virtue of honesty; if they want their people to be benevolent, these political leaders must first have the virtue of benevolent; if they want their people to be just, these political leaders must first have the virtue of justice.[25] In contrast, for Sandel and Aristotelianism, the virtues that political offices aim to honor, recognize, and reward their people for having are virtues or, rather, skills and abilities, of legislating, administering, and adjudicating laws that can make people virtuous (honest, benevolent, just, and so on). Sandel sometimes calls such virtues "civic virtue" (2009, 194), but I think he describes them more correctly when he calls them "statecraft as soulcraft" (1996, 326). One may defend the Aristotelian view that it is enough for political leaders, whose job is to make people virtuous, to have the effective soulcraft, by saying that even though this is not ideal, it is not necessary for them to be virtuous themselves, just as a CEO of an automobile company, for example, does not need to have any knowledge or ability either to make any part of the car or to assemble different parts together into a car. It is enough for him or her to have the knowledge, skills, and abilities necessary to manage different people doing different things in the most efficient ways.[26] Such a defense on Aristotle's behalf fails to notice an important difference between moral education and management or training of nonmoral things. If someone teaches me how to play basketball, the only thing I care about is whether they can teach me to play basketball better; whether that person can play basketball well is not my concern. However, if someone teaches me to be honest, benevolent, or just, but that person is dishonest, malevolent, and unjust, it is very unlikely that I will regard honesty, benevolence, and justice as virtues I should have, if I do not have them yet.

Let's now compare Confucius's and Sandel's Aristotelian views on justice in rectification. For a society to be just, what should it do when there are both virtuous people and vicious people in that society? I approach this question by developing a unique conception of justice of virtues from the Confucian perspective. Using the analogies of virtue with health and vice with disease, I claim that it is unjust that some people have more virtues than some others, and that a just society ought to redistribute these virtues so that everyone can be equally (and maximally) virtuous. We can see, interestingly, that this Confucian notion of justice of virtues, seen from a different perspective, can also be regarded as justice in rectification: Nonvirtuous or positively vicious persons are here seen as persons with defects, moral defects, analogous to people with physical defects. To distribute virtues to them— that is, to make them virtuous—is essentially to rectify them. It is here that we can see the fourth and the last contrast between Confucius and Aristotle.

Aristotle regards injustice as an inequality, and justice of rectification aims to restore the original (proportional) equality. Suppose there is originally a proportional equality between A and B. If A steals something from B, A gains what B loses, thus resulting in inequality. Rectificatory justice requires that A give that gain back to B to restore the original equality. Similarly, in cases "in which one has received and the other has inflicted a wound, or one has slain and the other is slain, the suffering and the action have been unequally distributed . . . the judge tries to equalize things by means of the penalty, taking away from the gain of the assailant" (Aristotle 1963, 1132a7–9), so that equality is brought back. Clearly, Aristotle holds what is now called a retributive theory of justice in rectification, which is in contrast to the utilitarian one.[27] If the retributive theory is backward looking (to restore the original equality disturbed by unjust acts), the utilitarian one is forward looking (to prevent future unjust acts from happening). In order to realize the utilitarian goal, it is not sufficient (and sometimes even unnecessary) to restore the original equality; it is necessary to require the party who has gained in the unjust transaction, the immoral person, the criminal, to give up more than the gain so that he, and other potential immoral persons and criminals, will be deterred from committing the same acts again.

As is well known, these two theories, with their respective strengths, have their respective weaknesses. Retribution cannot reliably perform the function of preventing future unjust acts, either by the same person or by other people, which is the strength of the utilitarian theory. The utilitarian theory has difficulty, however, justifying why a person who has done an unjust act should not only be asked to give up his undeserved gain but also be used as a tool, by being forced to give up more than gained, to deter not only his future self but, more problematically, other people, from committing the same acts. In this context we can see the significance of the Confucian justice of virtues. Taken as a theory of rectification, this Confucian view is neither retributive nor utilitarian but restorative, rehabilitative, or therapeutic.[28] The most unique feature of this view is that although it also aims at rectification, unlike the two familiar theories which aim to rectify the result of the unjust acts, it aims to rectify the source of the unjust acts, the immoral agent. This Confucian justice in rectification is superior to both retributive and utilitarian justice. When the immoral agent is rectified—that person's disease is cured and inner health is restored—the person not only will not commit the same immoral acts again, but will become a moral exemplar for others who may otherwise commit the same immoral acts. Thus, the utilitarian goal is realized without the use of utilitarian means. On the other hand, when the immoral agents' diseases are cured, their moral health is restored or rehabilitated, and thus they become moral agents, they will naturally seek to give up their undeserved gains and return them to their victims. In cases where their victims' loss cannot be restored (for example, if their immoral actions caused the loss of parts of their victims' bodies or even lives), they will try to make some appropriate compensation and will feel appropriate remorse, guilt, and regret for the immoral actions. Thus, the retributive goal is realized without the use of retributive means.

I have presented here a Confucian perspective on Sandel's neo-Aristotelian theory of justice, focusing on its two central features: justice as a virtue and justice according to virtues. To show the contributions Confucianism can make to the contemporary discourse on justice, I have mostly highlighted the differences between Confucianism and Aristotelianism. However, although there are still scholars, particularly those Confucian scholars in Taiwan and Hong Kong, who are deeply influenced by Mou Zongsan, perhaps the most influential contemporary Confucian, and thus think that Confucianism is better interpreted within the framework of Kantian moral philosophy, there are increasingly more people, including myself, who believe that Confucianism is congenial to Aristotelianism. It is possible that their differences are not as great as I have suggested in this paper, and that Aristotelianism, particularly Sandel's version of it, might be consistent with the Confucian view I have presented.[29] However, until I am convinced otherwise, I will side with Confucianism for the reasons I have given here.

Notes

I presented a draft of this paper at the International Conference on Michael Sandel and Chinese Philosophy, East China Normal University, Shanghai, March 2016. I benefited greatly from Sandel's challenging questions and comments. I am also grateful to Julia Driver, who at a later conference raised questions that improved this final version. I also benefited from conversations with Michael Slote. I thank Chenyang Li for his comments.

1. Although these are two different senses of teleology, it is also important to connect them in an appropriate way. The teleology related to a particular social practice has to be subordinated to the teleology related to human purpose, as it is the latter that determines whether a particular social practice should exist in the first place. Otherwise, one might try to distribute, for example, the leadership of a gang of thieves (as its telos is to steal, it would reward, honor, and recognize the character traits that are relevant to this telos). On this issue, Richard Kraut (2002) makes a very important comment: "Aristotle holds . . . that although merit is the basis on which distinctive questions should be resolved, the kind of merit that must be taken into account is a matter to be determined by looking to the common good of the whole community . . . The justice of an institution that distributes goods is a two-fold matter: first, the institution must contribute to the common good, and second, the distribution must be made in accordance with the criterion of merit that is appropriate, in light of the common good that is to be achieved. If an institution undermines the well-being of the community, then it does not serve the goal of justice, even if it succeeds in distributing goods according to the criterion of merit it uses" (147).

2. Although most examples Sandel uses are about rewarding the virtuous and not punishing the vicious, he does say that "greed that preys on human misery, we think, should be punished, not rewarded" (2009, 9).

3. On Sandel's view, though, the government bailout funds rewarded these CEOs not for their greed but for their failure.

4. It is in this sense that Michael Pakaluk (2005) points out: "The English word 'justice' can mean: (i) a just state of affairs, that is, an arrangement or situation which is just . . . (ii) the intention with which an action is performed . . . or (iii) the state of character, or virtue, which leads someone to aim at just states of affairs from a just intention . . . In Greek, there are separate words for each of these" (200).

5. Sandel (2011) seems to agree on this when he claims, "To achieve a just society, we have to reason together about the meaning of the good life, and to create a public culture hospitable to the disagreements that inevitably arise" (1310).

6. Of course, it may also be said that Rawls's principles of justice reflect or express the virtue of justice as understood by the person, Rawls in this case, who designs the original position as a procedure from which the principles of justice are derived. Clearly, however, Rawls does not rest his argument on this basis.

7. See Cohen 2002, chap. 8.

8. My argument in this section has exploited the analogy between laws and individual actions. Just as just actions reflect and express the agent's virtue of justice, just laws express and reflect the lawmakers' virtue of justice. However, there is a disanalogy: Just actions proceed from an individual person, whereas laws proceed from a group of people, lawmakers. This raises the issue of whether there is a sense in which we can talk about the virtue of a group of people, a so-called collective virtue or institutional virtue. For some interesting discussions on this topic, see Byerly and Byerly 2016; Gregory 2015; Fricker 2010; Sandin 2007; Ziv 2012.

9. For example, after raising the question of whether justice according to virtues is applicable only to honors and not to fruits of prosperity, Sandel states that "arguments about the rights and wrongs of economic arrangements often lead us back to Aristotle's question of what people morally deserve, and why" (2009, 13); and then he immediately turns to the discussion of the government bailout issue mentioned above.

10. David Keyt (1985) expresses a similar view when he says that "distributive justice for Aristotle is concerned primarily with the distribution of political authority . . . and only secondarily with the distribution of wealth" (24). Richard Kraut (2002) also says that "the principal question of justice, he [Aristotle] thinks, is: who should have powers" (147), and that it is for this reason that Aristotle "ignores the point that sometimes distributions are based not on merit, but on some other criterion. If food and other resources are available for distribution to the needy, then justice requires that larger amounts be given to those who have greater needs" (146).

11. Unlike the common view that in his *Ethics* Aristotle discusses two kinds of particular justice, distributive and rectificatory, Judith A. Swanson (2011) argues that Aristotle "recognizes three kinds: distributive, economic, and punitive. Government concerns distributive justice because it distributes offices and honors, rights and privileges" (1377). Although Swanson argues against Sandel and Keyt, among others, and claims that economic justice is a central concern of Aristotle's, she does claim that Aristotle's principle of economic justice is different from his principles of distributive justice and punitive justice.

12. Since it means to be an alternative to Sandel's justice according to virtues, the Confucian justice of virtues is similarly not concerned with the distribution of economic benefits.

13. Aristotle 1963, 1105b; see the end of chap. 4.

14. These two aspects, self-cultivation and moral education (of others), normally work together and even are inseparable in Confucianism. In this sense, although Slote's

view that self-cultivation is insufficient is correct, his view of Confucianism as being exclusively focused on self-cultivation, based on his reading of Tu Weiming and P. J. Ivanhoe, who regard moral self-cultivation as central to Confucianism, is not (see Slote 2016).

15. See, for example, Li 2007, 262.

16. See, for example, Li 1999, 339.

17. In another text Confucius is recorded as saying: "In the past, those who made strong remonstrations stopped with their effort when they died. There has never been one like Shi Yu, who, after death, remonstrated with his corpse. His loyalty transformed his ruler. How can it be not regarded as uprightness?" (*Kongzi Jiayu* 22.145).

18. See Huang 2013, 139–143.

19. I thank Julia Driver, one of whose comments prompted me to this issue.

20. It is only in this context that we can properly understand such *Analects* passages as "be strict with oneself and be lenient with others" (15.15); "the superior person makes demands upon oneself, while the inferior person makes demands upon others" (15.21); "attack your own faults, not those of others" (12.21); and while "happy in proclaiming merits of others" (16.5), "the superior person despises those who proclaim faults in others" (12.21). In all these passages, what Confucius means is not that we should not do anything to make others virtuous and it is enough for us to be virtuous; instead, Confucius means that we should blame ourselves for others' being not virtuous, as is clear when he quotes a saying supposedly by King Wu of Zhou: "If there are people with moral faults, I'm the only person to be responsible" (15.21).

21. Justice of virtues in this sense is not entirely alien to Aristotle, at least according to Marco Zingano's plausible interpretation. Because for Aristotle justice is equality, Zingano (2013) argues that Aristotle's answer to the question "What is to be equalized?" is virtue—and "moral virtue is the measure of justice in correct constitutions. In order to be spread over all the *polis*, the city must provide leisure and other prerequisites for the citizens" (209–210). To support his claim, Zingano cites the following passage from Aristotle: "The best life, both for individuals separately and for cities collectively, is a life of virtue sufficiently equipped with the resources needed to take part in virtuous actions" (*Politics* VII 1, 1323b40–24a2; in Zingano 2013, 209).

22. On other occasions Sandel makes claims that are more inclusive. For example, he says that the reason virtuous people "should hold the highest offices and honor is *not simply* that they will enact wise policies, making everyone better off. It is *also* that political community exists, at least in part, to honor and reward civic virtues" (2009, 195; emphasis added).

23. It is perhaps more properly regarded as consequential than as utilitarian, in the sense that Confucianism aims at the best consequence: to make as many people virtuous as possible. Thus, clearly, Confucianism overall is a virtue ethics, and consequentialism plays its role only within its overall framework of virtue ethics, which is teleological and not consequentialist.

24. Of course, they are not the only two ways of moral education in Confucianism. In other places Confucius mentions other measures. For example, he also says that moral

development "arises through *the Poetry*, established through *the Rites*, and completed through *the Music*" (*Analects* 8.8). Here, in addition to rules of propriety (the rites), Confucius also mentions poetry and music, both of which belong to sentimental education. In addition, Confucius is not absolutely against punitive laws, because he realizes that sometimes they are necessary. However, he thinks that such laws, in ideal situations, are merely present but not applied; when there is indeed a need to use them, they are merely supplemental and temporary. They should be not only preceded but also followed by other means of moral education.

25. This, of course, does not mean that moral virtues are the only things political leaders must have, for Confucianism. In addition to making people virtuous, a government also has it as a goal to make its society just, particularly to distribute economic benefits in a just way, which requires political leaders to have the relevant expertise. Still, for Confucianism, not only are moral virtues necessary and most important for political leaders, but such moral virtues will naturally lead political leaders to seek relevant expertise to govern their society justly and also efficiently.

26. I thank Julia Driver, whose comments prompted me to consider this issue.

27. Aristotle says that "men seek to return either evil for evil—and if they cannot do so, think their position mere slavery—or good for good—and if they cannot do so there is no exchange, but it is by exchange that they hold together" (1132b34–1123a2).

28. Here what's meant is something different from Sandel's therapeutic theory of criminal justice. In Sandel's case, the therapeutic procedure "treats punishment as a source of solace for the victim, a cathartic expression, a moment of closure. If the punishment is for the benefit of the victim, then the victim should have a say in what the punishment is" (Sandel 2005, 106). In Sandel's case the person who receives the therapy is the victim, whereas in Confucius's case it is the immoral agent who receives the therapy.

29. This is entirely possible, as Sandel sometimes does make similar claims. For example, in discussing the case of Callie Smartt, a popular freshman cheerleader, Sandel states that "in choosing its cheerleaders, the high school . . . makes a statement about the qualities it hopes students will *admire* and *emulate*" (2009, 186; emphasis added); and he also describes the Aristotelian approach to justice as "allocating goods to reward and *promote* virtue" (108; emphasis added). In this context, when Sandel says that political offices are to be distributed to honor, reward, and recognize relevant virtues, we should better understand him as saying that they are distributed to promote relevant virtues by honoring, recognizing, and rewarding those with relevant virtues, so that others will emulate them. If so, we might say that Sandel's view is after all the same as the Confucian view. However, even if this is the case (and it seems that it can be the case), we cannot fail to notice a couple of differences between them. On the one hand, in Sandel's version other people will emulate the virtuous because the virtuous hold political office. If they are not interested in such political office, they will lack the motivation to emulate the virtuous. On the Confucian model the virtuous should hold political office only because their exemplary behaviors can be better and more widely emulated by common people. On the other hand, we have to return to

the question of what relevant virtues these political leaders are to possess. On Sandel's Aristotelian model, the virtues those political offices are to reward, recognize, and honor, as we have seen, are those related to legislating laws, so they must also be virtues that the government promotes and encourage people to emulate. But is it really necessary for every citizen to have such virtues, given that only a small number of people are needed to make laws in any given society at any given time? In contrast, in the Confucian model, as we have seen, the virtues that political leaders ought to have and that they aim to make common people possess are moral virtues, virtues that everyone, whether a political leader or a common person, in order to be a healthy or nondeficient human being, must possess.

References

Analects. In *The Analects Annotated and Translated* 論語譯注, by Yang Bojun 楊伯峻. Beijing: Zhonghua Shuju.

Aristotle. 1963. *Nicomachean Ethics*. Translated by W. D. Ross. In *The Works of Aristotle*, vol. 9. Oxford: Oxford University Press.

Byerly, T. Ryan, and Meghan Byerly. 2016. "Collective Virtue." *Journal of Value Inquiry* 50:33–50.

Cohen, G. A. 2002. *If You're an Egalitarian, How Come You're So Rich?* Cambridge, MA: Harvard University Press.

Daodejing. In *Annotations and Interpretations of Laozi* 老子校釋. Beijing: Zhonghua Shuju.

Fricker, Miranda. 2010. "Can There Be Institutional Virtues?" *Oxford Studies in Epistemology* 3:235–252.

Gregory, James. 2015. "Engineering Compassion: The Institutional Structure of Virtue." *Journal of Social Philosophy* 44:339–356.

Huang, Yong. 2010. "The Self-Centeredness Objection to Virtue Ethics: Zhu Xi's Neo-Confucian Response." *American Catholic Philosophical Quarterly* 84:651–692.

————. 2013. *Confucius: A Guide for the Perplexed*. London: Bloomsbury.

Keyt, David. 1985. "Distributive Justice in Aristotle's *Ethics* and *Politics*." *Topoi* 4:23–45.

Kongzi Jiayu 孔子家語 (*Confucius's Family Sayings*). 2009. Beijing: Beijing Yanshan Chubanshe.

Kraut, Richard. 2002. *Aristotle: Political Philosophy*. Oxford: Oxford University Press.

LeBar, Mark. 2014. "The Virtue of Justice Revisited." In *The Handbook of Virtue Ethics*, edited by Stan van Hooft. Bristol, CT: Acumen.

Li, Ling 李零. 2007. *A Homeless Dog: My Reading of the* Analects 喪家狗：我讀《論語》. Taiyuan: Shanxi Renmin Chubanshe.

Li, Zehou 李澤厚. 1999. *A Contemporary Reading of the* Analects 《論語》今讀. Hong Kong: Tiandi Tushu.

Liji 禮記 (*The Book of Rites*). 2004. In *The Book of Rites Annotated and Translated* 禮記譯注, by Yang Tianyu 楊天宇. Shanghai: Shanghai Guji Chubanshe.

Mencius. 2005. In *The Mencius Annotated and Translated* 孟子譯註, by Yang Bojun 楊伯峻. Beijing: Zhonghua Shuju.

Pakaluk, Michael. 2005. *Nicomachean Ethics: An Introduction.* Cambridge: Cambridge University Press.

Rawls, John. 1999. *A Theory of Justice,* rev. ed. Cambridge, MA: Harvard University Press.

Sandel, Michael J. 1982. *Liberalism and the Limits of Justice.* Cambridge: Cambridge University Press.

———. 1996. *Democracy and Its Discontents: America in Search of a Public Philosophy.* Cambridge, MA: Harvard University Press.

———. 2005. *Public Philosophy: Essays on Morality in Politics.* Cambridge, MA: Harvard University Press.

———. 2009. *Justice: What's the Right Thing to Do?* New York: Farrar, Straus and Giroux.

———. 2011. "[Distinguished Lecture on] *Justice: What's the Right Thing to Do?*" *Boston University Law Review* 91:1303–1310.

Sandin, Per. 2007. "Collective Military Virtues." *Journal of Military Ethics* 6:303–314.

Slote, Michael. 2009. *Moral Sentimentalism.* Oxford: Oxford University Press.

———. 2016. "Moral Self-Cultivation East and West: A Critique." *Journal of Moral Education* 45 (2): 192–206.

Swanson, Judith A. 2011. "Michael J. Sandel's *Justice: What's the Right Thing to Do?:* A Response of Moral Reasoning in Kind, with Analysis of Aristotle's Examples." *Boston University Law Review* 91:1375–1403.

Wang, Yangming 王陽明. 1992. *The Complete Works of Wang Yangming* 王陽明全集. Shanghai 上海: Shanghai Guji Chubanshe 上海古籍出版社.

Zingano, Marco. 2013. "Natural, Ethical, and Political Justice." In *The Cambridge Companion to Aristotle's* Politics, edited by Marguerite Deslauriers and Pierre Destree. Cambridge: Cambridge University Press.

Ziv, Anita Konzelmann. 2012. "Institutional Virtue: How Consensus Matters." *Philosophical Studies* 161:87–96.

Zuozhuan 左傳. 1900. In *Annotations to the Zuo Commentary on the* Spring and Autumn Annals 春秋左傳注, by Yang Bojun 楊伯峻. Beijing: Zhonghua Shuju 中華書局.

II
Civic Virtue and Moral Education

— 4 —

Sandel's Ideas on Civic Virtue

ZHU HUILING

Michael Sandel's political theory has become a popular topic in China. From the 1990s up through the beginning of the twenty-first century, Chinese scholars who studied contemporary political philosophy focused largely on Sandel's criticisms of John Rawls's theory of justice. In particular, they zeroed in on Sandel's conception of the constitutive self, his prioritization of the good over the right, and his criticisms of neutrality. They also studied the debate between liberalism and communitarianism. In recent years, with the publications of *Democracy's Discontent, Public Philosophy, What Money Can't Buy: The Moral Limits of Markets,* and especially *Justice: What's the Right Thing to Do?,* Sandel's political philosophy has generated enormous publicity in China, in both academia and the public sphere. People began to reflect on what justice specifically means, what kind of justice we talk about and pursue, how to think about the moral dilemmas in our daily life, the harm of market reasoning and more generally, the moral defects inherent in a market-based society. In a word, Sandel's political philosophy has inspired both scholars and the lay public to think about day-to-day moral questions with the help of political theory. And the keen interest that the Chinese people have shown in Sandel's theory of justice springs from an emptiness and discontent in public philosophy here. With the rapid development of our burgeoning market economy, the Chinese need political theory and moral discourse in order to deal with the many problems that market-based reasoning brings with it.

Sandel's political philosophy has shown that it is capable of meeting these needs and enabling the public to realize and discuss those problems more deeply and efficiently.

However, most Chinese scholars still adhere to the "communitarian" label, thinking that Sandel is a communitarian and taking him to be one of the most prominent representatives of communitarianism: an ethico-political theory that emphasizes communal values, most prominently formulated in response to (and in part as a rejection of) John Rawls's theory of justice. While Sandel does emphasize the value of communities, what's more is that he is specifically trying to revive the tradition of civic republicanism in contemporary times. I have shown in several papers[1] that it is more appropriate to think of his political philosophy as a form of republicanism rather than communitarianism.

For one thing, his understanding of the common good is different from that found in communitarianism. Sandel asserts that values shared within a group may not fully realize or sustain their common good. What's more, the community's conception of the good does not only depend on whatever values happen to prevail in a particular community, but more importantly rely on public deliberation; and deliberation regarding the common good is not necessarily embodied in the community or in its shared tradition. Therefore, in Sandel's opinion, the conception of the common good could be in tension with the tradition of the community. The common good won't just accept the values that happen to be popular; on the contrary, it could offer a critical perspective on these values and the common good of the community and thus avoid the risk of majoritarianism inherent in the communitarian approach. Sandel's way of understanding the common good and his emphasis on deliberation conforms to the theory of republicanism more than it does communitarianism.

For another thing, he advocates the combination of politics and morality as a republican. He thinks that it is not only wrong-headed, but downright impossible to detach morality from politics. Rights cannot and should not be prior to the good, and it is neither desirable nor possible for the government to be neutral. For Sandel, this is the reason why contemporary citizens are discontent, feeling empty and lonely in their daily life (1998, 4). On the contrary, Sandel thinks that we should rebuild the relationship between politics and morality; that politics should be morally justified and that the government has the responsibility to advocate a way of good life. Meanwhile, politics and the citizens should pay more attention to the common good and civic virtue, citizens should participate in public affairs. In his political philosophy, civic participation is not an instrumental means of protecting individual rights, it is essential part of human nature, it is essential for being a citizen. Citizens should deliberate on the common good, and how to realize the common good and the kind of life that is worth living. Thus he takes freedom to denote participation in public affairs rather than the ability to perform or refrain from performing an action, where the decision is ultimately grounded in one's arbitrary and nonrational desires. Freedom is self-government, which requires resources such as civic participation, and deliberation about the common good and the good life.

Based on the above conceptions of the common good and freedom, along with his emphasis on civic participation, public deliberation, and disapproval of governmental neutrality, I think it is more appropriate to understand Sandel's political theory from the perspective of republicanism, and to read him as a republican who advocates a strong version of civic republicanism in particular, with the ultimate goal of replacing liberalism with civic republicanism in contemporary political philosophy.

The Importance of Civic Virtue in Sandel's Theory of Republicanism

As a Republican, Sandel pays much attention to civic virtue in his political philosophy. From *Democracy's Discontent* to *Justice: What's the Right Thing to Do?*, he has been emphasizing the importance of civic virtue. He has also proposed another kind of justice: specifically, a form of justice based on virtue, as opposed to a form grounded in utilitarianism or liberalism (Sandel 2009, 260). In fact, in Sandel's political theory, civic virtue is a key factor that it combines with other core ideas of civic republicanism such as common good, freedom, civic participation, and makes those essential ideas become a system.

Firstly, civic virtue is essential to the common good. Pursuing the common good is indeed one of the typical characteristics of civic republicanism. As I said above, Sandel emphasizes the common good, but he conceives of it in different terms than the sort of common good based on the shared value of communities advocated by communitarians. According to the elaboration by Iseult Honohan (2002, 150–152), there are four different understandings of what is meant by "the common good," the first three of which are: 1) the corporate good of a social group—a kind of unitary good of an organic or corporate whole directed toward a single purpose (e.g., Rousseau's general will); 2) the aggregate or sum of all individual goods; 3) the ensemble of conditions for individual goods. The third understanding of the common good is the sense in which liberals from Locke to Rawls have understood the common good. Some instrumental republicans (such as Quentin Skinner 1985) also approve of this sense of the common good, as they think that political participation and civic virtue are the necessary preconditions for the realization of diverse personal goods (Honohan 2002, 152). Honohan argues that this sense of common good entails an instrumental account of civic virtue. However, Sandel does not subscribe to any of the three conceptions of the common good listed above.

As a civic republican, Sandel resists the instrumental interpretation of the common good and thinks that this concept should not be translated directly into a "shared values" model, such as that advocated by communitarians. What's more, Sandel does not believe that the common good should be understood as a unitary, corporate good like the general will. Instead, he advocates what Honohan describes as the fourth kind of common good which is intersubjective and practical. According to Sandel and the Republican tradition, all citizens are interdependent and interconnected with each other, which is also why Sandel thinks that we are all constitutive selves: story-telling beings that bond with others. When understood in this way, the forming of the common good depends on shared values, while its realization depends on citizens pursuing the good life. For one thing, this form of the common good requires deliberation on the part of its members in order to prevent it from devolving into a "unitary" good, or one that is based on whatever values happen to prevail in the community. This implies that the realization of the common good depends on member participation. That is why civic virtue is important for achieving the common good: since active membership supports social practice, civic virtue is a necessary condition for sustaining the common good. It also equips citizens with the know-how necessary to deliberate on the common good and then realize it. Civic virtue emphasizes acting in a way that promotes the common good. Citizens who possess civic virtue would care more about the common good, and would consciously act in a way that prioritizes the common good over personal benefits. Civic virtue also helps citizens deliberate better on the nature of justice and the good life, and thus better reflect on social institutions such as the judicial system. As Sandel himself puts it, "when politics goes well, we can know a good in common . . . that we cannot know alone" (Sandel 1982, 183).

Secondly, freedom is in some sense a kind of civic virtue. People often think that freedom and civic virtue conflict with each other, since the former is believed to be about individual liberty and individual rights, while the latter connotes responsibility and social obligation. However, these two concepts are not in tension with each other in Sandel's brand of republicanism, since he subscribes to a different understanding of freedom that avoids the classical division between negative and positive freedom endemic to liberalism: namely, the tension between non-interference and self-mastery, respectively.

Instead, Sandel posits that mutual participation in self-government is itself the essence of freedom, and that freedom lay only in self-government and civic participation. Sandel writes: "The republican conception of freedom, unlike the liberal conception, requires a formative politics, a politics that cultivates in citizens the qualities of character that self-government requires" (2005, 10). Sandel argues against the liberal vision of freedom, criticizing it for lacking the civic resources to sustain self-government. Unlike other republicans such as Skinner and Philip Pettit, Sandel thinks self-government is essentially valuable, rather than merely instrumentally valuable. In other words, self-government is not valuable simply because it safeguards individual rights; it is a necessary condition for meaningful citizenship. Thus, Sandel doesn't understand freedom as denoting non-interference or non-domination, but as referring to self-government. He writes, "I am free insofar as I am a member of a political community that controls its own fate and is a participant in the decisions that govern its affairs . . . the republican sees liberty as internally connected to self-government and the civic virtue that sustain it" (Sandel 1998 25–27).

When we conceive of freedom as self-government, we understand that freedom is bound up with civic virtue, since the concept of civic virtue itself entails a commitment to self-government, and self-government is possible only when civic virtue prevails. For another thing, freedom requires civic virtue, given that freedom is not something one can achieve solely through individual effort, but a thing that must be cultivated and developed. The community as a whole plays a significant part in fostering self-government. Therefore, citizens who want to be self-governed or free ought to recognize that civic duty is what makes self-government possible in the first place.

Sandel follows Aristotle and Hannah Arendt in defining freedom in terms of political participation, and he sees participation as an intrinsic part of freedom. To realize freedom through civic participation, the common good cannot be fixed; if it is, and citizens are forced to act in accordance to some goal or common good, then they are not free.

Thus, Sandel's conception of freedom requires that citizens have enough civic virtues to better deliberate on the common good and participate in public affairs.

The third point is that civic virtue sustains civic participation. Civic participation is an essential part in Sandel's republicanism, as it is about deliberating on the common good, public affairs, and lastly realizing self-government. What's more, civic participation is itself a kind of civic virtue. Sandel's republicanism requires citizens to participate in public affairs. It is not solely concerned with protecting individual rights, but also demands a kind of political obligation or civic duty of every citizen. Civic virtue in republicanism includes political participation, since in the tradition of republicanism, virtue not only refers to something moral, but also connotes ability. To be "good" at something requires that one possess at least the ability to do that thing. Saying that someone is a good musician means that he or she is good at playing one or more musical instruments, and / or that he or she has the ability to play good music. Accordingly, Sandel says, when we say that a citizen possesses civic virtue, we are not only praising those citizens concerned with the common good, actively participating in public affairs or undertaking political obligations; more importantly, we say that citizens are good insofar as they display good abilities when participating. Civic virtue includes the meaning of "good" at deliberating about the common good, putting the common good prior to individual interest. Therefore, civic participation requires civic virtue in order to sustain it. Sandel thinks that the polity, the government, and society as a whole must cultivate civic virtue in order to sustain political participation. Because of this, he recommends that we stress the value and practice of civic education in order to equip citizens with civic virtue so that they could therefore participate in public affairs effectively.

Above all else, civic virtue is the most crucial component of Sandel's civic republicanism. It concerns the formation of the common good, is inextricably linked with freedom, and it sustains civic participation.

In other words, it takes the central ideas of civic republicanism and combines them to make a system.

However, while Sandel devotes much attention to civic virtue and believes it to be crucial to civic republicanism, the concept inevitably encounters some objections which challenge the very notion of civic virtue as well as the worth that republicans like Sandel ascribe to it.

Understanding Civic Virtue

One of the challenges to the idea of civic virtue is that civic virtue in republicanism is oppressive. It is worth noting here that civic virtue in republicanism differs from the concept as it appears in liberal thought. Some liberals also admit to the value of—and even promote—civic virtues such as tolerance, respect, reason, and a sense of justice (Rawls 1988, 263). Civic virtue in republicanism has a deep relationship with the common good. One the most typical characteristics of civic virtue is recognizing the common good and taking the common good to be prior to personal interests and promoting common good. But civic virtue in liberalism does not necessarily function the same way, some liberals even fight against this kind of prioritization. The common good could be unitary as in Rousseau's general will. If civic virtue is about forming and promoting this kind of common good, it could indeed be oppressive and dangerous, as well as do serious harm to individual rights and interests.

As I have shown, Sandel emphasizes civic virtue, but has not yet solved this challenge. Although he declares that the common good he emphasizes is totally different from Rousseau's general will, he does not answer certain questions effectively; questions such as: how can we form the common good in a pluralistic society? How can we guarantee that the common good is not unitary such that civic virtue is not oppressive? How can we promote civic education in a way that is not compulsory? Sandel mentions that he prefers Tocqueville's political theory to Rousseau's, and thinks that the former is able to evade the risk of oppression in a way that the latter is unable to do. Following Tocqueville, Sandel believes we can cultivate civic virtue via public holidays and celebrations, military and religious institutions, schools and certain public institutions. Local institutions and communities can play an important role in bringing citizens together and cultivating a sense of belonging (Sandel 1996, 347). However, Sandel does not go deeper here to illustrate how we can avoid the risk of uniformity or oppression, which could pose a particular sort of danger in cases like religious institutions or schools. Actually, it's a difficult problem that not only Sandel must face, but indeed all the contemporary Republicans who are presently attempting to revive the tradition of civic republicanism. Some republicans, such as Iseult Honohan (2002), define the common good according to interest or common concerns in the hope of avoiding the unitary of common good (158). However, I don't believe that we should conceive of the common good as synonymous with "common interests," since the common good is not only material, but also connotes virtue. So identifying the common good with interest is misguided, because understood in this way, the common good cannot avoid the danger of being reduced to a unitary or oppressive phenomenon. Meanwhile, the common good cannot be reduced to mere interest, otherwise the essence of common good will be changed. Republicans like Sandel need to think about this question and offer a more satisfying solution.

Civic virtue is distinct from general virtue; civic virtue explicitly concerns what citizens should do. In this sense, civic virtue is a role-related concept that refers to the citizen's virtues in the public sphere qua citizen, rather than in the capacity of a family member, friend, neighbor etc. In the tradition of republicanism and Sandel's political theory, civic virtue is the virtue and character that people show when deliberating about the common good and placing the common good over private goods in both action and deliberation. In the modern world, many political theories—especially liberalism—maintain that we should divide the social world into a public area and a private area. Accordingly, in the liberal way of thinking, civic virtue should also be limited to a certain field. Sandel is not unlike the liberal in that he also thinks that there will be a difference in the requirements for being a good citizen and a good person: "One need not to believe that civic virtue constitutes the whole of virtue in order to view it as an intrinsic good, and essential aspect of human flourishing" (1998, 325). That is to say, civic virtue is a kind of virtue which doesn't encompass all the virtues that a human can possess. As Honohan (2002) writes: "it has nothing to say about the accounts of family values, marital fidelity, religious belief, punctuality, industry or self-sufficiency" (164). In order to avoid the potentially oppressive aspect of civic virtue, Sandel does to some extent define civic virtue as explicitly political virtues present in the public arena. However, if republicanism insists on the division of private and public in its conception of civic virtue, it will confront a kind of dilemma. Since Sandel and his republicanism insist that we should not divide politics and morality as sharply as liberal thinkers have tended to do, maintaining the traditionally liberal divide proves to be an impossible feat. When people venture into the public arena to participate in public affairs, they cannot realistically be expected to suspend their backgrounds and moral values, which unavoidably influence their civic values. For this reason, civic virtue will inevitably be influenced by personal virtues. Can we reasonably expect a bad person to be a good citizen? This is the dilemma that Sandel and civic republicans face. On the one hand, they want to confine civic virtue to the private sphere in order to avoid the potential oppressiveness of the concept; yet it appears that such a project is not only dead on arrival, but inconsistent with their own objection to the division of public and private.

Though Sandel emphasizes the importance of civic virtue, he does not specify what civic virtue ought to entail. He does insist that solidarity and loyalty are most important civic virtues in the theory of civic republicanism, and civic virtue also includes civic abilities, such as the ability of judgment, the ability of deliberation, the ability of persuasion, and the ability of action. It seems that he thinks the spirit of republicanism could include many kinds of virtue, but he does not specify in detail the virtues civic republicanism needs, nor does he offer a definitive list of civic virtue, and these factors signal the problematic aspects of his civic republicanism. On one hand, to some extent he must accept some virtues like tolerance, reason, and so on. On the other hand, he must emphasize virtues such as solidarity and loyalty in order to distinguish his thought from that of liberal thinkers. It seems that his political theory intends to combine some of liberalism's more widely acknowledged virtues with virtues more typical of civic republicanism. Nancy Rosenblum defines contemporary civic republicanism as a kind of "Fusion Republicanism", indicating that the theory of contemporary civic republicanism is itself a hybrid theory combining many different key values or items taken from different political theories (Rosenblum 1998, 273). I don't think Sandel's theory of civic virtue is just a random fusion of different theories, however; based on his main concerns and assertions, he is genuinely trying to revive civic republicanism in contemporary political philosophy. However, Sandel does not deny this kind of combination, which shows that civic virtues in his theory have to face the prevailing values of liberalism, specify civic virtues, while keep its characteristic of republicanism at the same time.

In addition, there remains another unsolved question regarding solidarity and loyalty: Loyal to what? In other words, to what (and indeed to what extent) should citizens show their solidarity and loyalty while still laying claim to their personal rights and avoiding oppression on the part of the state or community? As Sandel insists, we belong to different communities, and possess different kinds of identities, but what if different obligations to different communities begin to compete with one another? How can we be loyal to one community without confronting the other identities that comprise us as people? These questions remain unanswered.

Note

1. See Li Yitian and Zhu Huiling 2014 and Zhu Huiling 2014a, 2014b.

References

Honohan, Iseult. 2002. *Civic Republicanism*. London: Routledge.

Li Yitian and Zhu Huiling. 2014. "Freedom, Rights and Virtues: The Core Ideas of Sandel's Civic Republicanism and Its Problem." *Jilin University Journal Social Sciences Edition* 4: 112–123.

Rawls, John. 1988. "The Priority of Right and Ideas of the Good." *Philosophy and Public
Affairs* 17 (4): 251–276.

Rosenblum, Nancy. 1998. "Fusion Republicanism." In *Debating Democracy's Discontent*,
edited by Regan Allen, 273–288. Oxford: Oxford University Press.

Sandel, Michael J. 1982. *Liberalism and the Limits of Justice*. Cambridge: Cambridge University Press.

———. 1996. "Easy Virtue." *New Republic* 2:23–28.

———. 1998. *Democracy's Discontent: America in Search of a Public Philosophy*. Cambridge, MA: Belknap Press of Harvard University Press.

———. 2005. *Public Philosophy: Essays on Morality in Politics*. Cambridge: Harvard University Press.

———. 2009. *Justice: What's the Right Thing to Do?* New York: Farrar, Straus and
Giroux.

Skinner, Quentin. 1985. "The Paradoxes of Political Liberty." In *The Tanner Lectures on
Human Values*, vol. 6, edited by Sterling M. McMurrin. Cambridge: Cambridge University Press.

Zhu Huiling. 2014a. "The Dilemma of Contemporary Republicanism and Sandel's Approach." *Philosophical Trends* 12: 77–81.

———. 2014b. "Sandel's Standpoint of Republicanism and Its Characteristic of Combination." *World Philosophy* 1: 92–98.

5

Sandel's *Democracy's Discontent* from a Confucian Perspective

CHEN LAI

In his book *Democracy's Discontent,* Michael Sandel presents various challenging reflections on American political history. In this paper I discuss several of these from a Confucian perspective.

The Moral Neutrality of Government

"From family to neighborhood to nation," writes Sandel, "the moral fabric of community is unraveling around us" (1996, 3). According to Sandel this situation has emerged due to the contemporary dominance of liberal political theory, especially the moral neutrality of government. The "central idea" of liberal political theory "is that government should be neutral toward the moral and religious views its citizens espouse" (4). Importantly, Sandel argues that historically such neutrality was not characteristic of the American political system, but instead developed only over the past half century (5). The republican tradition, on the other hand, has occupied an important position in the United States since the nation's founding.

Liberalism advocates government neutrality, and holds that moral beliefs should not be expressed in public life. The government should not provide moral guidance nor should it concern itself with cultivating qualities of character or civic virtue. Liberalism requires government only to guarantee the rights of individuals, which cannot be sacrificed for general interests (10). Sandel opposes liberalism and instead favors republican theory, which is centrally concerned with self-governance. Republicanism emphasizes the importance of negotiation among citizens regarding the common good and strives to mold the fate of the community. It moreover requires citizens to hold certain qualities of character or civic virtues, a sense of belonging, and concern for the collective, thereby stressing the moral link between citizen and community (5). Thus, the republican conception of the self is not isolated, individual, and without connections (it is not the unencumbered self). Instead, it emphasizes personal obligations, including obligations of solidarity (15). Sandel believes that the liberal position on obligation is too narrow; here Rawls serves as a good example of what Sandel is arguing against. For Rawls, obligations are either "natural duties," which we owe to others by virtue of being human, or they arise in agreements, which may be implicit or explicit. In the liberal view, "The average citizen is therefore without any special obligations to his or her fellow citizens, apart from the universal, natural duty not to commit injustice" (14). Here, not only do citizens have no obligations to one another, they also are without obligations to their community. This type of liberalism has difficulty explaining the basis of civic responsibility and loyalty. In Sandel's view, we are the particular persons we are [and cannot be meaningfully abstracted from our concreteness]. Our connections to a community of moral responsibility that arise in loyalty toward our family, city, state, and nation are extremely important, and cannot be explained through liberalism. We are "members of this family or city or nation or people" (14), and as such we have obligations of solidarity to the communities in which we live—moral responsibilities determined by our membership to them that are prior to our individual persons. Therefore, the moral duties that arise through such membership far surpass any "natural duties" we may possess. Sandel believes that the liberal conception of the person is too thin to support even the civic responsibility that the welfare state demands of its citizens.

Republicanism prioritizes its conception of the good society, and promotes a politics of the common good. It advocates the cultivation of qualities and virtues that are necessary to the common good of self-governance, including a sense of belonging, loyalty, and commitment, all of which are extremely important for realizing self-governance. Republicanism focuses on these moral virtues and does not see them as only private or personal matters (25). For example, in the Supreme Court's 1940 ruling on whether the requirement for schoolchildren to recite the Pledge of Allegiance violated religious freedom, Justice Felix Frankfurter wrote: "The ultimate foundation of a free society is the binding tie of cohesive sentiment. Such a sentiment is fostered by all those agencies of the mind and spirit which may serve to gather up the traditions of a people, transmit them from generation to generation, and thereby create the continuity of a treasured common life which constitutes a civilization" (Sandel 1996, 53). As a Confucian I agree with Sandel's criticism of the moral neutrality of liberalism, as well as his advocacy of republicanism's concern for the community. The Confucian position undoubtedly has an affinity with republicanism's promotion of virtues.

Civic Virtue

Republicanism responds in the affirmative to questions about whether or not government "should cultivate the qualities of character self-government requires" (Sandel 1996, 125) and whether or not morality ought to maintain a voice in public life. Sandel traces elements of republicanism throughout American political history. Drawing on political discourse in the United States since the eighteenth century, Sandel argues that throughout this history the civic virtues and a notion of the good have played an important role in American political thought. Regarding Virginia's 1784 Port Bill, George Mason wrote, "If virtue is the vital principle of a republic, and it cannot long exist, without frugality, probity and strictness of morals"; and Benjamin Franklin similarly asserted, "Only a virtuous people are capable of freedom" (Sandel 1996, 126). Worry over the loss of civic virtue is a long-standing theme of republicanism. Reforming the moral character of citizens and strengthening their commitment to the common good constitute two major republican ideals. John Adams wrote, "It is the part of a great politician to make the character of his people" (Sandel 1996, 127). This understanding is shared, at least in form, by the Confucian tradition, from the early Confucian text *The Great Learning* (*Da Xue* 大学) to Liang Qichao's 梁启超 (1873–1929) *New Citizen* essays (*Xin Min Shuo* 新民说). From a republican perspective, the American Revolution was inherently rooted in certain values. Sandel quotes Gordon S. Wood: "The sacrifice of individual interests to the greater good of the whole formed the essence of republicanism and comprehended for Americans the idealistic goal of their Revolution" (Sandel 1996, 127). For republicans, public interest is not simply a synthesis of personal interests, and the essence of politics does not consist in the pursuit of competing interests. Rather, politics transcends individual interests "to seek the good of the community as a whole" (127).

We thus see that republicanism opposes making pursuit of personal gain a core value, and instead believes that civic virtue can overcome personal interests or selfishness as well as protect freedom. Republicans believe that government should be controlled by persons of virtue and should aim for the common good, which transcends the sum of personal interests, and that, consistent with the traditional Aristotelean view, the government should help shape the moral character of its citizens. These aspects of republicanism all share common ground with Confucianism. However, republicanism approaches these principally through the notion of self-governance. "Central to the republican theory is the idea that liberty requires self-government, which depends in turn on civic virtue" (127).

Of course, republican thinkers differ in their conceptions of virtue. Alexander Hamilton, for instance, focused on the way patriotism shapes citizens, and was skeptical regarding whether or not selfless virtues could inspire loyalty to one's country. The qualities of character Hamilton aspired to cultivate among citizens do not lie in traditional civic virtue but rather in allegiance to one's nation. Hamilton writes, "The more the citizens are accustomed to meet with it in the common occurrences of their political life; the more it is familiarized to their sight and to their feelings; . . . the greater will be the probability that it will conciliate the respect and attachment of the community" (133). Republicanism does not, however, regard government as the primary instrument for enhancing the moral character of its citizens; instead it sees that role played by education, religion, and small communities. The virtues that the Federalists emphasized, in contrast, are largely conservative, including order, compliance, and restraint. They believed that the order and stability of a democratic government rely on religious and moral convictions. The early republican favor for agriculture and farmers sees a life of agrarian labor as the foundation of virtue. Sandel quotes Thomas Jefferson: "Cultivators of the earth are the most valuable citizens. They are the most vigorous, the most independent, the most virtuous, and they are tied to their country and wedded to its liberty and interest by the most lasting bonds" (144). In fact, it seems that the independent farming of early American agrarian society is the foundation of early republicanism. The virtues of classical republicanism are largely equivalent to those of nineteenth-century America's independent farmers. Republicans thus emphasized civic virtue's reliance on an agrarian economy and its lack of connection with urban life. Relatedly, they saw industry as standing in opposition to civic virtues and as a source of corruption, extravagance, and separation from the public good (161).

Beginning in the early twentieth century, republicanism began to increasingly identify public life with urban centers. The 1914 St. Louis pageant "sought to inspire among urban residents a sense of common citizenship and shared purpose" with the successful result that "there came over all the sense of sanctified citizenship, of interest and confidence in neighbor, of pride in the city" (Sandel 1996, 210). These Progressive reformers aimed to "mold a population of cultivated, moral, and socially responsible citizens" (209). Theodore Roosevelt stressed expanding the self-understanding of American citizens in order to instill a "spirit of broad and far-reaching nationalism" (218); Roosevelt believed that "the prime problem of our nation is to get the right type of good citizenship" (218). Sandel describes Roosevelt as holding that "democratic government could not be indifferent to the virtue of its people" and ought to inspire civic virtue of "strenuous dedication to duty" as well as virtues of "honesty, courage, and common sense," emphasizing the need to transcend concern with material benefit (218). Commenting on democracy and civic virtue, Sandel notes that Herbert Croly believed that "democracy had as its highest purpose the moral and civic improvement of the people"; that "the point of democracy was not to cater to people's desires but to elevate their character, broaden their sympathies, and enlarge their civic spirit"; and that "the principle of democracy is virtue" (220). On that view, not only does liberty rely on virtue, but democracy also takes virtue as its aim. This understanding of democracy easily finds resonance with Confucian political ideas.

It is worth noting that, more recently, in the Reagan era there was increased advocacy of the expansive functioning of free-market economics as well as emphasis on the role of morality in public life. The latter called for collective civil ethics, communal values, and familial, neighborly, and patriotic spirit, along with a nonindividualistic ideal of national civil community. This kind of policy received the support of cultural conservatives, who in this period emphasized government concern with citizens' quality of character. Jerry Falwell advocated the revival of Christian morality to save the United States, and George F. Will called statecraft "soulcraft" (Sandel 1996, 309). Arguing that the cultivation of virtue is the basis of free government, Will described this virtue as "good citizenship, whose principal components are moderation, social sympathy and willingness to sacrifice private desires for public ends" (310). Upon his reelection in 1984, Reagan stated, "We've begun to restore great American values—the dignity of work, the warmth of family, the strength of neighborhood" (312). Alongside the power of religion, these values included not only personal virtue, but also the cultural values of American society. "The warmth of family" is not a civic virtue, but a value. The three values that Regan lists are core values of American society, and we should note their alignment with republicanism's advocacy of prioritizing the community in personal values.

As Sandel discusses, republicanism focuses on the virtues of "self-governance" and "the common good" as its core and foundation. This type of virtue cannot but have its limitations, as self-governance seems also to be a political concept. This sense of virtue, like participation in governance, is also political and not purely moral. Looking at this issue from another perspective, we note that the tradition of self-governance is modeled on American rural agrarian or suburban communities. We can then ask whether this model suitable for city life. We can also ask how republicanism views qualities of character and virtues that are not based on a conception of self-governance. Additionally, although republicanism holds that the basis of a good citizen is self-governance, could there be a type of republicanism that does not take self-governance as its core value?

A More In-Depth Discussion of Civic Virtue

Throughout *Democracy's Discontent* the central term "civic virtue" arises frequently. However, Sandel does not make it clear whether civic virtue in this work refers exclusively to public morality or includes both public and private morality. Civic virtue is a requirement of virtue that arises through people being "citizens," whereas private morality refers to a moral requirement that arises through people being "human." Aristotle's *Politics* differentiates between the virtue of a good citizen and the virtue of a good man—the virtue of a good citizen is the morality one ought to possess as a citizen of a political community: "It is evident that there is not one single virtue of the good citizen which is perfect virtue. But we say that the good man is he who has one single virtue which is perfect virtue. Hence it is evident that the good citizen need not of necessity possess the virtue which makes a good man" (III.IV). Aristotle further concludes, "The virtue of the citizen and of the good man cannot coincide" (III.IV). From this we see that the education required for becoming a good person is not equivalent to that required of ordinary citizens. The virtue of the good person, or the virtue of the Confucian moral exemplar (*junzi* 君子), is higher and broader in scope than that of the good citizen, and the requirements of virtue for the citizen are comparatively low. Therefore, it is important to ask whether the republican virtues Sandel describes correspond to Aristotle's virtue of the citizen or virtue of the good man, and whether or not government ought to promote the virtue of the good person.

In modern Western thought there is a distinction between individual morality and social morality. This is seen in Jeremy Bentham's differentiation between private and public ethics, and then in John Stuart Mill's *On Liberty,* which distinguishes "self-regarding virtues" from "the social" (Mill 2003, 148). Influenced by these ideas, Japan became focused on discussions of public morality during the second and third decades of the Meiji period (1888–1908). Modern Chinese thinker Liang Qichao left for Japan following the Hundred Days Reform (1898) and was in turn affected by this. Liang himself distinguishes between public and private morality, arguing that private morality concerns personal character and moral cultivation, whereas public morality refers to virtue that benefits the state and society. In other words, public virtue is virtue that benefits the community and private virtue is virtue of personal perfection. Liang's starting point is patriotic nationalism, and he sees the core of public virtue as the person's conscious understanding of obligations to the community. This is closely related to the demand of the times— times when China desired to strengthen itself but found itself under external oppression—to save the Chinese nation.[1] Similar examples are found in republicanism. For example, Alexander Hamilton emphasized loyalty to the state, but overlooked the significance of "general selfless virtues," seeming to imagine too sharp a separation between political and social life. In contrast, Paul Boyer's discussion of "cultivated, moral, and socially responsible citizens" possesses relatively broad inclusivity. Indeed, the cultivation of virtue advocated by Roosevelt, Croly, and Will includes aspects that stretch beyond the self-government of citizens, such as honesty, bravery, and humility. Thus, if republican virtue is limited to public virtue, then there are a number of questions that republicanism must answer. How should private virtue be recognized and cultivated? How should we understand the relationship between public and private virtue? Should government in modern societies promote the cultivation of private virtues?

In *Democracy's Discontent* Sandel shows that some liberals admit we might be restricted by certain obligations; however, they insist that these obligations only apply to private life and are not politically significant. But even if these obligations carry no obvious political significance, it does not follow that their only significance is to private life. They can also be meaningful for social and cultural life. In line with Sandel, we can then ask: Why should we maintain a separation between the way we think of ourselves as citizens and the way we think of ourselves as people? Why should we separate civic virtue from more general human virtues, and only focus on cultivating civic virtue? In addition to promoting personal virtue, what other values does republicanism support?

Sandel discusses how Thomas Pangle asserts American republicanism to have consistently emphasized twenty-three civic virtues, reminiscent of Benjamin Franklin's thirteen virtues.[2] These virtues seem to be dominated by Protestant ethics or Puritan virtues, which raises the question whether American republicanism's two-centuries-long advocacy of virtue is connected with a certain religious background. Franklin's thirteen virtues were of great interest to Max Weber, who saw them as representative of Protestant ethics. If the virtues of American republicanism are mainly Protestant virtues—or are virtues that belong to the "spirit of capitalism" and are suitable for acquiring personal success in modern society like those Franklin promotes, and therefore cannot be equated with the virtue of the good person advocated in the Judeo-Christian tradition generally—then does this type of republican virtue have its limitations?

From *Democracy's Discontent* we see that the virtues primarily emphasized in American republicanism have historically included hard work, frugality, loyalty, and community. The first two are related to the Protestant work ethic, and the latter two are virtues of self-governing communities or communitarianism. These four virtues can all be said to be virtues suited to modern society, yet from the perspective of virtue ethics they are limited in that they cannot be broadly involved with personal moral perfection. Confucian theories of virtue are comparatively thicker. From the Confucian perspective, the virtue promoted by republicanism is not thick enough.

Comparing republicanism to Chinese thought, especially from the perspective of Confucian virtue theory, we find that personal life in contemporary China principally requires three groups of virtues:

> Benevolence (*ren'ai* 仁爱), moral principle (*daoyi* 道义),
> honesty (*chengshi* 诚实), trustworthiness (*shouxin* 守信),
> filialness (*xiaoshun* 孝顺), harmoniousness (*hemu* 和睦)
>
> Self-improvement (*ziqiang* 自强), industriousness (*qinfen* 勤奋),
> courage (*yonggan* 勇敢), uprightness (*zhengzhi* 正直),
> fidelity (*zhongshi* 忠实), sense of shame (*lianchi* 廉耻)

Patriotism (*aiguo* 爱国), abidance by the law (*shoufa* 守法),
orientation toward collective interest (*liqun* 利群), etiquette
(*zunli* 尊礼),
engagement in public affairs (*fenggong* 奉公), devotion to one's
profession (*jingye* 敬业)[3]

The first two groups of virtues belong to "private virtue," and assert fundamental personal morals for the individual. In ancient Confucianism these are considered the virtues of the moral exemplar. The third group can be categorized as "public virtue," and constitutes fundamental public morals for the individual. In contrast to these, freedom and equality are social values, and not morals for the individual. Comparatively speaking, the virtues advocated by Confucianism are relatively thick. In non-Confucian countries, the individual's fundamental personal morals most often are cultivated through religious teachings and not through government involvement. But in China, Confucian values have been the predominant values of traditional society and culture for more than 2,000 years. These values are Chinese civilization's own tradition. Confucian scholar-officials were the moral educators who served as the inheritors and bearers of this civilization— and yet Confucianism most certainly is not a religion.

The Great Learning opens, "The Way of great learning consists in manifesting clear character, loving the people, and abiding in the highest good."[4] Here we see that Chinese culture has always seen the government as representative of the community and bearing responsibility for the civil education and moral edification of the people. This includes responsibility for molding values and elevating the moral character, spiritual outlook, cultural constitution, and general etiquette of its citizens. This view still influences the contemporary Chinese government's understanding of politics and is a major part of what makes present-day China's political situation unique in the modern world.

Virtues and Rights

If the central principles of Western political thought lie in the prioritization of individual rights and personal freedom, and if we believe that the demands associated with notions of the common good violate basic individual freedoms, then Confucianism can never affirm such prioritization of the right. Confucianism and Western religious ethics both emphasize the common social good, social responsibility, and virtues benefiting the public interest. Therefore, Confucianism can accept the content of the International Covenant on Economic, Social and Cultural Rights and the International Covenant on Civil and Political Rights, but it can affirm this only within the background and framework of responsibilities, obligations, and the common good. Therefore, the ordering of civil, political, economic, and social rights differs between Confucianism and Western culture on the logical level, in the sequence of their realization (which is closely connected with historical circumstance), and especially in terms of the fundamental relationship between responsibility and rights. Here, the Confucian position certainly grants priority neither to rights nor to the individual.

The highest embodiment of the concept of the right is human rights. Human rights have become generally accepted values and ideals throughout the world. But the status of the concept of human rights varies in different cultures. In modern Western countries, especially America, human rights have become one of the most important parts of education. China, however, does not have a historical background of fleeing religious persecution or a history of struggle for independence from a colonial power, nor does it have a history of struggle between average citizens and aristocracy. Since ancient times, and especially within the Confucian tradition, China has not given primacy to the individual's rights and demands on the state. Confucianism asserts that it is the duty of rulers and government to safeguard the well-being of the people, but its focus in this regard is on economic and social rights.

Throughout several millennia Confucian thought has been predominantly the thought of scholar-officials (*shidaifu* 士大夫), who are both intellectuals and members of government. This has led Confucian thought to always and inherently prioritize the demand for responsibility toward society, virtue, and concern for public affairs. Moreover, the Confucian belief in the notion of "rootedness in the people" (*minbenzhuyi* 民本主义) further has required that these scholar-officials maintain a high level of concern for the people's well-being (*minsheng* 民生). In this way, concern for the state and concern for the people (*you guo you min* 忧国忧民) have become the inherent concern and spiritual tradition of Confucian intellectuals. Since the mid-nineteenth century, facing external shock and oppression, this spirit of Chinese intellectuals has only strengthened. Because of this, Chinese intellectuals, who resided in a developing country and were influenced by the Confucian tradition, have been happy to endorse the idea of human rights. However, this acceptance and endorsement will not surpass their established ethical attitude of prioritizing social consciousness and notions of responsibility associated with the concern for the state and concern for the people. Therefore, the concept of human rights will not become an unconditional first principle, but instead will always exist in complex interaction with the Confucian tradition and Chinese cultural values. In fact, this is true of many of the world's great religions, making the Confucian tradition no exception. Such cultural pluralism is the premise and background for the contemporary promotion of global ethics and dialogue between civilizations, and is worth our attention and respect.

Ideal Confucian politics are a politics based in virtue, with a special emphasis on the inseparability of political affairs from virtue. In terms of the relationship between politics and morality, Confucius held that politics could not be disconnected from morality, and thus here there exists no political neutrality. Politics must be founded on ethical principles. Politics separated from ethics or moral concepts are no longer politics. Politics must be comprehended within the context of value judgments of good and evil. Modern political philosophy asserts the independence of politics from morality. That is, it sees political positions, institutions, and principles as separable from society's moral culture, and holds that government should not advocate any moral or ethical principles.[5] This is hypocritical, and the transformation of politics into something amoral is quite dangerous. This changes politics into simply an electoral game where each person gets a vote, and leaves politics without commitment to society, order, ethics, or morality. The result is an absence of morality in social political life. Without the support of a traditional moral force, politics may throw society into moral confusion. The government may not necessarily have to be connected to a specific school of thought or religion, but it must clearly affirm and promote basic norms of social life, human virtues, and fundamental traditional values. Without these, not only are we left without political legitimacy, but politics itself even becomes problematic.

Chinese civilization is the only civilization in world history to maintain [a significant degree of] its continuity into the present day. In light of this, rather than describing China as a "nation state" in the Western sense, we would better call it a "civilization state." After a turbulent and difficult previous century, today China is working toward a renaissance of Chinese civilization [and its more traditional values]. The Chinese government is pushing for the preservation of traditional Chinese values and promotion of traditional Chinese virtues. Aspects of this are comparable to American republicanism, but even more so this push manifests the self-consciousness of a civilization. The virtues being advocated are not limited to civic virtue and political participation, but are more comprehensively oriented toward Confucian virtues and seek to carry out creative development of the practice of these virtues in times of change. Republicanism focuses on community, which empirically can be seen as family, local communities, race, and the state. The population in contemporary China includes dozens of ethic groups, and the construction of the Chinese political community developed along with the resistance to [the later] imperialist oppression that followed the first Opium War (1840–1842). Because of this, the community emphasized in contemporary China must primarily be a political community that transcends ethnicity— that is, the political state. Of course, as Charles Taylor tells us, if the idea of "the state" presents too strong a presence in the process of reconstructing cultural identity following a revolution, this will lessen the role of identification with "society," which is not conducive to the reconstruction of identity. This requires increased attention. These points are all central to a comprehensive understanding of contemporary Chinese political culture.

Notes

Translation by R. A. Carleo III and Paul J. D'Ambrosio.
1. See Chen Lai 2013.
2. See Sandel 1998, 372.
3. See Chen Lai 2014, 467.
4. Wing-Tsit Chan 1963, 86, with slight alterations.
5. See Wan Junren 2008, 152–153.

References

Aristotle. 2000. *Politics*. Translated by Benjamin Jowett. New York: Dover Publications.

Chen Lai. 2013. "Liang Qichao de Side Shuo" 梁启超的私德说 [Liang Qichao's position on private virtue]. *Journal of Tsinghua University* 28 (1): 1–21.

———. 2014. "The Inheritance and Transformation of Confucian Virtue" (*Rujia Meide de Chuancheng yu Zhuanhua* 儒家美德的传承与转化). In *Renxue Bentilun* 仁学本体论 [An Ontology of Humaneness]. Beijing: SDJ Joint Publishing.

Mill, John Stuart. 2003. *On Liberty* (1859). In *Utilitarianism and On Liberty*, edited by Mary Warnock. Malden, MA: Blackwell.

Sandel, Michael. 1996. *Democracy's Discontent*. Cambridge, MA: Belknap Press of Harvard University Press.

———. 1998. "Reply to Critics." In *Debating Democracy's Discontent: Essay's on American Politics, Law, and Public Philosophy*. Oxford: Oxford University Press.

Wan Junren 万俊人. 2008. *Zhengzhi Zhexue de Shiye* 政治哲学的视野 [Horizons of political philosophy]. Zhengzhou: Zhengzhou Daxue Chubanshe.

Wing-Tsit Chan, trans. 1963. *A Source Book in Chinese Philosophy*. Princeton, NJ: Princeton University Press.

III
Pluralism and Perfection: Sandel and the Daoist Tradition

6

Gender, Moral Disagreements, and Freedom

Sandel's Politics of Common Good in Chinese Contexts

ROBIN R. WANG

Having wrestled with the philosophical arguments about justice and the public good from Immanuel Kant to John Rawls and from libertarianism to utilitarianism, the contemporary political philosopher Michael Sandel has considered the ways in which these arguments have played out in the public sphere and concludes, "I do not think that freedom of choice—even freedom of choice under fair conditions—is an adequate basis for a just society" (2009, 220). According to him, "Justice is not only about the right way to distribute things. It is also about the right way to value things" (261).

Sandel's views go back to what he considers the very roots of a just society, which is organized through human values and is inescapably bound up with community. Sandel points out, "A just society cannot be achieved simply by maximizing utility or by securing freedom of choice. To achieve a just society we have to reason together about the meaning of the good life, and to create a public culture hospitable to the disagreements that will inevitably arise" (261). Any theory of justice needs to rest on a certain conception of the good life, because "justice involves cultivating virtue and reasoning about the common good" (260). To further his justice theory, Sandel challenges the viability of the notion of "moral individualism."[1] In its place he promotes a new politics of the common good that has these two possible themes: (1) "A just society requires a strong sense of community and must find a way to cultivate in citizens a concern for the whole, a dedication to the common good" (263), and (2) "A more robust public engagement with our moral disagreements could provide a stronger, not a weaker, basis for mutual respect" (268).

Developing his theories by applying them to such issues as abortion, stem cell research, and same-sex marriage, Sandel claims that such debates cannot be resolved without taking a position on the underlying moral and religious beliefs at play in these controversies and that our position must be openly argued. He asks us to "imagine a politics that takes moral and spiritual questions seriously, but brings them to bear on broad economic and civic concerns, not only on sex and abortion" (262).

Sandel's construction of the politics of the common good resonates with many of the central themes found in traditional Chinese thought and culture. In this essay I will triangulate Sandel's view on the connection between the common good and civic life with the Confucian promotion of moral cultivation for women as represented in the *Lienü Zhuan* 列女傳 (*Categorized Biographies of Women*) by Han scholar Liu Xiang 劉向 (77 B.C.) and with the Daoist celebration of human diversity represented by Zhuangzi 莊子 (369–289).[2] I will also situate all my findings within the framework of traditional Chinese *yinyang* thinking. By weaving together this triangle with a single gender thread, I will show that Sandel's suggestions for a just society can be supported through Chinese understandings of the human body, human society, and the natural world. In other words, both Liu Xiang's Confucian book on women's moral cultivation and Zhuangzi's Daoist ideas on the recognition and elevation of multiple human perspectives serve equally to specify a kind of cultural evidence for Sandel's endeavor.

A more overarching goal of this essay is to provide an adequate response to these questions raised by Sandel: "Is it possible to reason about the good in public without lapsing into wars of religion? What would a more morally engaged public discourse look like, and how would it differ from the kind of political argument to which we've become accustomed?" (2009, 243).

How do we see the role of moral disagreements? Why do we need a moral disagreement for a just society? Sandel does not provide a sufficient philosophical reason for why we need to engage in a moral disagreement. One possible reason might be that he takes moral disagreement for granted, because public engagement and moral disagreements are a part of the deep-seated Western notion of self-government. But is this a self-evident truth? When we turn to traditional Chinese thought to explore the reasons or justifications for a public engagement in moral disagreements for a just society, the different cultural standpoints and approaches can be tricky and complicated. At a conceptual level traced back to the ancient texts, we will see that moral disagreements are actually justified and encouraged, but not really at practical level. It is important to recognize this because in China's modern times moral disagreements, or the freedom to be different from others, seem to be difficult and discouraged.

Inspired by Sandel's vision, in this essay I revisit some old Chinese wisdom that upholds diversity as a mode of social existence, a wisdom that also cherished multiplicity and that can lead to a deepening of the range of human experience. One of my underlying assumptions is that people can be different and society should give a space for those who want to be different. Perhaps this will offer a different angle for responding to Sandel's inquiry: "So how is it possible to acknowledge the moral weight of community while still giving scope to human freedom?" (221). This dialogue between Sandel and traditional Chinese thought might expose a critical and significant value for a just society (not just in the United States but also in China) that can find its place in the political and social climate of our time. We can ask: Can Sandel make Chinese women happy?

Women's Contribution to the Common
Good in the *Lienü Zhuan*

Within the Chinese context, the inherent complexity of human society together with the social issues generated from it can be, like all things under heaven, classified and interpreted in terms of either *yin* or *yang* within their mutual interactions (Wang 2012). The complexities of gender represent another outstanding example. While scholars in the West have argued that gender tends to be dualistic, with gender construction reflecting institutional male dominance, in traditional China gender was correlative and constructed on notions of interdependence and complementarity that are modeled *yin* and *yang,* earth and heaven, inner and outer. This style of constructing gender provided a social space that allowed women a great range of opportunity (Hall and Ames 2001, 84).

The most important aspect of the *yinyang* matrix is that it protected a wide spectrum for differences within a general context of relatedness, connection, and mutual influence. *Yinyang* can be applied to all things that can be seen as opposites, contraries, or poles. As a result of the *yinyang* matrix, in early Chinese thought there was little exclusion of women or separation between men and women. There had always been the woman, female, and femininity as long as there had been the man, male, and masculinity. Both together constituted the wholeness of human existence and understanding. Man and woman lived in the same space and formed a unified horizon. One of the earliest descriptions of the gender division appears in *Shijing* 詩經 (the *Book of Songs*): *nangeng nüzhi* 男耕女织 (men plow and women weave). This can be translated as "The men are ploughing and planting while the women are weaving and spinning." All these activities are necessary parts of human existence and are highly valued, and the gendered division of labors exhibited a relationship of complementariness rather than subordination. Sericulture gave women a constructive economic role that empowered them within both the family and the state.

The "Xinshu" chapter of the *Guanzi* also states: "The ancients said: 'If even one man has to abandon agriculture the people become hungry, while if even one woman has to stop weaving the people are left cold'" (古人曰：一夫不耕或為之飢；一婦不織或為之寒). Women's work is considered a necessary and imperative part of human life; it was not only fundamental to the well-being of the family and the strength of the state, but it also offered great insights and metaphors on how men should govern and be effective leaders. Women represent a cosmic *yin* force next to men as a cosmic *yang* force. In the words of French feminist Luce Irigaray (2012), "Everything is born with her efforts, which are based on her interaction with the male, masculinity, or man" (130).[3]

This *yinyang* matrix can open new vistas for a better understanding of modern social dynamics, including those involving gender, in terms of a vision based on wholeness and complementarity and that could perhaps be employed in the construction of the kind of justice society envisioned by Sandel. One way that this can be conceived, or one way that it has been presented in traditional China, is through stories.

Interestingly, Sandel (2009) holds the view that "human beings are storytelling beings. We live our lives as narrative quests. I can only answer the question 'What I am to do?' if I can answer the prior question 'Of what story or stories do I find myself a part.' . . . To live a life is to enact a narrative quest that aspires to a certain unity or coherence. When confronted with competing paths, I try to figure out which path will best make sense of my life as a whole, and of the things I care about" (221).

In discussing the common good for a just society, Sandel strongly advocates for the role of civic education: "It can't be indifferent to the attitudes and dispositions, the 'habits of the heart' that citizens bring to public life. It must find a way to lean against purely privatized notions of the good life, and cultivate civic virtue" (263–264). Although it is not exactly the same as (but is very close to) civic education, traditional Chinese culture has always paid a great deal of attention to the cultivation of the virtues of its members and their contributions to the common good. Again let's take the gender issue as an example.

Traditional Chinese culture has long held that the actions of women can either support or weaken the health and well-being of men, the family, or the state. Women from all walks of life have been recognized as contributing to the public life of society in their own unique ways. Liu Xiang compiled 125 biographies of women from legendary times to the Han Dynasty in a work called the *Lienü Zhuan* 列女傳 (*Categorized Biographies of Women*), and his work evokes and commemorates an ideal of womanhood that Chinese culture has embraced since its historical beginnings. This is the earliest existing Chinese book that is solely devoted to the moral education of women, and it seeks, as Anne Behnke Kinney (2014) puts it, "to shape the entire female population in Confucian mold" (xxvi).

In the *Lienü Zhuan*, women as daughters, wives, or mothers are generally portrayed as agents in response to some form of conflict, crisis, or dangerous trend that threatens men, family, or state, and it endeavors to show that women's roles and dispositions can have a far-reaching effect on the welfare and common good of society. It values and praises women for their cultivated moral dispositions, and it recognizes their privileged position in shaping the person, family, and state. One goal of the *Lienü Zhuan* is to provide a set of guidelines for the moral education of women, to encourage the cultivation of their virtue, and to compel them to contribute to the common good. Since the time of Liu Xiang"s groundbreaking effort in the Han Dynasty, the stories have permeated all aspects of women's lives throughout Chinese history. From such stories was gradually fashioned a celebrated, sustainable, and enduring tradition of *lienü* 列女 (exemplary women) (Wang 2006, 93–115).

As biography is always determined by acts of representation as well as by acts of construction, so Liu Xiang defines and constructs a normative standard for women (*what ought to be the case*) through stories of women that claim to be descriptive of real lives (*what is the case*). Liu Xiang organized the biographies by placing them into one of seven categories. Six of these exemplify desirable virtues, namely "Maternal Rectitude" (*muyi* 母儀), "Sagely Intelligence" (*xianming* 賢明), "Benevolent Wisdom" (*renzhi* 仁智), "Chaste Obedience" (*zhenshun* 貞順), "Pure Righteousness" (*jieyi* 節義), and "Rhetorical Competence" (*biantong* 辯通). The last chapter, "Vicious and Depraved" (*niebi* 孽嬖), consists of cautionary tales against the vices of women. Each category is supported by fifteen to twenty stories. To better approach these stories, we can construct three distinctive and culturally significant contexts relating to the education of women (Wang 2006, 93–115): virtue (*de* 德), talent (*cai* 才), and beauty (*se* 色). Virtue (*de*) is primarily represented by maternal rectitude (*muyi*), benevolent wisdom (*renzhi*), chaste obedience (*zhenshun*), and pure righteousness (*jieyi*). Talent (*cai*) is represented by sagely intelligence (*xianming*) and rhetorical competence (*biantong*). Finally, beauty (*se*) is represented by a broad but brief presentation of rhetorical competence (*biantong*), as well as in the cautionary tales from the final chapter.

These biographies of the *Lienü Zhuan* reveal a kind of gender distinction that is different from Aristotle's male-female distinction, which he describes as requiring an excitation by the masculine on the feminine, the active upon the passive (Bianch 2014, 2). Aristotle understands the material or female body in terms of a mute passivity or essence that awaits activation by a male form or intelligence; for him, woman is a sign of lack. There is no such connotation with the female in the Chinese context. Kinney writes that the *Lienü Zhuan* demonstrates "how the actions of women either support or weaken the health and reputation of a family or dynasty," but women do this through their own moral agency involving their gendered duties as well as their ability to influence (Kinney 2014, xxviii).

In addition, the *Lienü Zhuan* reinforces the belief that the permutations of *yin*, identified with female power, and *yang*, identified with male power, produce all things and events. There is a danger that the *yin* force will be too strong and come to dominate *yang*—which ultimately is subject to the emperor's rightful authority. So there is a great need or imperative to curtail female influence and mold it to a Confucian value system. Kinney (2014) writes, "The rise and fall of dynasties was at least partly due to the good or destructive influence of the ruler's consort [who was] an essential component in dynastic stability. The right sort of woman would support the imperial house; the wrong sort would topple it" (xviii).

Let's look at a story from chapter 4, "Pure Righteousness" (*jieyi*), in the *Lienü Zhuan*. While walking in the country of Lu, Lady Luyi was seen carrying a little child in her arms while holding hands with an older child. When soldiers from an outside state attacked Lu and were about to descend on her, Luyi put down the younger child, grabbed the older child, and attempted to make a getaway. The younger child cried out, "Mommy, Mommy!" Luyi, however, did not even turn her head while continuing to flee. The soldier asked the little child, "Who is your mother holding?" The little child answered, "I don't know." The soldiers command Luyi to stop or else they would use the bow to shoot her. She did stop, and the soldiers confronted her. "Whose is the child you are holding?" Luyi replied, "It is my brother's child. I saw you coming and, knowing that I have no ability to protect two, I dropped the one and picked up the other one." The soldiers are very confused with Luyi's action, and they said, "A child is naturally most cherished by its own mother. Mothers will be affected deeply if anything happens to their own child. How could you leave your own child and take another's child?" Luyi explained, "Love for my own child is a private love (*si ai* 私愛), but taking care of my brother's child is public righteousness (*gongyi* 公義). I can't act against public righteousness for the sake of a private love. Even if I saved my own child by doing this, no one will accept me in the future, and I will have no place to stay. So I am willing to endure the pain of losing my own child, if that is what it takes to follow righteousness. I can't survive without righteousness." When the military commander heard Luyi's reasoning, he reported it to his king and urged him to stop the invasion of Lu. He said, "We can't invade Lu. Even the women in Lu know how to preserve virtue and act according to righteousness. They are not selfish, but they protect public righteousness. If the women in Lu can do this, then their leaders must be exemplary too. Please withdraw our troops." The king accepted this request and rewarded Luyi with a hundred bolts of cloth and named her the "righteous sister" (*yimei* 義姊). This story illustrates how women exercise their public responsibilities primarily by maintaining their virtue in the immediacy of family life.

This story also portrays one woman's value system, and how she adjudicates among conflicting values. She draws a clear distinction between her own feelings and sentiments, and the righteous action. Yet this and other tales from the *Lienü Zhuan* are also puzzling, and we can reasonably ask why these women do such things. What do they actually have in mind? A possible answer might emerge from a feminist lens. According to Robin S. Dillon (1995), any feminist conception of self-respect must be built on a foundation of relatedness, "for recognition of self-respect involves recognizing one's place in the moral community, as a person among persons, understanding that and how one is related to all other persons. It is this more encompassing vision of the self-in-relation-to others that distinguishes self-respect from the more narrowly focused self-love" (300).

This conception of self-respect highlights the fact that our ability to comprehend and value ourselves as persons depends on being acknowledged and respected by others. The women in the *Lienü Zhuan* attain self-respect because they are honored and esteemed by others, and their identity as moral agents is bound to the community they inhabit. Dillon thus makes it easier to perceive the link between self-sacrifice and a feminist concept of self-respect. She writes, "Self-sacrifice in and of itself is not oppressive or denigrating or incompatible with self-respect. For it is possible to give up pursuing my self-interest, even to give up myself, in a self-respecting manner—knowing what I am worth and so knowing the extent and meaning of my sacrifice" (300). Such insights may unravel the enigma contained in many of these stories. Though deliberately posed in extreme terms, the moral dilemmas faced by these "exemplary women" permit us to glimpse how self-sacrifice may be a significant condition for maintaining their self-respect and self-worth. If they resolve their dilemmas by favoring their private loves, they risk forfeiting not only their public righteousness, but their own basic sense of self as a fully human person. The loss of moral identity equates to an irreparable breach of self-esteem, at least in these stories, and it is more painful than any other loss, no matter how close to their natural desires.

This early Chinese view anticipates Sandel's notion of obligations of solidarity or membership. He writes that, "Unlike natural duties, obligations of solidarity are particular, not universal; they involve moral responsibilities we owe, not to rational beings as such but to those with whom we share a certain story" (2009, 225).

In the West, many female protagonists in fairy tales, such as Snow White and Sleeping Beauty, are unimportant and devoid of any moral agency until their princes come to awaken them. Cinderella endures her suffering until her prince places the glass slipper on her foot and rescues her from cruelty. In Liu Xiang's stories, however, the reason many slaves or ugly women turn out to be empresses or noble in any other way is because of their own inner beauty or virtue (de 德). Does this not imply that a woman can be her own savior and liberator without a man to do it for her? Any woman can be empowered by understanding that cultivating her own inner moral character can bring her a better life, a good reputation, and a lasting legacy. Women can thereby be valued and praised for their own cultivated dispositions and effectiveness, and enjoy a privileged position based on their own merit. Even Mao Zedong recognized that "women hold half the sky." Therefore, Chinese women do not just subordinate themselves to men; more importantly, they are perceived as an important force able to sustain or destroy dynastic power, or even family prestige.

Moral Disagreement and Epistemological
Arguments in Zhuangzi

Sandel (2009) claims, "A more robust public engagement with our moral disagreements could provide a stronger, not a weaker, basis for mutual respect . . . A politics of moral engagement is not only a more inspiring ideal than a politics of avoidance. It is also a more promising basis for a just society" (268–269). But how can we validate the claim that moral disagreement is an important feature of a just society? In other words, what can account for the generation of moral disagreement in the first place? Is this a question of epistemology, or is it a more basic ontological question that comes down to how we understand the mechanics of generation?

Ontologically speaking, only interaction and diversity can lead to generation, and only with generation can there be development, which in turn can lead to flourishing. The *yinyang* matrix is constructed from structures of interactive relationships and the dynamic tendencies that compel them, rather than on the individual characteristics of things in themselves with their own unchanging essences. Newton's laws of motion show the universe to be an immanently ordered place in which the behavior of moving objects, whether observed in the laboratory, or out in the world, or in the far reaches of the universe, obey calculable laws that allow for prediction. Those laws imply that the universe operates with the stability and reliability of a perfect clock. The legitimacy of a universe that works like clockwork is "the idea that things tomorrow, the day after, and the day after that are completely determined from things now through a set of simple rules and nothing else" (Laughlin 2005, 24). Yet the model of a precise, predictable, and orderly clock cannot solve the issue of the generation of the myriad things of the universe: How do the myriad things come into being? As Peter Corning (2002) puts it, "Rules or laws have no causal efficacy; they do not in fact generate anything" (25). The clock metaphor alludes to a metaphysical system that imposes a rational order on both thought and reality. This model of nature can accept only those objects that fit into its own mechanical scheme and must cast out any other type of alternative functionality within a network of interactions. Its result is "the methodological desideratum of reductionism" (Schonfeld 2008, 168).[4]

Traditional Chinese thought has attended to the issue of "generation" (*sheng* 生) to a superlative degree, and in fact *sheng* is one of the most central notions to be found in all of Chinese philosophy. In that tradition, the generation of the world and its myriad things are often understood through the lens of what I have called the *yinyang* matrix of complementary interaction. When it attends to the origin of the myriad things, its use of the term "generation" (*sheng*) simultaneously encompasses the meanings of "life," "birth," and "transformation."

One foundational example of this is seen in chapter 42 of the *Daodejing*, which gives a specific account of the origination of the world from "generation":

> Dao generates [or "gives birth to," *sheng*] One.
> One generates Two.
> Two generates Three.
> Three generates the myriad things.
> The myriad things carry *yin* on their backs and embrace *yang*.
> Through the blending of *qi* they arrive at a state of harmony.[5]

Thomas Michael (2005) writes, "This short passage sets forth the most influential portrayal of the supremely Daoist vision of the stages of the cosmology through its depiction of the sequence of the original emergence of the world from the pristine Dao" (56). Here, then, Dao generates primordial *qi* as one; *qi* separates into *yin* and *yang* as two; pure *yin* congeals below as Earth, pure *yang* congeals above as Heaven, leaving a middle area in which *yin* and *yang* mix and which is called Human; this is three. From within this universe, Dao generates all the myriad things. The conception of the emergence of the world and the existence of the myriad things directly reverberates in all Daoist perceptions of the world, and particularly those that have anything to say about moral disagreement. And Zhuangzi's ideas provide a prime example of this.

Zhuangzi draws a sharp distinction between the actual existences of the myriad things of the world and our own epistemological interpretations of them, and this is where his ideas on moral disagreement become apropos. For him, the ability to disagree is precisely what can assist our efforts to close the gap between ontological actuality and epistemological interpretation. Being able to disagree and freely argue allows us to better calibrate our efforts to fit objects and situations into an internal matrix of what reality should look like, and disagreement about this is inevitable. Nonetheless, these disagreements, if they are honest and public in the spirit of openness, ideally will allow us to appreciate the wide diversity of people, societies, and even our own individual understandings of reality. This openness is what he calls "the equalization of all things" (*qi wu lun* 齊物論)—a state where all things or beings are equally existent but do not value one thing or being over any other; each being, thing, and event has its own distinctive value and merit. The qualifications of size, age, rank, and other worldly classifications are meaningless to him.

Zhuangzi's views start with a basic epistemological cry against "this-that" (*bi shi* 彼是) distinctions: "There is no being that is not 'That.' There is no being that is not 'This.' But one cannot be seeing these from the perspective of 'that': one knows them only from 'this' [that is, from one's own perspective]. Thus, we can say: 'That' emerges form 'this,' and 'this' follows from 'that.' This is the theory of the simultaneous generation of 'this' and 'that.' But by the same token, their simultaneous generation is their simultaneous destruction, and vice versa" (Ziporyn 2009, 12).

Zhuangzi recognizes the inherent values and intrinsic functions of diversity, and he articulates the need for us to be open to alternative perspectives that will shake our common fixed conceptual categories and values. He sees this as a good thing that compels us to take ever higher perspectives that strive for "the axis of all courses" (*daoshu* 道樞) (which can also be translated as "the pivot of the Dao"). When one attains this perspective, one can then respond to all things without limit in a spirit of freedom, unshackled from the epistemological confines of the "this-that" (*bi shi*) paradigm. Through this *daoshu* perspective, one perceives "the illumination of the obvious" (*mo ruo yi ming* 莫若以明).

According to Zhuangzi, each being innately inhabits its own unique place in the greater horizon of all things, and each perspective also has its own inherent right to be taken. The force of his argument is in its compulsion to appreciate the uniqueness of each and every one of the myriad things in the world, and by calling out the situational conditioning of human judgments and concerns to make us aware of them. Once aware of them, we can take responsibility to create a better social space for all citizens and embrace a more subtle understanding of the otherness and differences of all others from ourselves, because every perspective is special to its own situation and speaker. While Zhuangzi has often been accused of being a skeptic, he has a point in that there is no single fixed view of truth that is the possession of a single person's single perspective, and one should overcome the limitations of right-wrong dualistic thinking.

Allowing for multiple perspectives elevates the human mind and allows it to reach for higher horizons (and this is *daoshu*). Zhuangzi writes, "The sage is dim and dense, standing shoulder to shoulder with the sun and moon, scooping up time and space and smooching them all together, leaving them all to their own slippery mush so that every enslavement is also an ennobling. He is there taking part in the diversity of ten thousand harvests, but in each he tastes one and the same purity of fully formed maturation" (Ziporyn 2009, 12).

This orientation leads to a meta-perspective and opens the way to be flexible, tolerant, and aware of the infinite range of possible ways to lead a flourishing life. It requires an open-mindedness that can avoid those blind spots cohering around the "this-that" paradigm.

A Dao-based (*daoshu*) vision of life relinquishes personal, one-sided perspectives and appreciates, even celebrates, different ways of looking at reality that allow for differences, alternative functions, and even personal preferences. Seeing things from the perspective of the Dao is a very difficult challenge; it requires both the ability to appreciate diversified views and the ability to see bigger and more panoramic patterns of the world. Zhuangzi attempts to convey this in his remarks about the cosmic vision of the "True Person" (*zhenren* 真人). Livia Kohn (2014) summarizes: "The True Person observes, looking at things from his unique perspective and understanding what his particular viewpoint is; he witnesses, watching the flow of reality from a detached position; he examines, detecting relations between things and seeing hidden strands of connections; and he comprehends, opening himself to the full clarity and brightness of totalizing knowledge" (45).

Sandel's Question and Chinese Philosophy's Answer

Sandel's discussion on bringing conceptions of the good life into public discourse—a discussion that also certainly involves notions of justice and rightness—compels us to ask another question: How can we discuss the good life in a pluralistic society where people disagree about the best way to live? In his words, "So how is it possible to acknowledge the moral weight of community while still giving scope to human freedom?" (2009, 221).

Because the *yinyang* matrix can serve as a link for relating traditional Chinese thought to Sandel's ideas about the just society, let's return to it once again—particularly in regards to the ways allows a certain conceptualization of the body—in the attempt to formulate an answer to Sandel's question.

One reason for the noteworthiness of traditional Chinese philosophy is that when it ponders the ultimate questions about existence, it often does so by thinking through the human body, and even the natural and social worlds are typically conceived of in terms of an organic human body. One staple feature of this way of thinking is that it holds that any understanding rests on the assumption that it shares the same categorical structure (*xianglei* 相類) with heaven, earth, and the myriad things. The value of the human body is not very different from the value of human well-being as it is discussed in Western philosophy, namely in terms of its position at the foundation of, and ultimate source for, all social issues. To think about a harmonious political order and a just society, one still needs to reason from the position of a harmonious and healthy human body. The human body is often understood as a structurally and functionally complex system that cannot be reduced to simple quantitative or linear descriptions, and this is very much like human society. While both are naturally taken as organic and interrelated wholes based on the human mind's ability to understand the complex schemes of interdependence between any two parts, metaphors of the body are both more primordial and more primary. Traditional Chinese thought sees the basic movements of the body as compelled by the excitations of *yang* and the restraints of *yin*.

Furthermore, in traditional Chinese thought, human society, just like the human body, comprises a vast network of *yinyang* interactions and operations that provides the structures in which all aspects of social practices take place. This understanding offers a way to grasp the complicated connections and continual changes between society's common good and individual freedom.

Much like the interactions of *yin* and *yang* applied to the progress of any given society, the measures of common good and individual freedom can be tracked in their own specific interplays, interactions, and mutual integrations (or the absence or failure thereof; tyranny and despotism are also undeniable features of human history). Like the inherent interplay of *yin* and *yang*, the common good cannot exist without individual freedom, and individual freedom cannot be fully expressed without the common good. When individual freedom flourishes smoothly, then the common good augments steadily, and in an ideal world, one that thinkers both Chinese and Western have imagined since the birth of philosophy, both will naturally regulate the other in the maintenance of their mutually interdependent connections. Neither the common good nor individual freedom exists in isolation; they exist, rather, in a dynamic field of mutual interaction.

Traditional Chinese thought has constructed its own highest understanding of the common good in the strict terms of harmony (*he* 和); it has denoted a distinctive Chinese value applicable to all aspects of human life from the most ancient of times to the present. In traditional Chinese thought, harmony (*he*) directly refers to the common good, but it is anything but sameness or uniformity (*tong* 同). For example, we can find many examples of this in the text of the *Guoyu* (*Discourses of the States*), a fourth-century BC Chinese philosophical writing. In the chapter entitled "Zhengyu" (Discourses of Zheng), the minister Shi Bo (571–475 BCE) is recorded as saying:

> Harmony [*he*] generates things, but sameness [*tong*] leads to replication. Using one thing to balance the other is called harmony [*he*], whereby things come together and flourish. If, however, one applies sameness [*tong*] to sameness [*tong*], then things will necessarily diminish. Therefore, the ancient kings mixed earth with metal, wood, water, and fire to produce the myriad variety of things. They harmonized [*he*] the five spices to adjust the taste of foods, they strengthened the four limbs to protect body; they harmonized [*he*] the six notes to attune ears; they straightened the seven organs to serve the heart / mind, they balanced the eight body parts to complete the person, they laid down the nine regulations to establish pure virtue, and they set up the ten bureaus to regulate the multitudes . . . The ancient kings achieved the highest degree of harmony [*he*].[6]

But the minister Shi Bo is not quite finished, and he goes on to situate this, one of the very earliest recorded discussions of harmony (*he*) in the entire Chinese tradition, in terms of the harmonizing of fla-vors and sounds, saying, "A single sound is not musical, a single color does not constitute a beautiful pattern, a single flavor does not make a delicious dish, and a single thing does not make harmony" (Chenyang Li 2014, 25). Chengyang Li notes that the heterogeneity that follows from Shi Bo's ideas, which is not to be confused with "sameness" (*tong*), is a central feature of harmony that is nevertheless achieved through the wisdom of the ancient kings in their ability to mix and har-monize diversity (25). Like the ancient kings, a good cook, a skilled musician, or a creative artist will all share the same magnificent talent or ability: to mingle, balance, or harmonize very different and opposing elements into an organic whole.

At the practical level, these recognitions should enhance our will-ingness to maintain a space (which some might consider indispensable) for the current social and personal debates surrounding gender issues in our own time (both in the United States and in China). Men and women approach their own circumstances as bearers of a particular social and cultural identity, and this is, in part, what gives our lives their unique particularity; and then there is also gender to be reckoned with. To apply gender considerations to the *yinyang* matrix is to identify and recognize differences that will not always and necessarily secure an equal male and female partnership, even while we intend that matrix to work on a standard of complementarity. In other words, a comple-mentary relationship does not guarantee one of equality. Therefore, the *yinyang* matrix can be easily misused, and it remains much more compli-cated than any mechanistic division of elements because it necessitates a particular frame of reference, namely one of complementarity. Ideally, the gender dynamics accounted for by the *yinyang* matrix should be able to deal with diversity and creativity in all of its many displays, and this will go hand in hand with understandings of what it means for a living body to live in a balanced way.

Chinese women are more than qualified to negotiate their natural rights to inhabit their own spaces, either separately from men or together with them, and securing such a space, to exert their strong influences through a value system that is their unique prerogative. But we must also recognize that there is no individual woman (or man) who can succeed within or through any social structure if it is devoid of the freedom to also allow them to engage in dispute or disagreement, or even to allow them to work across all boundaries of difference, in order to promote social justice.

In terms of the *yinyang* matrix and with respect to its understandings of the human body, gender is ever transformative in the interaction and transformation between men and women: it allows for a person to be male, or female, or both, or none. This means that *yin* is not simply equated with being a female, and that *yang* is not simply equated with being a male. A man has a man's *yin* and *yang*, but in both he remains a "male"; similarly, a woman remains female in both of her *yin* and *yang* aspects. The most valuable and unique contribution that the *yinyang* matrix can offer to understandings of gender construction is that they are always dynamic and fluid. One no longer has to live up to what it means to be a "woman" or "man." A husband and wife can participate in a harmonious relationship of wholeness without having to limit themselves to any static conceptions of gender expectation.

The real significance of the *yinyang* matrix for understanding gender lies in its structural ability to respect gender as dynamic, as something that is subject to the influence exerted by each part(ner) within any own organic whole and that accepts change and transformation at any moment of its functioning.

The *yinyang* matrix recognizes the diversity of women's needs and experiences, as well those of men; it is without bias. It does not assert any single solution, or any one kind of ideal woman, which might be promoted by traditional Confucian ideology, even though that ideology does tend to give priority to "good wives and loving mothers" (*xianqi liangmu*) that will be adequate and fitting for all. In some important ways, the *yinyang* matrix resembles Hans-Georg Gadamer's conception of using interpretative horizons to illuminate our lived experience of, responses to, and reasoning about the world. Both represent efforts to account for the inevitably congealed and framing assumptions that we bring to our perceptions and understandings of lived experience.

We learn something from Zhuangzi about how to become a "True Person" (*zhenren*) with his attention to the notion of *du* 獨 ("solitude" or "aloneness" or even "uniqueness") as an important component that should be integrated into our lives. As we read in the chapter "Under Heaven" (*Tianxia* 天下), "But now Master Mo alone, would have no singing in life" 今墨子獨生不歌, and "In the solitude of one's individuality to dwell with the spirit-like and intelligent" 澹然獨與神明居; we also read, "I will receive the scouring of the world. Men all choose fullness; he alone chooses emptiness . . . Men all seek for happiness, but he feels complete in his imperfect condition . . ." 己獨取後曰: 受天下之垢. 人皆取實, 己獨取虛 . . . 人皆求福, 己獨曲全; finally, we read, "He chiefly cared to occupy himself with the spirit-like operation of heaven and earth" 獨與天地精神往.[7]

In these passages Zhuangzi confirms the idea that any man or woman can come to an understanding of his or her self that is not limited to conventional roles. In the story of the "shrine" (*she* 社) tree, Zhuangzi describes how a particular tree goes along with the social designations that others have applied to it (namely, as a shrine tree), and yet it does not limit its own self-identity to those designations. The tree allows itself to be viewed as a shrine, and that is all; it is happy to just go on being a tree. The social designations applied to it have no significant impact on how it views itself, and even less on how it actually lives. This story is entirely in line with the *Zhuangzi*'s general approach of advocating a view of oneself that is not limited to conventional roles, or even concrete actions. As one possible attitude to be embraced, *du* does not necessarily imply a rejection of social roles or even social values; rather, it offers the opportunity to undertake a critical reflection on them (D'Ambrosio 2012, 2014).

The attitude of *du* offers the possibility of viewing oneself outside of and apart from one's conventional social roles, and it opens avenues for a person to surpass or transcend everyday cultural constraints. For less proactive feminists as well as for oppressed peoples all over the world, it can be a very useful attitude (especially in today's China), but this does not entail self-sacrifice on a par with the kind of self-sacrifice that we have seen in the *Lienü Zhuan*. In fact, this attitude of *du* can motivate—for example, it can motivate one to stand up for one's right to be heard in public debate. For Zhuangzi, *du* is anything but self-pity; it can, nevertheless, allow a person to feel at home with the knowledge that no conventional roles can perfectly fit with the difference that each of us, or even each of the myriad things in the world, embodies, simply by the fact of our existence.

Other ways to view the *yinyang* dynamic in terms of gender is that *yin* is an individual self, whether male or female, and *yang* is a social structure that the individual must confront. The *yin*-self has to create and craft a free space within *yang*-social power.[8]

Instead of having an internal matrix of a gender identification that is male and female, a healthy social structure should allow sex *and* gender to have a space to play freely and appreciate what each person wants to be. This will lead to less frustration and fewer problems. For instance, when a little girl is allowed to freely choose to play with a doll or a truck, she does not have to feel constrained by social norms, or frustrated by certain restrictions. In the spirit of Zhuangzi, when we allow for gender playing, we can reach a spirited and easy state characterized by continuous willingness to be surprised and to be open to the enjoyment of being jolted. The key factor is awareness. One should remain vigilantly aware of the plurality of possibilities, the multiplicity of viewpoints, the continuity of change, and the complexity of circumstances. This leads to appropriate decision making, so one can learn, train, and perfect oneself fully in any environment.

Stimulated by Sandel's work, in this essay I have undertaken a journey to revisit some classical Chinese texts in order to pursue some of the pathways cleared by Sandel's ideas about the just society, but it does so with a road map that might surprise him. This map has led us through Confucian ideas about female virtue, Daoist ideas about the epistemological value of public disagreement, and more traditional Chinese ideas about "generation" and the *yinyang* matrix.

This discussion and application of the *yinyang* matrix to Sandel's thought comes down to a recognition of the value of openness in the face of difference, even if we only want to categorize that in the strict terms of moral disagreement. As Sandel has framed it, openness responds to any healthy, integral, or even imperative ethical stance that allows for not just entertaining difference but celebrating it. This is precisely the stance for which both Liu Xiang and Zhuangzi are trying to make us responsible.

Openness, in this sense, is a kind of ontological requirement for engaging with the processes of generation (*sheng*) of all the myriad becomings without predetermined ideas that would prevent them from bursting forth into the world. Opening our eyes and our hearts, our senses and our awareness, to these becomings is to accept the embodied experience of untamable entanglements, fraught alliances, and fuzzy boundaries that only openness can accept. This openness lets us be like curious children: honest, playful, and taking joy in the myriad things of the world.

The *yinyang* matrix is dynamic and fluid, and it celebrates, just like the interactions of *yin* with *yang*, the interaction of the common good with individual freedom. These interactions, whether they are between *yin* and *yang* or between the common good and individual freedom, are like using chopsticks instead of a fork and knife. The fork and knife require two hands, whereas moving the two chopsticks with only one hand is a kind of harmony in action. The fork and knife both penetrate food. Chopsticks keep it intact—they play only a supportive role in bringing food to your mouth, and they have to work in concert with each other. There is not any single correct way to use them as long as they bring the food to the intended destination, and when and if they do, then it is clear that they are in the proper position with regard to one another in a sort of rhythmical movement. Chopsticks appear outwardly identical, though each is used differently: one held straight, the other moving or yielding to the action of your forefinger or hand. But you can switch the chopsticks, and the one that was straight will now be the yielding one. It does not matter which goes in which position, so long as both work together harmoniously. To paraphrase the famous words of Zhuangzi's happy fish, is this not the happiness of the chopsticks?

In the end, we might indeed conclude that Sandel (or his views) should make Chinese women happy!

Notes

1. Sandel explains that "moral individualism" does not "assume that people are selfish. It is rather a claim about what it means to be free. For the moral individualist, to be free is to be subject only to obligations I voluntarily incur; whatever I owe others, I owe by virtue of some act of consent—a choice or a promise or an agreement I have made, be it tacit or explicit" (2009, 213).

2. All translations from Chinese are my own, unless otherwise noted.

3. Irigaray claims that *she* vanishes in a Western culture based on sameness: "Instead of saying: the world is born from her, and from my relation with her, Western philosophers say: there is Being, there are beings, which is, or are given without anyone who gives. There is, there are, without being born in a way, without any origin. There is, there are, mysteriously there. With the neutralization of his own being and of the whole of the universe, the Presocratic philosopher somewhat prepares our tradition for nihilism" (Irigaray 2012, 4). According to Irigaray, in Western culture man excludes the other: his split from his origin or from nature belongs then to his *logos* for being in control or being a master of things. To solve this problem Irigaray calls for respect for sexuate differentiation, where one recognizes the natural difference between a man and a woman and yet goes beyond this genealogy into a relational world.

4. Schonfeld (2008) also says there are two kinds of European views of nature in the Enlightenment period 1680–1780: "Through Newton and the Scottish Enlightenment, the English view of nature is somewhat like a clock; a machine; whose materials are passive, and whose motions are mechanical. Through Leibniz and the Eurasian Enlightenment, Europeans tend to look at nature more as a web; an organism, whose materials are active, and whose motions are dynamical" (208).

5. Michael 2015, 251–252; translation slightly modified.

6. *Guoyu*, my own translation

7. For a further discussion see D'Ambrosio 2012, 2014.

8. This can be modeled on the *yinyang* strategy of horse riding. This metaphor is from the *Huainanzi;* compare Wang 2012, 124.

References

Bianch, Emanuela. 2014. *The Feminine Symptom: Aleatory Matter in the Aristotelian Cosmos.* New York: Fordham University Press.

Chenyang Li. 2014. *The Confucian Philosophy of Harmony.* New York: Routledge.

Corning, Peter A. 2002. "The Re-Emergence of Emergence: A Venerable Concept in Search of a Theory." *Complexity* 7 (6): 18–30.

D'Ambrosio, Paul. 2012. "The Role of a Pretending Tree: Hermits, Social Constructs and 'Self' in the *Zhuangzi*." In *Identity in Eastern and Western Philosophies,* edited by Jason Dockstader, Hans-Georg Moeller, and Günter Wohlfart. Freiburg: Karl Alber.

———. 2014. "Going Along: A Daoist Alternative to Role Ethics." In *Landscape and Travelling East and West: A Philosophical Journey,* edited by Hans-Georg Moeller and Andrew Whitehead. London: Bloomsbury Academic.

Dillon, Robin S. 1995. *Dignity, Character and Self-Respect.* New York: Routledge.

Hall, David L., and Roger T. Ames. 2001. "Sexism, with Chinese Characteristics." In *The Sage and the Second Sex,* edited by Chenyang Li. Chicago: Open Court.

Irigaray, Luce. 2012. *In the Beginning She Was.* London: Bloomsbury.

Kinney, Anne Behnke, trans. and ed. 2014. *Exemplary Women of Early China: The Lienü zhuan of Liu Xiang.* New York: Columbia University Press.

Kohn, Livia. 2014. *Zhuangzi: Text and Context.* St. Petersburg, FL: Three Pines Press.

Laughlin, Robert. 2005. *A Different Universe: Reinventing Physics from the Bottom Down.* New York: Basic Books.

Michael, Thomas. 2015. *In the Shadows of the Dao: Laozi, the Sage, and the Daodejing.* Albany: SUNY Press.

Sandel, Michael J. 2009. *Justice: What's the Right Thing to Do?* New York: Farrar, Straus and Giroux.

Schonfeld, Martin. 2008. "The Kantian Blueprint of Climate Control." In *Global Warming and Climate Change: Ten Years after Kyoto,* edited by Velma Grover. Enfield, NH: Science Publishers.

Wang, Robin R. 2006. "Virtue, Talent, and Beauty: Authoring a Full-Fledged Womanhood in Lienuzhuan (Biographies of Women)." In *Confucian Cultures of Authority,* edited by Peter Hershock and Roger Ames. Albany: SUNY Press.

———. 2012. *Yinyang: The Way of Heaven and Earth in Chinese Thought and Culture.* Cambridge: Cambridge University Press.

Ziporyn, Brook, trans. 2009. *Zhuangzi: The Essential Writings with Selections from Traditional Commentaries.* Indianapolis: Hackett.

7

Satisfaction, Genuine Pretending, and Perfection

Sandel's The Case against Perfection *and Daoism*

PAUL J. D'AMBROSIO

> Take things as things, and do not be thinged by things.
> —*Zhuangzi* 20.1

In *The Case against Perfection*,[1] Michael Sandel provides a philosophical critique of bioengineering and genetic manipulation. Far from a wholesale rejection of such technologies, *The Case against Perfection* provokes readers to reflect on the types of attitudes these practices tend to foster when used for purposes of human enhancement. Sandel is particularly concerned with the way this genetic revolution promotes a "Promethean drive" toward "overreaching" and "mastery"—a drive that he believes erodes our appreciation of the "giftedness" of human talents and limitations. Moreover, he argues that the technologies in use today have already proven damaging to certain aspects of our moral landscape, especially in terms of humility, responsibility, and solidarity. These negative effects, Sandel warns, will broaden and deepen if the use of genetic enhancement is allowed to grow unfettered.

Others who share many of Sandel's general concerns, such as Francis Fukuyama, have advocated the implementation of concrete regulatory institutions "to control the pace and scope of technology development" (Fukuyama 2002, 183).[2] Sandel's objective—which in this regard is consistent with his work on democracy, markets, and justice—complements and informs the intuition-level arguments proposed by thinkers such as Fukuyama. Sandel's main goal is subtle and, with respect to Fukuyama, comparatively modest. In our times, Sandel argues, science sometimes moves faster than moral understanding. Accordingly, people can struggle to articulate their emotions, grasping for ethical reasoning that cannot fully account for their reactions. Sandel hopes to stimulate public debates (and in many cases he has already succeeded) by sharpening the moral issues at stake and providing a nuanced account of our moral intuitions and their accompanying moral reasoning—with the goal of creating space for better-informed discussions.[3]

Sandel (2007a) proposes two types of ethics to help frame relevant philosophical reflections: (1) the "ethics of giftedness," which invites us to acknowledge that our aptitudes and weaknesses are not wholly products of our own design, will, or ambition; and (2) the "ethics of restraint," which asks us, in our appreciation of giftedness, to rein in our drive toward mastery and domination over the "gifted character of human powers" (83). More recently, in an interview released in 2016, Sandel hones some aspects of his critique when responding to the view that biotechnology may be used to cure social inequality (Heijine and Sandel 2016). He notes that insofar as biotechnology aims at making people fit better into the social world, it distracts us from more fundamental issues. By appealing to our desire for social conformity, genetic enhancements and even modern medicines implicitly reaffirm the appropriateness of the status quo—the very institutions and norms responsible for creating inequality. We are then, to use the vocabulary of Chinese philosophy, *ben mo dao zhi* 本末倒置, or "confusing the root [of the problem] with [its] branches."

Much has already been said, both in this volume and elsewhere, about the parallels between Sandel's philosophy and Confucianism. Ruiping Fan (2010), Joseph Chan (2010), and Li Zehou (2014) have commented specifically on *The Case against Perfection* from a Confucian standpoint. Meanwhile, scholars have largely glossed over the surprising tendency of some of Sandel's arguments from *The Case against Perfection* and the more recent interview to resonate with traditional Daoist perspectives—even though the traditional understanding of Daoist reasoning differs markedly from Sandel's reasoning.[4] My goal in this essay is to explore ways in which that "black sheep" of the Chinese tradition, Daoism, can itself be put in dialogue with Sandel. In fact, Daoist reflections on some of the philosophical and moral questions raised by scientific developments in bioengineering and genetic manipulation may have even more to contribute to Sandel's case than their Confucian counterparts.

On the surface, a link between Sandel's critiques and Daoism seems unlikely. Sandel is a staunch moralist whose philosophy highlights the importance of the human community, whereas the Daoist philosophies of the *Laozi* 老子 (or *Daodejing* 道德經) and the *Zhuangzi* 莊子 are exceedingly skeptical of social institutions, explicitly anti-anthropocentric, and amoral. Yet Daoist philosophies can be seen as sympathetic to certain aspects of Sandel's call for a deep consideration of an "ethics of giftedness," an "ethics of restraint," and a critical consideration of the moral status of social organization.

There are three key concepts in Daoist thought that can be directly related to, and shine new light upon, Sandel's arguments. First is the rejection of the sort of procedural calculations traditionally associated with a utilitarian conception of social roles, virtue, and profit. This calculative way of thinking, which admittedly is born of the institutionalization (and probably misreading) of competing schools of thought in early China, is later summarized as "mechanical thinking," or more literally the "mechanical heart-mind" (*ji xin* 機心). The well-known Daoist ideals of "spontaneity" or "self-so" (*ziran* 自然) and "non-assertive action" or "non-interference" (*wu wei* 無為) can be viewed as proto-alternatives to this "mechanical heart-mind." They ask us to reflect on how we interact with other people, things, and nature, as well as on the attitudes that these interactions foster.

Second, "knowing satisfaction," "knowing what is enough," or "mastering satisfaction" (*zhi zu* 知足)[5] is an important part of the foundation for the critique of, and itself another alternative to, the "mechanical heart-mind." "Knowing satisfaction," especially as it appears in the *Laozi*, is a caution against overindulgence. It asks us to think about what we actually need, and to realize that excess only perpetuates a continual rising of one's expectations, which in turn shifts the focus from feelings of gratification to the desire to attain more and more.

The third concept is the description of the "*zhen*uine person" or "sage" (*zhen ren* 真人) in the *Zhuangzi*.[6] In my own interpretation of this term, which closely follows both traditional and contemporary Chinese commentary, an investigation of the *zhen*uine person reveals the Daoist philosophy of *genuine pretending* (D'Ambrosio 2012, 2014; Moeller and D'Ambrosio 2017). This concept, which should not be confused with mere pretense, describes the person's ability to maintain a critical distance from social norms and roles while performing them. In many ways, it is the existential application of "spontaneity," "non-assertive action," and "knowing satisfaction" in the social sphere.

My aim in this essay is to demonstrate how the Daoist philosophy of the *Laozi* and the *Zhuangzi* can provide new perspectives on Sandel's arguments against the use of genetic engineering for enhancement. Paradoxically, it is precisely the amoralism and deflation of human importance in Daoist philosophy that allow it to make considerable contributions. I will begin by outlining Sandel's critique of human bioengineering for the purposes of enhancement, as provided in his book *The Case against Perfection* and his interview as part of the series *The Perfect Human Being* (Heijine and Sandel 2016). Then I will discuss "mechanical heart-mind," "knowing satisfaction," and the Daoist philosophy of genuine pretending and put these perspectives in dialogue, arguing that Sandel's "case" is in line with, and can be further bolstered by, Daoist philosophy.

Sandel: Ethics of Giftedness, Restraint, and Social Intuitions

Sandel begins *The Case against Perfection* by rejecting some of the common liberal objections to cloning and genetic engineering. Responding first to the "autonomy objection," that "cloning is wrong because it violates the child's right to autonomy," Sandel argues that this objection "wrongly implies that, absent a designing parent, children are free to choose their physical characteristics for themselves" (Sandel 2007a, 6–7). Next he deals with objections based on an idea of "fairness." Some might claim that when only some people have access to drugs and technologies that enhance human abilities, they have an unfair advantage. But this reasoning is also flawed because it ignores the fact that there are always some who are naturally more talented than others. Sandel writes, "From the standpoint of fairness enhanced genetic differences are no worse than natural ones" (12–13). Thinking through both types of objections quickly reveals their shortcomings, and neither is able to adequately account for the moral hesitation we feel about genetic enhancement.

The above objections are more often the result of a desperate attempt to find a rational foundation for emotional grievances than the conclusion of well-thought-out arguments. Sandel then sets out to enrich public debate by replacing these concerns with ones that hold more moral weight. He constructs his investigation as a discussion of the threat to human dignity posed by enhancement practices. His basic question is this: "What aspects of human freedom or human flourishing do [enhancement technologies] threaten?" (24).

Discovering the moral force of this threat means probing the deeper sources of "our moral hesitation about people who seek genetic enhancements" (8). The analysis therefore begins from an emotional discomfort rather than a (purely) rational one. In fact, as the concrete starting point for critical reflection, nearly every aspect of Sandel's philosophy takes a serious look at the feelings we have, the commitments we hold dear, and the contradictions we unwittingly adhere to—about anything from mundane daily decisions to society's most pressing moral issues.[7] Moreover, instead of ignoring these factors, or laying them aside as if humans were purely rational calculating machines, Sandel's philosophy suggests that these emotional elements are deciding factors in moral reasoning.[8] In other words, our "moral hesitation" or "unease" toward genetic enhancements should be taken as important elements in philosophical debate (2007a, 8–9). Sandel's aim is to explain the moral issues behind feelings of apprehensiveness about biotechnological enhancements.

The major framework underlying Sandel's analysis can be directly attributed to his Aristotelian approach. He writes, "Arguments about the ethics of enhancement are always, at least in part, arguments about the telos" (38). Sports offer a concrete example. When deliberating on an issue in sports, Sandel argues, we turn to the "point, of the sport in question, and the virtues relevant to the game" (38). So when thinking about what makes people so upset about the illegal use of enhancement drugs in sports, it is important to first decide on the telos of the sport—which helps to clarify the reason behind people's emotions and, in turn, determine the exact problem. However, Sandel (as he openly admits) does not claim to know of any one fixed telos for human nature or human life. He has a much more dynamic understanding of human beings and human life—one that does not necessitate a single telos.

Instead of questioning whether, or to what extent, genetic manipulation may violate our human nature or its telos (a line of questioning that would require a definition of that nature), Sandel explores how these technologies transform our relationships to our bodies, others, society, and nature—particularly in terms of the accompanying attitudes those technologies implicitly foster. The hesitation he identifies and the arguments he proffers have more to do with the *treatment* of human nature than they do human nature itself. In this way, Sandel's discussion remains more or less silent on the nature-versus-nurture debate, and thus offers a perspective that remains theoretically compatible with positions on either extreme (such as biological determinism and Marxism).

Even though Sandel does not provide an exact description of human nature or the telos of human life, his talk about an "appreciation of giftedness" guides the orientation of his reasoning. Regarding embryonic gene identification and manipulation, or "designer children," Sandel writes, "To appreciate children as gifts is to accept them as they come, not as objects of our design or products of our will, or instruments of our ambition" (2007a, 45). And this appreciation works in a much wider context as well. From athletic aptitudes to creative capacities, the talents we have are not of our own choosing. Everything from our genes to our socioeconomic, political, and historical environments shapes the growth and development of our abilities. The "appreciation of giftedness" refers to recognizing the fact that many aspects of our lives are not freely chosen. When we do attempt to choose for ourselves, or for others, particular attributes, talents, or capacities that we find desirable, we tend toward an attitude of mastery. Sandel seeks to curb this mastery, urging an "ethics of restraint" to accompany the "ethics of giftedness."

Promoting restraint is a way of curtailing the drive toward controlling ourselves and others through biotechnologies. But this should not to be confused with the autonomy objection, which sees bioengineering as undermining human agency. When we actively dismiss giftedness, we come to take human life, and perhaps nature as well, as a cold series of calculations. The autonomy objection thus maintains that a "wholly mechanistic understanding of human action" is completely "at odds with human freedom and moral responsibility" (26). But for Sandel the problem is more nuanced. His concern is "not the drift to mechanism but the drive to mastery" (27). It is the hubris we encourage when we use biotechnology to enhance our lives. If we restrain ourselves from these activities, accepting instead that we are not wholly masters of human nature, then this positively informs critical aspects of our moral reasoning, which have influence well beyond issues of genetic engineering.

Sandel identifies humility, responsibility, and solidarity as "three key features of our moral landscape" that are transformed by the awareness of not being in full control of our own aptitudes (86). When we overlook giftedness, we undervalue humility and veer toward hubris, mastery, and the impulse to control our own lives or the lives of others (such as our children or our teammates). We then become responsible for a whole host of new issues, such as choosing the right genes for children, or deciding whether or not to dope up for the big game. And we can be scorned for failing in these obligations as well. Sandel calls this an "explosion of responsibility" that is accompanied by a "moral burden" (88). He provides an illustrative example: "Today when a basketball player misses a rebound, his coach can blame him for being out of position. Tomorrow the coach may blame him for being too short" (87). And the problem works in reverse as well. Children who feel they are not tall enough, attractive enough, or smart enough might blame their parents for these lacks. And as this mentality catches on, it will only diminish solidarity in larger circles as well.

Echoing his work on democracy, markets, and justice, in which solidarity plays a decisive role (this is part of the reason he has been labeled a communitarian), Sandel believes that the underappreciation of giftedness has an impact on solidarity that is far-reaching and damaging:

> If genetic engineering enabled us to override the results of genetic lottery, to replace chance with choice, the gifted character of human powers and achievements would recede, and with it, perhaps, our capacity to see ourselves as sharing a common fate. The successful would become even more likely than they are now to view themselves as self-made and self-sufficient, and hence wholly responsible for their success. The bottom of society would be viewed not as dis-

> advantaged, and so worthy of a measure of compensation, but as
> simply *unfit*, and so worthy of eugenic repair. The meritocracy, less
> chastened by chance, would become harder, less forgiving . . .
> [P]erfect genetic control would erode the actual solidarity that
> arises when men and women reflect on the contingency of their
> talents and fortunes. (Sandel 2007a, 91–92, emphasis added)

In other words, the drive toward mastery is already unraveling the moral fabric of society. The further devaluation involved in seeing our talents as being partially contingent will only tear at the fabric even harder. Restraining ourselves by resisting the tendency toward overreaching and mastery can enhance our humility, responsibility, and solidarity, rather than merely our genome.

Anticipating potential objections that an "appreciation of giftedness" and "ethics of restraint" may be "overly religious," Sandel claims his arguments can be accepted on completely secular grounds. One can recognize and be grateful for the various contingencies that constitute one's life or nature without feeling indebted to a God or any other supernatural power. Resolving ourselves to respect that our capacities are not of our own making—and correspondingly, respecting that they *should* not be—leaves room for an appreciation of the unknown. Drawing as he often does from everyday experience, Sandel makes a compelling case: "We commonly speak of an athlete's gift, or a musician's, without making any assumption about whether or not the gift comes from God. What we mean is simply that the talent in question is not wholly the athlete's or the musician's own doing; whether he has nature, fortune, or God to thank for it, the talent is an endowment that exceeds his control" (2007a, 91). Normally we do not presume to know everything about the way we think, feel, or act— or about our natural environment. While we can strive to understand more about ourselves and our world, we must do so responsibly. On the Internet forum *Big Think,* Sandel presents some fundamental questions that need to be considered when we think about the role of biotechnological enhancement in human society. He asks, "What is the proper stance of humans towards the given world? How should we understand our relation to the natural? What is the relation between moral and political reflection, on the one hand, and biology?" (2007b). We can consider these questions and arrive at an appreciation of giftedness and ethics of restraint without relying on religion.[9]

The second objection Sandel imagines is consequentialist. In cost-benefit terms, the above considerations are not necessarily persuasive. Many who advocate for the use of genetic enhancements, including those who directly object to Sandel's arguments, rest their arguments on consequentialist reasoning. But Sandel is not prepared to take such arguments on their own terms. He wants to look deeper. Specifically, Sandel is after at the type of thinking that goes on behind consequentialist reasoning, and the attitudes that this type thinking fosters. In one of his most important (and overlooked) arguments, he provides the following defense:

> My point is not that genetic engineering is objectionable simply because the social costs are likely to outweigh the benefits. Nor do I claim that people who bioengineer their children or themselves are necessarily motivated by a desire for master, and that this motive is a sin no good result could possibly outweigh. I am suggesting instead that the moral stakes in the enhancement debate are not fully captured by the familiar categories of autonomy and rights, on the one hand, and the calculation of costs and benefits, on the other. *My concern with enhancement is not as individual vice but as habit of mind and way of being.* (2007a, 95–96; emphasis added)

With respect to both moral emotions and moral reasoning, Sandel is concerned with the type of attitude that genetic engineering cultivates. His caution is against the way this kind of attitude or mode of being depreciates the giftedness of our lives and the world, feeds the Promethean drive to become masters of our own genetic fate, and promotes an unreflective acceptance of the social and moral institutions that structure our understanding of ourselves (and of perfection).

In a more recent interview, Sandel elaborates on how our understanding of perfection—or even enhancement, improvement, and "good"—is shaped by a shallow acceptance of social institutions. In other words, we do not fully realize the deep effects roles and norms have on the way we think of ourselves and others. He explains, "What these genetic enhancements aim at, fundamentally, is fitting ourselves into the social roles we have." It is disturbing, Sandel believes, "to change ourselves through biotechnology to fit the world and the social roles we have created rather than to question and debate whether we've designed the system of roles and rewards in a just way" (Heijine and Sandel 2016). Similar to the argument about the attitudes cultivated by enhancement practices, Sandel dismisses as superficial claims that enhancements might be used to "level the playing field." In fact, this kind of reasoning is exactly what hinders us from engaging in more penetrating discussions. Sandel says, "I think one of the dangers of seeing biotechnology as a cure for inequality or disadvantage or for poverty, is that it distracts us from reflecting critically on the way we've organized our societies and our economies, and simply treats those who lose out as *unfit*" (Heijine and Sandel 2016, emphasis added).

Pressure to conform to one's social roles has only increased in recent decades. Sandel observes that drug use today reflects this trend: "Unlike the drugs of the sixties and seventies, Ritalin and Adderall are not for checking out but for buckling down, not for beholding the world and taking it in, but for molding to the world and fitting in. We used to speak of nonmedical drug use as 'recreational.' That term no longer applies. The steroids and stimulants that figure in the enhancement debate are not a source of recreation but a bid for compliance, a way of answering a competitive society's demand to improve our performance and perfect our nature" (2007a, 60–61). Ritalin and Adderall are perfect examples of striving for perfection. These drugs are used to keep one awake and concentrated on the task at hand.

They are supposed to enhance one's ability to study, perform on tests, and maybe even write philosophy articles. In essence, these drugs are a bid for greater compliance, greater fulfillment, and a better fit to social institutions. But before we get the other half of children on prescription drugs, or prescribe growth hormones to everyone below average height, Sandel suggests that we think seriously about the very institutions we are implicitly promoting.

Appreciating giftedness, maintaining an ethics of restraint, and critically reflecting on our social roles and institutions are mutually supporting actions that speak to the hesitation many people feel toward the use of biotechnology for the purpose of human enhancement. And they are issues that should be publically debated so that we can decide, as a society, how to regulate these technologies. While Sandel's challenges stand well on their own, they can be further bolstered, and perhaps made more global, by being put in dialogue with Chinese philosophy, particularly some concepts in Daoism that overlap and can be used to enhance Sandel's case against perfection.

Daoism: Spontaneity, Satisfaction, and Genuine Pretending

Early Daoist texts, namely the *Laozi* and the *Zhuangzi,* were likely written in response to proto-Confucian ideas, the *Lunyu* 論語 or *Analects (of Confucius),* and perhaps most importantly the institutionalization of Confucian conceptions of the person, social roles, and ethics. One general argument Daoism has made against (at least some versions of) Confucianism, as well as other influential schools of thought such as the Mohists, can be well encapsulated in the pejorative term "mechanical heart-mind" (*jixin* 機心). Although the expression is completely absent in the *Laozi,* and appears only once in the so-called "outer chapters" (which are no longer generally perceived by scholars to be less "authentic" than the inner chapters) of the *Zhuangzi,* it nevertheless provides a very accurate and concise il-

lustration of particular ways of thinking these texts oppose. Specifically, the term is often used by later Daoist thinkers to illustrate the
type of thinking that can be contrasted with the "self-so" (*ziran* 自然)
or "non-assertive" (*wu wei* 無為) ideals that characterize the Daoist
tradition.

"Self-so" or "non-assertive" action actually refers more to a type
of attitude one maintains when interacting with others or things, rather
than to any specific practice.[10] According to classical Daoist thought,
it is best to approach situations without preconceived plans, fixed
ideas, or an "already made-up mind" (*cheng xin* 成心). One moves
most effectively in the world when one "goes by what is obvious" (*yi
ming* 以明), "accords with what is the case" (*yin shi* 因是), and / or
"follows natural patterns" (*yi hu tian li* 以乎天理). The "mechanical heart-mind" represents one type of antithesis to the more spontaneous attitudes Daoists expound. A mechanical heart-mind is overly
concerned with profit and reputation: it imposes calculations for these
things on the world, and ultimately ends up imprinting them on one's
own mind as well.

Broadly similar to Heidegger's critique of "Calculative Thinking,"
the criticism of the "mechanical heart-mind" in the *Zhuangzi* asks us
to seriously deliberate on why we use machines and how using them
influences our own thoughts and attitudes (Heidegger 1966). When
people become infatuated by machines and calculations, they tend to
operate like machines—simply working toward a quantitative goal
without considering qualitative aspects, or as the *Zhuangzi* poetically
warns, they "become thinged" (*Zhuangzi* 20.1).[11] The "mechanical
heart-mind" is thus associated with an overwhelmingly utilitarian consideration for profit, reputation, and material goods.

In the *Zhuangzi* the "mechanical heart-mind" is described in a dialogue between an old Daoist gardener and Zigong, one of Confucius's
disciples portrayed in the *Analects*. The scene opens with the old Daoist
carrying a pail of water to his garden, when he is suddenly approached
by Zigong. Seeing the amount of labor the man puts in to transporting

just a few liters of water, Zigong proudly tells the gardener about a device that could move much more water with about the same amount of effort. A hundred plots, Zigong proudly explains, could be watered in a single day. With an angry look on his face the Daoist then changes his countenance and laughingly rejects Zigong's proposal. Mechanical things, the gardener says, only lead to a mechanical heart-mind. He claims that he can do the work just fine and has no need for so much water. Having more water would mean that he should have more plants. Although in doing so he could certainly turn some profits, and perhaps some prestige as well, he is simply not interested in either (*Zhuangzi* 12.11).

Importantly, Zigong's advice itself is not problematic. The only objection the gardener makes is to a particular type of procedural teleological thinking that pines over benefits purely for their own sake, without meditating on the work at hand and its qualitative value. In other words, he is scoffing at Zigong's mechanical heart-mind, which divorces potential benefits from the gardener's actual desires or needs (which are not known to Zigong) and, more importantly, from the act of gardening itself. In fact, Zigong's description of his ingenious device is already reflective of his mechanical heart-mind; he assumes that this water pump will serve the Daoist well without first knowing why the gardener is gardening in the first place. From the gardener's own reactions we may conclude that either the gardener does not desire to grow more plants because he does not want, or perhaps does not need, the surplus income he could gain from selling them at the market, or that he simply enjoys the act of gardening, or both. What is obvious is that for the Daoist gardener, selling his plants for profit would be an entirely different activity. Thus, the problem with Zigong is his wildly incorrect assumption that the gardener would naturally want to engage in buying and selling for profit. The end, meaning, or "good" of gardening drastically transforms when it goes from being enjoyed for its own sake to being a mere means to an end. And this move is precisely where our attention is drawn in the critical reflection on the coldly calculating mechanical heart-mind.[12] The Daoist implicitly asks us to consider what we actually need, to satisfy our needs, and not to engage in a constant striving for more (which, as we shall see, can be broadly applied to the social realm as well).

The concern with satisfying needs and desires, which appears quite early in the Daoist cannon, prefigures the skeptical view of a "mechanical heart-mind." The word *zhi zu* 知足, or "knowing satisfaction," is used four times in the *Laozi,* and once in the *Zhuangzi.* The *Zhuangzi* says that those who "know satisfaction" will not tire themselves over the pursuit of benefits—that is, they do not have a mechanical heart-mind (*Zhuangzi* 28.11). In the *Laozi,* knowing satisfaction is specifically linked with *zhi zhi* 知止, literally "knowing when to stop." Translated more poetically, *zhi zhi* can be read as "mastering cessation." *Zhi zu* can likewise be rendered as "mastering satisfaction." Both ideas fundamentally refer to appreciating what one has by stifling the constant craving to continually attain more. Satisfaction in this sense is not measured by gaining possessions to gratify desires. Knowing or mastering satisfaction is the opposite of indulgence; it is about matching one's expectations with what one actually needs as well as one's concrete situation. The twelfth chapter of the *Laozi* warns against indulgence and gives a brief description of "mastering satisfaction":

> The five colors bring blindness to the eyes
> The five notes bring deafness to the ears
> The five flavors bring tastelessness to the mouth
> Galloping and hunting make the heart-mind crazy
> Goods that are difficult to come by hinder one's actions
> Thereby, the sage satisfies his belly, not his eyes
> Thus he eschews one and attains the other.

Here the *Laozi* argues that excess only perpetuates a continual increase in one's expectations. For example, if one who enjoys spicy food persists in eating spicier and spicier food, this will only increase on that person's tolerance for spicy food. Over time the same amount of spice will no longer be appreciated, and consequently one's standard for spicy food will rise. It may even be the case that this person becomes "blind" to other potentially delicious flavors. Things that are not spicy, or not spicy enough, will no longer be enjoyable.[13] Knowing when to be satisfied and when to stop adding spices leaves one more open to an appreciation of a wider variety of options, whereas feeding desires only serves to impoverish one's sensibilities.

The *Laozi* notes that sages are masters at avoiding this situation because they satisfy their bellies rather than their eyes. The analogy speaks to the fact that stomachs can easily be filled, but eyes tend to wander, and if given free rein they do so endlessly. Like Zigong's mechanical heart-mind, which thinks only of prestige and profit, the desires of the eyes can never be completely satiated. But the cravings of the belly, the *Laozi* argues, are more like the Daoist gardener in that they are easily contented. Moreover, trying to fulfill the incessant desires of wandering eyes can easily distract one from more important things, such as filling their belly. This is why Zigong's mechanical considerations allow him to completely ignore what the Daoist gardener is actually concerned with in his gardening—Zigong is simply distracted from making qualitative considerations. Here the sage is like the gardener in that they both take an unattached "matter of fact" approach to their cravings; they aim to satisfy them so that they cease to exist, at least temporarily. Once they have gotten what they need, these Daoists simply move on. Sages are not preoccupied with fast horses, exciting hunting trips, or luxury goods, says the *Laozi*.

The *Zhuangzi* gives the "sage" of the *Laozi* a new name: the "*zhe-*nuine person" (*zhen ren* 真人). In addition to being unperturbed by her or his own desires, the *zhen*uine person of the *Zhuangzi* maintains and extends this attitude to the social realm. In direct response to the Confucian sage or exemplar, who seeks to develop and cultivate his "self" through social roles and personal relationships, the *zhen*uine person is cautious about getting carried away by social influences.[14] In the same way that the Laozian sage engages with his desires but does not become obsessed with them, the *zhen*uine person is involved in social norms, roles, and relationships, but only to a certain extent. In the first descriptions of this ideal personality type, the *Zhuangzi* begins by warning against a person who sees his or her own self through a social lens:

> Thereby, if someone's understanding is effective for a certain job, or if their actions can be applied in a certain village, or if their virtuosity is liked by a certain ruler, he may win over a certain country. This person will see themselves just like this [that is, as the others see him, as fitting a specific job or role]. But Song Rongzi would have a laugh at such a person. Even if the whole world praised Song he would not be persuaded, and if the whole world scorned him he would not be upset. He fixed the distinction between the inner and outer, and distinguished the place of honor and disgrace. Nothing more can be done than this. He did not worry himself over worldly matters, and remained poised—though he was not firmly planted.[15] (*Zhuangzi* 1.3)

According to the *Zhuangzi*, one should not take too much pride in one's career. Whether someone is appointed to some position is highly contingent upon the circumstances surrounding their situation. Having a particular type or capacity for knowledge may allow one to work successfully at one job or another, just as one's physical aptitudes or likeability may have a significant impact on one's accomplishments in society. One should not, however, get carried away by thinking that they are especially great, or especially terrible, because of their role, status, or position.

The *Zhuangzi* then presents Song Rongzi as representing the first step on the path to becoming a *zhen*uine person. Song is someone who is unattached to his social standing; he does not allow the way others see him to impact the way he understands himself. Song recognizes that honor and disgrace are determined mainly by his social environment, and he deals with his roles and reputation in the same way the sage of the *Laozi* handles his desires. By knowing what is enough, becoming a master of preventing himself from getting carried away, and not making calculations with a mechanical heart-mind, Song is able to maintain a fixed distinction between his internal nature and external evaluations. As the *Zhuangzi* states elsewhere, "The *zhen*uine person of old . . . [does] not use what is human to assist nature" (*Zhuangzi* 6.1).

As this passage in the *Zhuangzi* continues, we are told of the next step toward becoming a *zhen*uine person. Liezi, whose ability to ride the wind enables him to avoid walking, is offered as an example. "Walking" and "riding the wind" are analogies for Liezi's expertise at dealing with norms and customs, which makes him more of a *zhen*uine person than Song Rongzi. Here the word "walk" is *xing* 行, which is "actions" in the first lines of the passage ("if their actions can be applied in a certain village"). Clearly, the *Zhuangzi* is playing on the multiple meanings of *xing*, describing Liezi as someone who is even less absorbed in external evaluations. The word for "wind," literally *feng* 風, can also mean norms or customs. Liezi is thus presented as even less preoccupied with social contingencies, and thereby much better at dealing with them, than Song. Liezi is still not, however, at the highest level; the *Zhuangzi* criticizes him for "relying" (*dai* 待) on something (namely, the wind).

This gradual unfolding of the *zhen*uine person culminates in one of the most famous sentences of the text: "Therefore it is said: the utmost person has no self, the mystical person has no achievements, and the sage has no name."[16] The religious Daoist tradition, Buddhist commentators, and contemporary scholars have sometimes taken this sentence literally—that is, as advocating some type of esoteric self-less person—but read in the context of the entire passage, and especially in light of the philosophical and historical setting of the *Zhuangzi*, it can also be interpreted as something much more mundane. Having no self, no achievements, and no name actually refers to the lack of a need to rely on, become attached to, or identify with one's self, achievements, or name.[17] More importantly, these aspects must be interpreted against the historical Confucian background the *Zhuangzi* was partly written in reaction to. The Confucian "self" is constituted by—if not entirely, as Ames and Rosemont read it, then at least largely, as Tu Weiming admits—a person's network of social roles, relationships, and their accompanying responsibilities. Accordingly, "achievements" are successes and accomplishments that are, again, associated with one's position in society. And "name" (*ming* 名) is another term for one's reputation. Having no self, achievements, or name is then used to describe the *zhen*uine person's ability to remain unattached to their public roles and social standing.

Analogous to the way the sages of the *Laozi* satisfy and therefore do not become engrossed in their desires, the *zhen*uine person in the *Zhuangzi* does not identify with social norms and expectations. *Zhen*uine persons treat their roles in a spontaneous non-calculative manner, which allows them to act (or refrain from acting) in accordance with them. Devoid of an "already made-up mind" or a calculative heart-mind, they live in the world by "going by what is obvious," "according with what is the case," and "following natural patterns." Whatever they do is, in the Confucian sense, "impersonal" (*bu ren* 不人) and "inhumane" (*bu ren* 不仁), because they act in a provisional manner and do not cultivate any fixed notions of self. The *Zhuangzi* provocatively illustrates this point by trading on two cardinal Confucian virtues: "The sages of old borrowed the [Confucian] way of humaneness (*ren* 仁), and temporarily lodged in duty (*yi* 義)" (*Zhuangzi* 14.5). Importantly, however, the Daoist sages do remain genuine in their borrowed lodgings.

Paradoxically, it is precisely the lack of any fixed ideas or self that allows the *zhen*uine person to be genuine. Their inner thoughts and feelings can completely, although only temporarily, match whatever they do. Nothing is in conflict with "who they are," because they are not attached to their self, achievements, or reputation. From the

Confucian perspective, in which one ought to cultivate one's self according to one's role in the community, relationships with others, and moral norms, the *zhen*uine person is a pretender. Confucians argue strongly that in order for a person to be considered sincere, that person's inner psychology and external behavior must both be in accord with norms or virtues.[18] Because the Daoist sage only "borrows" or "temporarily lodges" in roles and morals, his actions are considered deceptive. But from the Daoist perspective, the pretense that Confucians point to is more like the sort of play a child would engage in.[19] Just as the Laozian sage engages in desires but is not defined by them, the *Zhuangzi*ian *zhen*uine person can perform roles without becoming overly attached to them. Like a child, the *zhen*uine person can play someone different in a completely innocent manner, without any deceptive intentions or devious goals. The term "genuine pretender" can thus be used to describe the way the Daoist sage engages in society while maintaining a critical distance from norms, roles, and other various social expectations.

Sandel and Daoism: Appreciating Nature

The "mechanical heart-mind" or a "wholly mechanistic understanding of human action" is problematic for both Daoism and Sandel, but the related drive to mastery is a far more pressing issue. Sandel counters the impulse to control our genes and biology by invoking an appreciation of our talents, nature, and the world as gifts. The aim is to cultivate humility, which relieves the pressure of being wholly responsible for our capacities and promotes solidarity. This discussion is mostly negative for Sandel, and he leaves room for a more constructive conversation about what this kind of attitude might look like in actual practice. The Daoist tradition can be quite useful in this regard. The *Laozi* and *Zhuangzi* contain many descriptions of "self-so" or "non-assertive" spontaneous action, thus providing an account of what appreciating giftedness might look like in practice.

Promoting spontaneity, especially as it is further defined in the *Zhuangzi* as "going by what is obvious," "according with what is the case" and / or "following natural patterns," is a way of downplaying the (supposed) importance of human agency by going along with patterns of relationships in the world. Acting spontaneously thus implies a strong resistance to any type of hubris or a "Promethean drive" to mastery. The "self-so" Daoist does not impose her will on the world, but instead finds a way to incorporate her intentions with what is "already the case." The story of Cook Ding, one of the best-known passages in the *Zhuangzi*, provides a clear illustration:

> Cook Ding was carving an ox for King Hui of Liang. Wherever his hand touched, wherever his shoulder leaned, wherever his foot trod, and wherever his knee braced, the sound of skin, bone, and meat separating, and the beat of the knife's cut were all in tune, matching the "Mulberry Tree" dance, or the "Jing Shou" song.
>
> King Hui of Liang exclaimed: "Wow! Magnificent! Can skill really reach such perfection?"
>
> Cook Ding laid aside his blade saying, "I am fond of the Dao, it goes beyond skill. When I started cutting oxen, I did not see the ox. After three years I did not see the entire ox. Now when I look, I do not rely on my eyes and am able to see the spirit in the ox. The knowledge from my senses ends, and the spirit seeks to move. Relying on the natural patterns [of the body], I stab into the larger holes, and cut along the wide crevices. I go along with what is already there. I never cut through joints, much less big bones! A skilled cook changes his knife once a year, he cuts; most cooks change their knife every month, they slash. I've already been using this knife for nineteen years, having cut thousands of oxen, and my blade is as sharp as on the day it was made. Joints have spaces

between them, and the edge of the blade has no width, using what has no width to enter where there are spaces, it has lots of room to play around in, and there must even be extra space! That's why my knife has not dulled at all over the past nineteen years. Although, there are times when I come across a difficult part, I get nervous and cautious, I stop looking [with my eyes] and my motions are slowed. I move the knife slightly, and suddenly it's done, the ox is cut, on the ground like so much soil. I lift the knife and look all around me, I think about it and am in total admiration, I wipe the knife and put it away.

King Hui of Liang replied "Wow! I have heard Cook Ding's words and learned how to nourish life!"

It is important to note that when asked about his skill, Cook Ding spends most of the time discussing his knife. His own will or agency plays only a minor role in his description. Tasked with carving the ox, he does approach the situation with a particular goal, but he conducts his duty by working out a harmonious relationship between the knife, the carcass, and himself. By his own admission, he does little more than "rely on natural patterns" by "going along with what is already there." When things get difficult, he does not become frustrated or resort to calculations, but simply slows down and allows his knife to move along the spaces in the ox. Cook Ding is "skilled" at orchestrating his relationship with things and the environment, and this skill arises from his ability to refrain from asserting his own will. And this is the message King Hui walks away with.

The story of Cook Ding relates to Sandel's proposed ethics of giftedness in two ways. Firstly, despite possessing a high-level skill, Ding maintains his humility. He feels neither pride nor responsibility for his ability. In fact, he claims that what he does has little to do with his own skill. "Fondness for the Dao," which can also be read as "fondness for the way" or "fondness for nature," is what allows Cook Ding to reach perfection in the art of butchering. Secondly, Dao, way, or nature (*dao* 道) is, in this context, closely related to Sandel's giftedness. It is an ineffable "way" of the world, by which things attain (*de* 得) their qualities and talents (*de* 德) as well as their potentials or "nature" (*xing* 性). Furthermore, Daoist texts are well known for respecting the mysterious nature of the Dao while remaining wholly secular. For example, the opening chapter of the received *Laozi* reads: "A Dao that can be named is not the constant Dao . . . Darker than darkness, Gate of the myriad mysteries."

Dao is something that one seeks to align themselves with, but it is never fully revealed. It is always particular and context-dependent. Cook Ding navigates *this* carcass well with *this* knife. But with a different blade he would have to follow different spaces in the meat, and a different ox would have its own unique spaces. Likewise, another butcher might carve (or hack) completely different lines. Approaching the world from this standpoint, one not only maintains a great amount of respect for the world as mysterious in some sense, but also naturally resists the temptation to master it. Cook Ding is concerned with finding his place in the relationship between himself, the knife, and the ox, all while not controlling it. Cultivating this type of attitude as a way of "nourishing life" would have a significant impact on the way people interact with things, others, and the natural world. It would also promote a nonreligious reverence for our aptitudes. Daoism thus offers a more concrete account of what an ethics of giftedness might look like, and in a way that makes no appeal to the divine.

Sandel and Daoism: Restraint and Satisfaction

Sandel argues that a respect for the fact that we are not masters of our potentials and abilities "restrains our tendency towards hubris" (2007a, 86). In other words, we should resist the temptation to shape and direct our biological development. Employing Daoist notions of "mastering satisfaction" and "mastering cessation" in this context offers a slightly different outlook. Holding one's desires back is not as effective, the Daoists argue, as figuring out how to appropriately satisfy them, and when to stop. When these methods are applied to our "tendency towards hubris" or "drive to mastery," they may help encourage a type of attitude that is both more appreciative of giftedness *and* more satisfying.

For the Daoist, respecting the mystery of the Dao and fulfilling one's desires work in a kind of constant feedback look. The more one realizes that not only one's nature and potentials, but also one's desires and impulses, arise from the Dao, the less likely one is to try to manipulate one's tendencies. Instead, one fosters a more humble approach. Just as Cook Ding manages his relationship with the knife and ox by not aggressively inserting his own will, the Daoist seeks to regulate her desires rather than dominate them.

Barring certain role-based moral elements, a rather emblematic example of dealing tactfully with desires occurs in the Confucian text *Mengzi* 孟子 (*Mencius*).[20] Here King Xuan of Qi admits to Mencius that he cannot carry out moral governance because he is too fond of sexual pleasures (*hao se* 好色). Mencius does not, however, reprimand the king for his sinful desires or for having a character flaw. For Mencius, the main problem is King Xuan's misunderstanding of what it means to be a king. In order to govern well, the king should acknowledge that everyone is fond of sex, but that this fondness is best exercised in the form of love, marriage, and having children (*Mengzi* 1B12). As an individual, there is nothing wrong with King Xuan. He does not need to undergo psychotherapeutic treatment, and no medicine is needed to curb his sexual drive. Mencius claims that all people are born with the same desires. Problems come about when these desires are not properly nurtured and grow irregularly. Once the king realizes that his "perversion" is based on unhealthy social practices, he can correct his thoughts, feelings, and behavior, find more appropriate ways of interacting with others, and practice moral governance.

Although this is a Confucian story, certain elements of it exemplify the Daoist notions of mastering satisfaction and cessation. When Mencius proposes that the king channel his desires in the right way rather than attempt to suppress them, he is talking about mastering desires with satisfaction and cessation. King Xuan should accept his fondness for sex, fulfill his desires, and simply move on. In this way he will not be distracted by it. Once he figures out the appropriate way to be sexual, he can be both sexually gratified and a better ruler. This is exactly the message the *Laozi* conveys about desires. Chapter 33 reads, "One who knows how to be satisfied [with his lot] is rich" (*Laozi* 33).

In addition to the appreciation of giftedness, taking this attitude toward the tendency to control our own biology would mean recognizing that this tendency exists, and seeking to satisfy rather than repress it. Sandel is more interested in curbing our Promethean impulse, but the Daoist approach may yield outlets that keep the drive both satisfied and in check.

Sandel and Daoism: Maintaining Distance

Although the Daoists are not particularly keen on reorganizing or improving social institutions, the way the *zhen*uine person (or "genuine pretender") in the *Zhuangzi* deals with social norms, roles, and expectations provides an attitude that can be used to reflect critically on these issues. By attaching oneself only temporarily to what one does or what is asked, the genuine pretender creates a space that could, in light of Sandel's concerns, provide a model by which we could "question and debate whether we've designed the system of roles and rewards in a just way" (Heijine and Sandel 2016).

In his famous class "Justice," which has attracted over 20 million online viewers in China (on websites such as sina.com), Sandel challenges his students' most central moral views—not by presenting them with an alternative set of "true" moral beliefs, but by creating space for students to reflect critically on their moral reasoning through discussions based on actual situations and controversial cases. Sandel ends his first day of class with a cautionary statement:

> [Reading philosophy] as an exercise in self-knowledge carries certain risks. Risks that are both personal and political . . . These risks spring from the fact that philosophy teaches us and unsettles us by confronting us with what we already know. There is an irony: The difficulty of this course consists in the fact that it teaches what you already know. It works by taking what we know from familiar unquestioned settings and making it strange . . . Philosophy estranges us from the familiar, not by supplying new information, but by inviting and provoking a new way of seeing. (2009a)

These "risks" that Sandel warns his students about are the very heart of his case against perfection. To have reservations about genetic enhancements, believing that their primary aim is to "fit ourselves into the social roles we have" (Heijine and Sandel 2016), is to have reservations about our "system of roles and rewards." But in order to question and debate our social institutions, we need to become "estranged" not only from them, but from ourselves as well. Insofar as we automatically see certain traits as being "good," and insofar as we are, as Sandel argues, largely encumbered by the communities we participate in, thoroughly questioning and debating these beliefs requires that we do not identify with them (or our "selves")—at least temporarily.

To take two examples used in *The Case against Perfection,* being tall and being intelligent are often unreflectively considered "good." However, for a gymnast a shorter stature is often a plus, and it is certainly possible to be "too smart for one's own good."[21] Appreciating the advantages of being shorter than average or a bit "simple" requires that we detach ourselves from the ways we might normally think.[22] Sandel does an excellent job of guiding his students and readers to a space where their preconceived notions of the good are confronted with challenges both external and internal. The Daoist philosophy of genuine pretending further expands this space. Here conventional ideas fall away, making room for an even more robust reflection on the status quo.

In chapter 4 of the *Zhuangzi*, titled "In the Human World" (*ren jian shi* 人間世), we are given an account of what a genuine pretender thinks about customary notions of "the good" or, more precisely in ancient Chinese, "the useful." The story begins with a carpenter named Shi who is traveling with his apprentice. One day they pass through a village where an enormous chestnut tree serves as its ceremonial *she* 社 shrine. Though this massive tree could easily be carved into numerous boats, coffins, and tools, carpenter Shi ignores it, telling his disciple that its wood is useless. He says, "This is a talentless, worthless tree. It is precisely because it has 'no-use' that it has lived so long" (Ziporyn 2009, 30).[23] That night, the tree spoke to carpenter Shi in a dream:

> What do you want to compare me to, one of those *cultivated* trees? The hawthorn, the pear, the orange . . . when their fruit is ripe they get plucked, and that is an insult. Thus do their abilities embitter their lives. That is why they die young, failing to fully live out their natural life spans. They batter themselves with the vulgar conventions of the world—and all other creatures do the same. As for me, I've been working on being useless for a long time. It almost killed me, but I've finally managed it—and it is of great use to me! If I were useful, do you think I could have grown to be so great? Moreover, you and I are both (members of the same class, namely), *beings*—is either of us in a position to classify and evaluate the other? (*Zhuangzi* 4.5; Ziporyn 2009, 30)

At this point carpenter Shi wakes up and tells his apprentice about the dream. The apprentice reacts: "If it's trying to be useless, what's it doing with a shrine around it?" (*Zhuangzi* 4.5; Ziporyn 2009, 30). Carpenter Shi then scolds his apprentice:

> Hush! Don't talk like that! Those people came to it for refuge of their own accord. In fact, the tree considers it a great disgrace to be surrounded by this uncomprehending crowd. If they hadn't made it a shrine, they could have easily gone the other way and started carving away at it. What it values is not what they value. Is it not absurd to judge it by whether it does what is or is not called for by its position, by what role it happens to play? (*Zhuangzi* 4.5; Ziporyn 2009, 30–31)

Like Song Rongzi, the tree does not see itself through the eyes of others. It has no problem playing along with being the shrine, but it does not identify with its role.[24] More importantly, however, it came to be dubbed "shrine" only through its uncertain attitude toward what is commonly considered "good" or "useful." Cultivated trees, ones that bear fruit or produce valuable wood, are trees that live up to the expectations of "vulgar conventions"; they are therefore abused and cut down before their "natural life spans." Having taken on the philosophy of genuine pretending, the tree was able to critically distance itself from expectations and, to borrow Sandel's phrasing, evaluate its "habit of mind and way of being." But as the carpenter notes, the tree's philosophy of genuine pretending also "carries certain risks." The people could have just as easily gotten rid of this "useless" tree.

Coupled with Sandel's concern that we might unreflectively aim to "fit ourselves into the social roles we have," the philosophy of genuine pretending allows us to take a deeper look at conventions, expectations, and what is commonly considered "good."

Roger Ames and Li Zehou have both noted—independently of one another, it seems—that one fundamental distinction between the philosophical backgrounds of mainstream Chinese and Western traditions can be ascribed to the difference between "one-world theory" versus "two-world theory" metaphysics.[25] According to a (Western) two-world theory, there is another world independent of this one—a world of Platonic forms, or of the Christian God, or perhaps of Kantian noumena—that this world merely reflects or emulates. The (Chinese) one-world theory makes no such assumptions, opting instead for metaphysical monism and complete immanence. This platform can be used to interpret the distinction between general philosophical issues such as the Dao and God, but it can also be useful for understanding more mundane phenomena. For example, the English word "perfect" is not often used to describe actual concrete things, and it cannot be put in superlative or comparative forms (we do not say "more perfect" or "perfecter"). In Mandarin, on the other hand, the word for "perfect"—*wanmei* 完美 (or *wanshan* 完善)—is much more commonly used than its English counterpart, and it is often qualified. In China today one can frequently hear "this is very perfect" (*hen wanmei / ting wanmei* 很完美 / 挺完美) or "this is more perfect" (*geng wanmei / bijiao hai wanmei* 更完美 / 比較完美). In this one-world sense we can say, with the Daoists, that this world is perfect—not because there are no problems, but instead because we can—as the *Laozi* and the *Zhuangzi* suggest—be satisfied with the problems, and come to appreciate things as they are. To borrow the process vocabulary of Ames and Hall (2003), we might say that the world is "perfect-ing."[26]

This does not, however, imply the rejection of change. Both the *Laozi* and the *Zhuangzi* celebrate change and transformation as constants in our world. To understand the world as perfect then means to appreciate the "perfectness" of the world, and to participate in change with a healthy (non-calculative) attitude. The *Zhuangzi* especially stresses both an appreciation of the way things are and a simultaneous enjoyment of transformation:

> Suddenly, Ziyu took ill . . . He hobbled over to the well to get a look at his reflection. "Wow!" he said. "The Creator of Things has really gone and tangled me up!"
>
> Ziji said, "Do you dislike it?"

> Ziyu said, "Not at all. What is there to dislike? Perhaps he will
> transform my left arm into a rooster; thereby I'll be announcing the
> dawn. Perhaps he will transform my right arm into a crossbow
> pellet; thereby I'll be seeking out an owl to roast. Perhaps he will
> transform my ass into a wheel and my spirit into a horse; thereby
> I'll be riding along. (*Zhuangzi* 6.5; Ziporyn 2009, 45)

This is, in many ways, similar to the type of mentality Sandel promotes with his "ethics of giftedness" and "ethics of restraint." Both Daoism and Sandel promote an appreciation of the world and human life by reining in our desire for mastery and maintaining a philosophical distance from social norms, roles, and fixed notions of "perfect."

There are, of course, crucial differences as well. In many readings of Daoism, the constraining of our desire for mastery extends well beyond what Sandel describes, into the social and political realm. It is difficult to imagine Sandel being on board with the broader implications of Daoism's quietistic tendencies. Likewise, Sandel's notion of "giftedness," at least in terms of some of some of the religious baggage it brings, is perhaps not a good way of thinking about the Daoist appreciation of the Dao. Yet despite these differences (and many others), a number of substantial connections can be drawn between the two.[27] And they can be productive participants in a collaborative approach to some of today's most pressing philosophical problems and moral issues.

Biotechnology, genetic engineering, and transhumanism are emerging fields, and they are only going to occupy more of the front page as time goes on. Some of the moral questions that Sandel raises are, in part, concerns for what is on the horizon. This leaves us in a unique position to engage with these issues in public debate either prior to or concurrent with the development of these technologies. But if our debates are to cross national, religious, and cultural boundaries, then they will need to incorporate non-Western perspectives—not simply through comparisons, but through collaborations that allow different traditions to contribute their own perspectives. There is a particular need for this kind of approach if, following Fukuyama's suggestions, we are to establish international regulatory pacts and institutions to govern new biotechnologies. And although Confucianism often dominates philosophical discourse (especially when it comes to contemporary issues), this is one area where Western engagement with Daoist philosophy in particular will prove especially invaluable for shaping the future of this imminent—and unavoidable—global debate.

Notes

I want to thank Hans-Georg Moeller, Seth Crownover, and Robert Carleo for comments, suggestions, and corrections on earlier drafts of this paper. All translations from Chinese are my own, unless otherwise noted.

1. Research for *The Case against Perfection* began in 2001 when Michael Sandel was invited to serve on the President's Council on Bioethics. In 2004 Sandel published in *The Atlantic* an article titled "The Case against Perfection," which he expanded into the short book (2007a).

2. Fukuyama and Sandel both served on the President's Council on Bioethics from 2002 to 2005.

3. Others, such as Ruiping Fan (2010), have argued that Sandel gives a "once-and-for-all conclusion" on this issue (68). Fan writes, "Although he never states it straightforwardly, his conclusion is obviously that humans should not conduct any genetic enhancement" (64). While Sandel certainly limits the scope of the argument, his discussions are clearly attempts to set up the parameters of dialogue—that is, narrowing the relevant issues—rather than to give a final answer.

4. In his closing remarks at the conference that inspired this volume, Sandel said, "It seems to me it is not easy to explain what is wrong with genetic engineering to improve our children or ourselves, or picking and choosing designer babies on standard utilitarian or atomic-based terms alone . . . I think the moral heart of the objection has to do [with the] hubris of a parent who would exercise such mastery and dominion over his or her child, it would be a kind of overreaching . . . I do not claim to have worked out the adequate account of nature . . . But it seems to me the fourth theme [genetic enhancement] could possibly be a fruitful bridge for discussion with the Chinese tradition—a reflection on nature and humanity" (Sandel 2016).

5. I have borrowed the term "mastering" from Hans-Georg Moeller. For a more detailed analysis of this issue, see Moeller 2006, 2007.

6. The term "*zhen*uine person," which Hans-Georg Moeller and I have used (Moeller and D'Ambrosio 2017) and which was suggested to us by Robert Carleo, is more than a play on words. "*Zhen*uine" and "genuine" are almost identical in pronunciation, and indeed "genuine person" has often been used as a translation, but the use of "*zhen*uine" distinguishes the "*zhen* person" from the "genuine person." Simply put, the *zhen*uine person is not someone who has returned to a "genuine" root self. The details of this argument will be clear below, and are also found in Moeller and D'Ambrosio 2017.

7. In his book *Justice: What's the Right Thing to Do?*, Sandel quickly identifies "outrage" as our natural response to what we find unjust (2009b, 7). In *The Case against Perfection*, he outlines the problem people have with the use of biotechnologies for enhancement, pointing to feelings of "moral hesitation" and "unease" (2007a, 8–9).

8. The philosophical consideration of moral emotions is a characteristic feature of Chinese thought and a major point of overlap between Chinese philosophy and Michael Sandel. (See D'Ambrosio 2016.)

9. In fact, one of the central issues in Chinese philosophy concerns the relationship between humans and nature (or "heaven"), which is debated without reference to religious ideas. This discussion, usually given as "the unification of humans and nature" (*tian ren he yi* 天人合一), could also serve as an interesting point of comparison, and as a potential resource for Sandel's arguments.

10. "Self-so" is sometimes understood as "natural" or "spontaneous"; and "non-assertive action" has been translated as "non-doing" or "non-interference."

11. When referring to passages from classic Chinese texts, I cite the chapter and section number as they appear in the online versions on the Chinese Text Project website (www.ctext.org).

12. I discuss this story and its relation to environmentalism in more detail in D'Ambrosio 2013.

13. I have borrowed this example from Moeller 2006, 92–93.

14. For a more thorough description of the Confucian person, see the essays in Part IV of this volume.

15. Translation from D'Ambrosio 2014.

16. "Utmost person," "mystical person," and "sage" are all terms the *Zhuangzi* uses to describe the ideal Daoist person. They are synonymous with one another and with the "*zhen*uine person."

17. For an expanded version of this argument, see D'Ambrosio 2014.

18. See Chapters 8 and 9, this volume.

19. The *Zhuangzi* itself includes several imaginary stories where this type of person is criticized (mostly from a Confucian perspective) as a pretender (*Zhuangzi* 4.5, 6.7).

20. The *Mencius* is a Confucian text, but there are many overlaps between Daoist and Confucian themes, especially when they are contrasted with Western philosophy.

21. A similar case in China would be the preference for having baby boys. After the introduction of ultrasonography in China, so many female fetuses were aborted that an estimated 55 million Chinese men will not be able to find a spouse.

22. In the Chinese tradition, the appreciation of being "simple" is exemplified in Zheng Banqiao's (1693–1765) famous calligraphy *nan de hutu* 難得糊塗—"it is difficult to be muddled."

23. This line has been adapted from Ziporyn with minor changes.

24. For a more detailed discussion of this passage and how it expresses the philosophy of genuine pretending, see D'Ambrosio 2012.

25. Ames and Li Zehou have very similar arguments about one-world and two-world theories, but both claim to have been unaware of the other's argument when writing their own. To describe the main difference between Western and Chinese philosophy in this way is certainly a generalization, and it does not hold true for everyone in either tradition—and neither Ames nor Li argues that it does. However, if we compare some texts, such as Plato's *Republic* with the *Lunyu* or *Zhuangzi*, the one-world and two-world distinction does seem to hold.

26. It seems that Sandel's own understanding of perfection is similarly process-based. In the dedication to *The Case against Perfection* he writes, "I dedicate this book to our sons, Adam and Aaron, who are perfect just as they are."

27. There is much room for further comparative research on Sandel's criticism of biotechnology and Daoism. For example, the Daoist appreciation of "nature" (as either *tian* 天 or *dao* 道) could be elaborated on, and "fate" or "contingency" (*ming* 命), the "usefulness of the useless," and the famous stories of the cripple all provide great resources for expanding on the Daoist case against perfection, and double as comparisons to Sandel's own case.

References

Ames, Roger, and David Hall. 2003. *Dao De Jing: "Making This Life Significant"; A Philosophical Translation*. New York: Ballantine Books.

Chan, Joseph. 2010. "Concerns beyond the Family." *American Journal of Bioethics* 10 (4): 82–84.

Chen Guying 陳鼓應. 2008. *Lao-Zhuang Xin Lun* 老莊新論 [New theories on Laozi and Zhuangzi]. Revised edition. Beijing: Commercial Press.

D'Ambrosio, Paul. 2012. "The Role of a Pretending Tree: Hermits, Social Constructs and 'Self' in the *Zhuangzi*." In *Identity in Eastern and Western Philosophies*, edited by Jason Dockstader, Hans-Georg Moeller, and Günter Wohlfart. Freiburg: Karl Alber.

———. 2013. "Rethinking Environmental Issues in a Daoist Context: Why Daoism Is and Is Not Environmentalism." *Environmental Ethics* 35 (Winter): 401–417.

———. 2014. "Going Along: A Daoist Alternative to Role Ethics." In *Landscape and Travelling East and West: A Philosophical Journey*, edited by Hans-Georg Moeller and Andrew Whitehead. London: Bloomsbury Academic.

———. 2016. "Approaches to Global Ethics: Michael Sandel's Justice and Li Zehou's Harmony." *Philosophy East and West* 66 (3): 720–738.

Fan, Ruiping. 2010. "A Confucian Reflection on Genetic Enhancement." *American Journal of Bioethics* 10 (4): 62–70.

Fukuyama, Francis. 2002. *Our Posthuman Future: Consequences of the Biotechnological Revolution.* New York: Farrar, Straus and Giroux.

Heidegger, Martin. 1966. *Discourse on Thinking.* Translated by John M. Anderson and E. Hans Freund. New York: Harper & Row Publishers.

Heijine, Bas, and Michael Sandel. 2016. "The Perfect Human Being." YouTube video, 13:17. https://www.youtube.com/watch?v=tK3GyjnA3Yc.

Li Zehou 李澤厚. 2014. *Huiying Sangdeer ji Qita* 回應桑德爾及其他 [A response to Michael Sandel and other matters]. Beijing: Sanlian Shudian.

Moeller, Hans-Georg. 2006. *The Philosophy of the Daodejing.* New York: Columbia University Press.

———. 2007. *Daodejing (Laoẓi): A Complete Translation and Commentary.* Chicago: Open Court.

Moeller, Hans-Georg, and Paul J. D'Ambrosio. 2017. *Genuine Pretending: On the Philosophy of the* Zhuangzi. New York: Columbia University Press.

Sandel, Michael. 2007a. *The Case against Perfection.* Cambridge, MA: Belknap Press of Harvard University Press.

———. 2007b. "Michael Sandel Frames the Stem Cell Debate." *Big Think* video, 3:57. June 6, 2007. http://bigthink.com/videos/michael-sandel-frames-the-stem-cell-debate.

———. 2009a. "Episode 01: The Moral Side of Murder." *Justice: What's the Right Thing to Do?* YouTube video, 54:56. https://www.youtube.com/watch?v=kBdfcR-8hEY.

———. 2009b. *Justice: What's the Right Thing to Do?* New York: Farrar, Straus and Giroux.

———. 2016. "Closing Remarks." Presented at the International Conference on Michael Sandel and Chinese Philosophy, East China Normal University, Shanghai, March 10.

Ziporyn, Brook. 2009. *Zhuangẓi: The Essential Writings with Selections from Traditional Commentaries.* Indianapolis: Hackett.

IV

Conceptions of the Person: Sandel and the Confucian Tradition

8

Theorizing the "Person" in Confucian Ethics

ROGER T. AMES

In the introduction to his *Encyclopaedia Logic,* G. W. F. Hegel famously observes that one of the most difficult problems in any philosophical investigation is the question of where to begin. This concern is not lost on Michael Sandel. As early as *Liberalism and the Limits of Justice,* Sandel has been strongly critical of the deracinated self that serves as starting point for the Kantian-cum-Rawlsian deontological conception of the individual. Sandel (1982) describes the Rawlsian deontological self in the following terms:

> We can locate this individualism and identify the conceptions of the goods it excludes by recalling that the Rawlsian self is not only a subject of possession, but an antecedently individuated subject, standing always at a certain distance from the interests it has. One consequence of this distance is to put the self beyond the reach of experience, to make it invulnerable, to fix its identity once and for all. (62)

And Sandel is clear about the perceived limitations and the consequences of beginning from and embracing such an anemic conception of individual identity:

> But a self so thoroughly independent as this rules out any conception of the good (or the bad) bound up with possession in the

constitutive sense. It rules out the possibility of any attachment (or obsession) able to reach beyond our values and sentiments to engage our identity itself. It rules out the possibility of a public life in which for good or ill, the identity as well as the interests of the participants could be at stake. And it rules out the possibility that common purposes and ends could inspire more or less expansive self-understandings and so define a community in the constitutive sense, a community describing the subject and not just the objects of shared aspirations. (62)

Sandel (1982) characterizes an alternative, "intersubjective," if not "intrasubjective," conception of self that the Rawlsian position by implication clearly rules out:

Intrasubjective conceptions, on the other hand, allow that for certain purposes, the appropriate description of the moral subject may refer to a plurality of selves within a single individual human being, as when we account for inner deliberation in terms of the pull of competing identities, or moments of introspection in terms of occluded self-knowledge, or when we absolve someone from responsibility for the heretical beliefs "he" held before his religious conversion. (63)

Sandel certainly sees this intrasubjective conception of person as potentially more productive than the deontological self, but he still has a sustained worry that there is the danger of it becoming so defused as to lose a sufficiently robust sense of choice, unity, and identity. Over the years Sandel has appealed to a range of philosophers such as Aristotle and Hegel, and more recently to the Jewish tradition, in his attempt to formulate an adequately intrasubjective conception of person that allows for a communally constitutive identity while at the same time retaining a sufficiently strong sense of personal unity and autonomy.

Sandel's Challenge: Theorizing the
Intrasubjective Person

In many ways, in this project, Sandel has embraced the philosophical problem of our time. Almost a century ago John Dewey in his *Individualism Old and New* (1962) rued the degeneration of unique individuality—the real possibilities and promise of realizing an American Emersonian soul—into a self-interested and contentious ideology of individualism that produces a zero-sum culture of winners and losers: "The spiritual factor of our tradition, equal opportunity and free association and intercommunication, is obscured and crowded out. Instead of the development of individualities which it prophetically set forth, there is a perversion of the whole ideal of individualism to conform to the practices of a pecuniary culture. It has become the source and justification of inequalities and oppressions" (18). Dewey goes on to encourage, if not to exhort, philosophers to step up to the challenge of formulating a new "individuality" that would be consistent with his idea of democracy, in which personal realization and communal realization are coterminous and mutually entailing: "The problem of constructing a new individuality consonant with the objective conditions under which we live is the deepest problem of our time" (32).

In this essay I join John Dewey and Michael Sandel in common cause in recommending that we take full advantage of all of our cultural resources, Asian as well as European, in formulating an adequate conception of the intrasubjective person. We might want to give Confucius and his relationally constituted conception of person a seat at the table in this continuing quest for an adequate alternative to the discrete, exclusive, and foundational individualism that has become default in most liberal conceptions of person.

But then, Confucius in the current literature is not one thing. While many, if not most, scholars of Confucian ethics would choose to categorize this tradition as a variation on virtue ethics, I and my collaborators—Henry Rosemont in particular—have contended that only in allowing that Confucius offers us a *sui generis* role ethic are we able to appreciate the important contribution Confucian ethics has to make to contemporary ethical discourse (Ames 2011; Rosemont 2015; Rosemont and Ames 2016). And on the issue of "intrasubjective person" in particular, we argue that the appropriateness of categorizing Confucian ethics as either role ethics or virtue ethics turns largely on the conception of person that is presupposed within the interpretive context of classical Chinese philosophy.[1] If our goal is to take the Confucian tradition on its own terms and to let it speak with its own voice without overwriting it with what we in our own culture take to be important, we must begin by first self-consciously and critically theorizing the Confucian conception of person as the starting point of Confucian ethics, and only then introduce this notion of person into our contemporary discourse.

Making Responsible Comparisons: "It's a Poor Sort of Memory That Only Works Backwards"

This entrenched problem of using Western categories to theorize Confucian philosophy is an old and persistent story. Kwong-loi Shun (2009) has recently made much of this asymmetry in how we make our cultural comparisons: "There is a trend in comparative studies to approach Chinese thought from a Western philosophical perspective, by reference to frameworks, concepts, or issues found in Western philosophical discussions. This trend is seen not only in works published in the English language, but also in those published in Chinese. Conversely, in the contemporary literature, we rarely find attempts to approach Western philosophical thought by reference to frameworks, concepts, or issues found in Chinese philosophical discussions" (470).

Perhaps an immediate example of this problem, is the fact that most of our most influential scholars on Chinese ethics—such as Fung You-lan and Guo Qiyong—early on proffered a principle-based interpretation of this tradition. But when Elizabeth Anscombe in her 1958 essay "Modern Moral Philosophy" challenged deontology and utilitarianism for being legalistic and for lacking any moral psychology (33), and precipitated a revisionist direction in Western ethical discourse with publications such as Alasdair MacIntyre's *After Virtue* (1981), our interpretation of Chinese ethics changed too. That is, our own turn from principle-based ethics to virtue ethics in Western normative theory occasioned by Anscombe's challenge is also the story of an interpretive turn in our reading of Confucian ethics, where we too have come to embrace virtue ethics as the most apposite reading of this antique tradition. Said another way, remembering the White Queen's musing that "it's a poor sort of memory that only works backwards," for Confucian ethics to be thus "remembered" by its unfolding encounter with Western ethical theory might be a good example of this putatively "better" kind of memory.

In our own time, but with deep roots in the classical Greek philosophical narrative, individualism has become a default, commonsense assumption, if not an ideology. That is, in our post-Marxist, post-collectivist era, the ideology of individualism has garnered a monopoly on human consciousness without any serious alternative to challenge it. I will argue that the language of virtue ethics, broadly understood, in appealing as it does to the vocabulary of agents, acts, generic virtues, character traits, autonomy, motivation, reasons, choices, freedom, principles, consequences, and so on, introduces distinctions that assume this foundational individualism as its starting point.

And further, I will claim that Confucian ethics by contrast begins from the wholeness of experience, and is formulated by invoking a radically different focus-field cluster of terms and distinctions with fundamentally different assumptions about how personal identities emerge in our human narratives, and how moral competence is expressed as an achieved virtuosity in the roles and relationships that come to constitute us. To fail to distinguish what I will call individual human "beings" from relationally constituted "humane becomings," then, would mean that we have willy-nilly insinuated a contemporary and decidedly foreign notion of person into our investigation before it has even begun.

Angus Graham on Abjuring Ontology and Teleology in Theorizing the Confucian Person

"If in classical Confucian philosophy human beings are not individuals, then what are they?" seems to be the obvious, operative question from which to begin. But is it? Angus Graham (1990) first echoes the Saussurian distinction between *langue* and *parole* that ascribes unique conceptual structures to different cultural traditions, and like many of us, is persuaded that different cultures appeal to different categories in their thinking and living: "That people of another culture are somehow thinking in other categories is a familiar idea, almost a commonplace, but one very difficult to pin down as a topic for fruitful discussion" (360).

Like Saussure, Nietzsche (1966) is also persuaded that a particular worldview is sedimented into the languages of the family of Indo-European cultures and the systematic structure of their concepts, and as a consequence encourages certain philosophical possibilities while discouraging others: "The strange family resemblance of all Indian, Greek, and German philosophizing is explained easily enough. Where there is an affinity of languages, it cannot fail, owing to the common philosophy of grammar—I mean owing to the unconscious domination and guidance by similar grammatical functions—that everything is prepared at the outset for a similar development and sequence of philosophical systems; just as the way seems barred against certain other possibilities of world-interpretation" (20).

Graham, like Nietzsche and Saussure, looks to what language reveals to get at the issue of cultures "thinking in other categories" by recognizing that the way we formulate our questions—for example, our asking "What is a human being?"—already prompts a particular kind of answer. That is, we might be able to discern important conceptual differences (and perhaps different conceptions of the human being) if we go back to the different questions being asked. As Graham (1990) observes: "Since every philosophical answer is shaped by the posing of the question, it may be suspected that the categories within which we think correspond to the basic words available in the language for asking the questions . . . Can we use the interrogative words to trace differences between Chinese and Western categories?" (3).

Graham (1991) warns us broadly that serious equivocations emerge when we elide the distinction between classical Greek ontological assumptions that privilege "being *per se*" and its attendant dualisms, with those assumptions grounding a classical Chinese procreative cosmology that gives privilege to "becoming" and the vital, interdependent *yinyang* categories needed to "speak" about process: "In the Chinese cosmos all things are interdependent, without transcendent principles by which to explain them or a transcendent origin from which they derive . . . A novelty in this position which greatly impresses me is that it exposes a preconception of Western interpreters that such concepts as *Tian* 'Heaven' and *Dao* 'Way' must have the transcendence of our own ultimate principles; it is hard for us to grasp that even the Way is interdependent with man" (287).

What does Graham's wariness about importing teleology and formal causes into Chinese cosmology mean when the investigation is directed specifically at how classical Confucians understood human beings and the human experience? Sandel (1982) underscores the weight of idealism and teleology that is pervasive within our own common sense: "To speak of human nature is often to suggest a classical teleological conception, associated with the notion of a universal human essence, invariant in all times and places" (50).[2] A case in point is when Graham (1991) opines that this imposition of such foreign teleological assumptions on the Mencian notion of person is precisely the problem we have had in reading Mencius on "human nature," where "the translation of *xing* 性 by 'nature' predisposes us to mistake it for a transcendent origin, which in Mencian doctrine would also be a transcendent end" (287).

By contrast, the generative and open-ended conception of human "becoming" in the Confucian tradition requires us to register how the evolving personal identity emerges *pari passu* within the unfolding narrative context—that is, person and narrative are a coterminous and mutually entailing process *in media res*. Neither particular persons nor humanity as a species has a discrete beginning or any final end. Graham (1991) observes: "*Xing* is conceived in terms of spontaneous development in a certain direction rather than of its origin or goal . . . The *cheng* 成 'completion' of a thing's development which in man is his *cheng* 誠 "integrity," is the interdependent [context] becoming integral rather than the realization of an end" (288). Graham is keenly aware here of a fundamental contrast between closure and disclosure: between the potential and actualization of a teleologically driven and substantive human "being" on the one hand, and the continuing emergence of a narratively nested humane "becoming" on the other—a continuing process wherein progenitors live on in their progeny.

Asking the Right Questions

Long before Hegel, Aristotle was also concerned about where to begin. The *Categories* is the first fascicle in the standard *Corpus Aristotelicum* translated as the *Oxford Complete Works of Aristotle,* and the ontological question "What is a man?" is the first and primary question in the *Categories.* In his several formulations of his predications, Aristotle delineates the questions we must ask to give an exhaustive description of the "subject," with his own concrete example of this subject being "the man in the market-place." He begins by introducing an ontological disparity in identifying the essence or substance of the subject (Gk. *ousia*, L. *substantia*)—what someone "is"—as opposed to this person's various contingent attributes. "To give a rough idea, examples of substance are man, horse; of quantity: four-foot, five-foot; of qualification: white, grammatical; of a relative: double, half, larger; of where: in the Lyceum, in the market-place; of when: yesterday, last-year; of being-in-a-position: is-lying, is-sitting; of having: has-shoes-on, has-armour-on; of doing: cutting, burning; of being-affected: being-cut, being-burned" (Aristotle 1984, 1a25–2b4). And for Aristotle, it is the primacy of the "what" question that provides us with the essential predicate: what is said "of" a subject that identifies the underlying substance of what the man *is*. The remaining secondary conditions and the questions that prompt them—quantity, quality, relation, place, time, position, state, action, and affection—provide us with the full complement of attributes that are "in" a subject as contingent and conditional predicates that cannot exist without this subject. It is important to note that Aristotle's questions do not include "how" or "why." He assumes that asking after a complete description can be undertaken separately from an explanation, an assumption that we will see is untenable in Chinese process cosmology.

In reflecting on Aristotle's strategy for complete description and what it reveals about his categories, Graham (1990) observes: "Aristotle's procedure is to isolate one thing from others, treating even transitive verbs ('cuts,' 'burns') as objectless, and even the relative ('half,' 'bigger') as not relating two things but said of one with reference to the other" (380). One of the commonsense corollaries to an Aristotelian ontology that gives privilege to an isolated, individual subject is to experience the world as being populated by discrete things or objects that "object" to us in standing off independent of us. And a second corollary to this substance ontology is the assumed doctrine of external relations: that these various objects, each having its own essential integrity, are first-order as discrete things, and any relations that might conjoin them are second-order contingent relations that they subsequently contract. Graham reflects on the question forms that shape Aristotle's answers and the way in which this substance ontology buys into the notion of simple location and discrete individuality and by implication precludes the notion of person as an event: "Aristotle's thinking is noun-centered; he starts with the substance identified as man, and before introducing any verb but 'to be'" can already ask 'When was he in the market-place?' and 'Where was he yesterday?' but not 'Whence?' or 'Whither?'" (391).

A Doctrine of Internal, Constitutive Relations

Graham (1990) sees this commonsense understanding of the discrete and substantial individual as standing in stark contrast to a classical Chinese process cosmology in which the world is characterized by the interdependence of "things" (or better, "events"), and thus requires a doctrine of intrinsic, constitutive relations to describe them: "In Chinese thought on the contrary things appear not as independent but as interdependent . . . and the questions that isolate things from each other have no primacy over those which relate them" (391).

For Graham the human being as a dynamic, gerundive concept references a continuing developmental process that is spontaneous and realizes its own potentialities when it is properly nourished and unimpeded. But given that Graham's understanding of early Confucian cosmology assumes a doctrine of internal relations constitutive of putative "things" rather than external relations that merely conjoin discrete and independent things, his interpretation of "its own potentialities" would make potential particularist, emergent, and genealogical rather than front-loaded as the latent and internal qualities or abilities of discrete persons. Graham (1991), in his clarification of the nature of "relations" that is relevant to this Chinese cosmology, introduces precisely this distinction: "As for 'relationships,' relation is no doubt an indispensable concept in exposition of Chinese thought, which generally impresses a Western as more concerned with the relations between things than with their qualities; but the concern is with concrete patterns rather than relations abstracted from them" (288–289).

Peter Hershock (2006) offers a rather clear and uncontroversial account of internal, constitutive relations in diagnosing the problem we have in our recalcitrant habit of seeing the world as being composed of preexisting, discrete "things" that then enter into external relations among themselves: "Autonomous subjects and objects are, finally, only artifacts of abstraction . . . What we refer to as 'things'—whether mountains, human beings, or complex phenomena like histories—are simply the experienced results of having established relatively constant horizons of value or relevance ('things'). They are not, as common sense insists, natural occurring realities or [things]. Indeed, what we take to be *objects* existing independently of ourselves are, in actuality, simply a function of habitual patterns of relationships" (140). Hershock goes on to offer us an intellectual cure for our culturally bound, default assumption that "things" are primary, allowing us to see "through the conceit that relations are second-order realities contingent upon pre-existing actors." A doctrine of internal relations requires of us a different common sense: "This amounts to an ontological gestalt shift from taking independent and dependent actors to be first order realities and relations among them as second order, to seeing relationality as first order (or ultimate) reality and all individual actors as (conventionally) abstracted or derived from them" (147).

Asking Different Questions: Whence and Whither?

The world of classical Chinese cosmology is thus better described in terms of interpenetrating "events" than as a spectrum of individual "things." In such a world, "whence" and "whither," which would assay *an event over time,* become the primary questions, whereas "where" and "when," as *points in place and time,* are merely conventional abstractions from and even distortions of what in fact comes to us as both continuous and eventful in our experience. In appealing to a narrative, processual, and generative understanding of persons, with all of the transitivity and conjunctions that are integral to their identity, Confucian persons are thus to be more likened to historical events than to marbles in a jar or spoons in a drawer.

And when we ask after such historical events—the Civil War, for example—we are likely to ask, not "what" is the Civil War, but "how did it come about" and "what were its consequences"—that is, the narrative "whence" and "whither" of the event. And in order to provide an adequate description of such an event, the explanatory "why" and "how" questions are immediately relevant. Indeed, in the case of events, the "what" question provides perhaps the least satisfying answer, arresting and delimiting a temporal and spatial event that is itself holistic and specious in the Jamesian sense of having implicated within it all of the history that has preceded it, and all of the history that follows from it.

Understanding the human "becoming" more as a verb than as a noun, Graham (1990) offers us a holographic world in which radically situated persons cannot be extricated from the temporality and fluid locale of their continuing narratives:

> If on the contrary one starts from the action, then duration and direction are already inherent in the verb; action is as much *from* and *to* as *in,* and as much *to, from* and *in* things and persons as places [italics added] . . . We may link this asymmetry with the verb-centeredness of Chinese language and thought . . . One notices the special interest of Chinese thinkers in the circumstances one "happens on" (*yu* 遇) and the action which is "timely" (*shih* [*shi*] used verbally). The categorical distinction which emerges from the question forms would seem to be between, not places and times, but the way (*tao* [*dao*] 道) one is on, coming from and proceeding along, and the times (*shih*) [*shi* 時] that one meets on the way. (391)[3]

In this process, cosmology, time, and place are not separate dimensions that can be parsed as discrete moments and simple locations of individuated things, but are inseparable "aspects" within the ceaseless flow of the always unique human experience. And the temporal and spatial terms we require in describing the events of this world are "aspectual" in proceeding from the assumption that we are identifying different yet mutually entailing ways to talk about the same phenomenon.[4] What this means is that person, place, and time are simply three among many perspectives on the same unfolding event, the same unique quantum of human experience.

Perhaps the one supplementary qualification we might want to make here, beyond Graham's noting Chinese thinkers' interest in what they "happen upon" within the unfolding of the "times," is to qualify the putative contingency of the human journey with the assumed importance of the deliberate resolution that must attend our capacity for "broadening and extending our way" through life (*hongdao* 弘道), and the aspiration to a timeliness in our activities that is required to make this shared pathway harmonious and fully our own (*zhonghe* 中和).[5] Way-making for this Confucian person is living deliberately and with musicality.

Graham offers us what we might call a "narrative" understanding of "human nature" (*xing*) in which person and world evolve together in a dynamic, contrapuntal relationship. The identities of persons are certainly grounded in their native beginnings within family, community, and environing relationships that need to be both nurtured and protected from loss or injury, but such identities emerge only in the process of these relationships achieving thick resolution as they are cultivated, grown, and consummated over their lifetimes. Their potential, far from being a given, in fact emerges contrapuntally in the always transactional events that in sum constitute lives lived in the world.

That is, even though there certainly are important initial conditions to be registered as the "potential" for becoming human, such conditions are not the idealist "beginnings" or the teleological "end"—something inborn "within" the persons exclusive of context and family relations, or the ineluctable actualization of some predetermined end. In the first place, in this natural cosmology there are no such deracinated persons. Persons do not exist inside their skins; they exist only in their associations. And because persons in their nested, narratives-within-narratives are constituted by these evolving, eventful relations, the "potential" of persons and their achieved identities in fact emerge *pari passu* out of the specific, contingent transactions of their lives. Thus, the best sense we can make of "potential" here is this: Potential, rather than being wholly antecedent as a set of given conditions, is also prospective and evolves within ever-changing circumstances; rather than being generic or universal, such potential is always unique to the career of this specific relational person; and rather than existing simply as an inherent and defining endowment, one's potential can be known only post hoc, after the unfolding of the particular narrative.

"Human *Beings*" or "Humane *Becomings*"?

What is a human "being"? This was the perennial Greek question asked in both Plato's *Phaedo* and Aristotle's *De Anima*. And the most persistent answer from the time of Pythagoras has been an ontological one: The "being" of a human being is a permanent, ready-made, and self-sufficient soul. And "know thyself"—the signature exhortation of Socrates—is to know this soul. Each of us *is* a person, and from conception, has the integrity of *being* a person.

How or *in what way* (*dao* 道) do persons in their roles *become* consummately humane (*ren* 仁)? This was the perennial Confucian question asked explicitly in all of the Four Books: in *The Great Learning,* in the *Analects of Confucius,* in the *Mencius,* and again in the *Zhongyong.* And from the time of Confucius onward, the answer was a moral, aesthetic, and ultimately religious one. Persons (necessarily plural) *become* humane by cultivating those thick, intrinsic relations that constitute our initial conditions and that locate the trajectory of our life narrative—its whence and whither—within family, community, and cosmos.[6] "Cultivate your persons"—*xiushen* 修身— the signature exhortation of the Confucian canon—is the ground of the Confucian project of becoming consummate as persons (*ren*): it is to cultivate our conduct assiduously as it is expressed through those family, community, and cosmic roles and relations that we live. And in this Confucian tradition, the "I" is irreducibly "we" in the sense that we need each other to become persons. That is, if there is only one person, there are no persons.[7] Becoming consummate in our conduct (*ren*) is something that we *do,* and that we do either together or not at all.

What is at stake here is the answer to perhaps our most basic and important philosophical question: How should we understand what it means to become fully human? How do we explain birth, life, and growth of the human "being"?—by reduplicative causal accounts (the infant is a ready-made adult), by teleological accounts (the infant is simply preliminary to the existing ideal), or in terms of humane "becomings" that appeal to a contextual, narrative account available to us through a phenomenology of deliberate personal action? How do we define what it means to be a human "being"? In terms of speculative assumptions about innate, isolatable causes that locate persons outside of the roles and relations in which they live their lives, or alternatively, as having "become" humane by taking account of the initial, native conditions and context within in which persons are inextricably embedded, and then by assaying the full aggregation of consequent, deliberate action as their life stories unfold?

As I have observed above, in our own world a foundational "individualism" has become an ideology without any robust alternatives. We must ask whether the bandwidth of our own seemingly default commonsense assumptions about *individual* human "beings" are consistent with the Confucian project as it was situated and developed within the natural process cosmology that serves this tradition as the context for such personal growth.

The Confucian Project: Persons as an Achieved Relational Virtuosity

Although this Confucian project certainly has important theoretical implications, what is compelling about it is that it proceeds from a relatively straightforward account of actual human experience. It is a pragmatic naturalism in the sense that, rather than appealing to ontological assumptions or supernatural speculations, it focuses instead on the possibilities for enhancing personal worth available to us here and now through enchanting the ordinary affairs of the day. A grandmother's love for her grandchild is at once the most ordinary of things, and at the same time, is the most extraordinary of things.

By developing his insights around the most basic and enduring aspects of the ordinary human experience—personal cultivation in family and communal roles, family reverence, deference to others, friendship, a cultivated sense of shame, education, community, a human-centered religiousness, and so on—Confucius has guaranteed their continuing relevance. In addition to being focused on perennial issues, one further characteristic of Confucianism that is certainly there in the words of Confucius himself, and that has made his teachings so resilient in this living tradition, is the porousness and adaptability of his teachings. His contribution was simply to strive to take full ownership of the cultural legacy of his time, to adapt the wisdom of the past to his own present historical moment, and then to recommend to future generations that they continue to do the same.[8]

The personal model of Confucius that is remembered in the *Analects* does not purport to lay out a generic formula by which everyone should live their lives. Instead, the text recalls the narrative of one special person: how he in his relations with others cultivated his humanity, and how he lived a fulfilling life, much to the admiration of those around him. Indeed, in reading the *Analects* we encounter the relationally constituted Confucius making his way through life by living his many roles as best he can: as a caring family member, as a strict teacher and mentor, as a scrupulous and incorruptible scholar-official, as a concerned neighbor and member of the community, as an always critical political consultant, as the grateful progeny of his progenitors, as an enthusiastic heir to a specific cultural legacy, and indeed, as a member of a chorus of joyful boys and men singing their way home after a happy day on the river Yi (*Analects* 11.26). In his teachings, he favors historical models over principles, analogies over theories, and exhortations over imperatives. The power and lasting value of his insights lie in the fact that, as I will endeavor to show, these ideas are intuitively persuasive and readily adaptable to the conditions of ensuing generations, including our own.

Indeed, what makes Confucianism more empirical than empiricism, that is, what makes Confucianism a *radical* empiricism, is the fact that it is prospective in respecting the uniqueness of the particular—in this case, the particular narrative of this one special person, Confucius, who lived an exemplary life. Rather than advancing universal principles and assuming a taxonomy of natural kinds grounded in a notion of strict identity, Confucianism proceeds from analogy with and always provisional generalizations derived from those *particular* historical instances of successful living, the specific events recounted in the narrative of Confucius himself being one case in point. And as an exemplar within the tradition, Confucius is "corporate" as ensuing generations continue to defer to this model in the way in which they live their lives.

Confucian Role Ethics and a Narrative
Understanding of Persons

What we are calling Confucian role ethics begins from the primacy of vital relationality—of lived roles and relations. Stated simply, it assumes the bare fact of associated living. The claim here is that no one and nothing and does anything by itself. All physical and conscious activity is collaborative and transactional. But where association is merely descriptive, roles are normative. A person's specific roles—daughter, grandfather, teacher, neighbor, shopkeeper, lover, and so on—are simply stipulated kinds of association that in their specificity take on a clear normative cast: Am I a good daughter? Am I a good teacher?

Role ethics is a properly "gerundive" and holistic, focus-field reading of this tradition that resists our seemingly default assumption that individuals as discrete entities are concrete existents rather than second-order abstractions from their narratives, and that they can be accurately described, analyzed, and evaluated independently of their contextualizing environments, including first and foremost their dealings other human beings. Role ethics begins from the assumption that, in any interesting moral or political sense, persons cannot be understood apart from the other persons with whom they interact, and that in fact persons are best described and evaluated in terms of the specific roles that guide their actions in their transactions with these specific others. Simply put, what is moral is conduct that conduces to growth and flourishing in the roles and relations we live together with others, and what is immoral is the opposite.

Virtue ethics, which appeals to the language of agents, acts, generic virtues, character traits, autonomy, motivation, reasons, choices, freedom, principles, consequences, and so on, assumes the individual human being as its starting point. Confucian role ethics, in contrast, is grounded in a more holistic and eventful "narrative" understanding of persons. As David B. Wong 黄百銳 reports: "The *Analects* thus shows a group with Confucius at the center, engaged in moral cultivation, each with a different configuration of strengths and weaknesses, not theorizing about it or giving philosophical justifications for it, but rather through their interactions providing a basis and inspiration for subsequent theorizing and justification by Confucius' successors in the Chinese philosophical tradition" (2014, 175). This being the case, Confucian role ethics is not so much an alternative "ethical theory" but a more capaciousness, *sui generis* vision of the moral life that begins from, and ultimately seeks its warrant in, the relatively straightforward account of the human experience that we find in the *Analects* and other early Confucian texts. I will argue that the normativity of role ethics arises from whole persons aspiring to live whole lives. I will make this argument for the scope of Confucian role ethics by responding to several fellow travelers—David Wong, Karyn Lai, and Steve Angle—who have offered welcome comments on and who have requested clarification about certain aspects of a Confucian roles ethics as we continue to search for the language to provide a sufficiently coherent account.

What Is the Term for "Role Ethics" in the Classical Chinese Canon?

Henry Rosemont and I have worked at formulating this Confucian position.[9] A starting point for us is the stubborn ambiguity that attends the key philosophical term *ren* 仁 as it first occurs, and is then is developed, in the *Analects of Confucius*.[10] It seems that *ren* will not give itself up to the "what" question. In the more than one hundred instances in which *ren* appears in the *Analects*, there seems to be a persistent eliding of a set of familiar, rather useful distinctions guaranteed at least in part by the grammar and inflections of our own English language. The function of these distinctions, in service to clarity and precision, is to abstract and isolate one or more aspects of persons from the unity of concrete experience: that is, an inner self from an outer world, agents from their actions, selves from others, a singular self from a field of selves, the means from the ends, mind from body, a person's character from the whole person, virtuous character traits from an exemplary life, psychological dispositions from the behaviors that are informed by them, the specific virtuosic actions from a general and characteristic habitude, the abstract concept itself from the concrete narrative from which it is derived, specific instances of conduct from higher-order generalizations made from them, and more.

Most, if not all, of these overlapping linguistic distinctions that fragment the continuity of personal experience make good sense to us because of our penchant for separating persons from each other as individuals, and then again separating them from what they do. As we have seen, this habit of thinking has deep roots in the ontology of our philosophical narratives. Such a deracination of persons and their conduct is a persistent, uncritical assumption for those who would argue that Confucianism offers a virtue ethics with Chinese characteristics—that the early Confucian counterpart of the term "virtue" (*aretē*) can be found in the term *de* 德, and thus that the core ethical terminology in early Confucian ethical writings can be rendered into an aretaic vocabulary.

But as we can see with the term *ren*, the *Analects* seem to eschew severe distinctions between persons as individuals and between persons and their conduct. No one can become *ren* by themselves, nor can anyone become *ren* by doing a generic and reduplicable *ren* action. The significance of *ren* is not only different for different people and for different situations, but we even find cases in which the very opposite of what is recommended as *ren* in one case is encouraged in another.

For example, staying with one of Wong's examples, we might compare the Master's answer to Yan Hui's question—when "Yan Hui inquired about *ren* (颜渊问仁)" (12.1)—with the answers he gives to exactly the same question—What does *ren* mean?—when it is asked by Zhonggong (12.2), Sima Niu (12.3 and 4), Fan Chi (12.22), and Zigong (15.10). They are very different answers. But Confucius sees Yan Hui and the others as very different students, and his answers mirror these perceived differences. In another case, when Confucius is asked the same question by Ranyou and Zilu (11.22)—"On learning something, should one act upon it?"—Confucius gives them opposite answers—"yes" to Ranyou and "no" to Zilu. When asked why he would give clearly contradictory counsel to these two students, Confucius says that his response is appropriate to the demonstrated habituated capacities of the questioner: "Ranyou is diffident, and so I urged him on. But Zilu has the energy of two, and so I sought to rein him in." *Ren* seems to be situation-and-person-specific, and to reference virtuosity in the conduct of the roles that we live. Indeed, I would argue that this holistic, specific, normative, and narrative meaning of *ren* allows us to claim that it is precisely this term *ren* that references role ethics in classical Confucianism.

And if we would defer to early Chinese cosmology as providing an alternative interpretive context for reading the *Analects* and the other classical Confucian texts—that is, an alternative cosmology that first and foremost gives primacy to vital relationality rather than to substance—we must question the relevance of our own commonsense distinctions about persons as individuals and their conduct to the extent that they violate the fundamental unity of experience entailed when we begin from this primacy of relationality. Said another way, the narrative ground of all ethical discourse in Confucian philosophy renders such distinctions between agents and actions always post hoc abstractions made from concrete and continuous episodes of associated conduct. What we are inclined to distinguish as erstwhile "individuals" and their "virtuous actions," or "concepts" and their "narrative sources and applications," are manifested in actuality as inseparable and nonanalytic aspects of the same experience.

Confucian Role Ethics and Moral Artistry

In her article "*Ren* 仁: An Exemplary Life," Karyn Lai (2014) is perhaps making a similar point in arguing that *ren* should be understood as an expansive, always context-specific quality of conduct discernible in those morally exemplary lives that have in common a commitment to the well-being of others, and hence that are lived in such a way as to foster growth in relations. Such persons develop and come to express this quality of conduct biographically in the roles and behaviors that are first associated with a family environment and that are then extended to the community more broadly. Lai insists on an underlying holism that brings unity to the different and various capacities of such persons as they are evidenced in their conduct. She contrasts this organic, situational, and dynamic reading of *ren* with Tu Wei-ming's more analytic, theoretical, and abstract understanding, where *ren* for Tu is "a higher-order concept" and "an inner morality." Lai (2014) argues that Tu's reductionistic descriptions of *ren* that invoke such fragmenting distinctions tend to individuate, theorize, and psychologize what she takes to be irreducibly concrete and thus always specific qualities of lives lived well.

Lai's understanding of *ren* requires that such exemplary lives be ultimately evaluated by appeal to more holistic, inclusive aesthetic criteria rather than by invoking abstract and reductionistic standards of conduct such as appeal to specific principles, the calculation of goods, or the cultivation of generic virtues. When we reflect on our exemplary teachers, for example, we are more inclined to remember particular situations or specific events as emblematic of their virtuosity rather than invoking anemic character traits such as honesty or courage: "We loved old Angus dearly, he was such a temperate man" is an unlikely thought (and especially so with Angus), whereas "Do you remember when Angus . . ." is all too familiar.

Evaluating Roles in Confucian Role Ethics

Steve Angle (2014) provides a fair-minded, generous, and yet still critical evaluation of the argument Rosemont and I offer that Confucian role ethics is sufficiently distinctive to resist collapsing it into existing Western moral theories. As Angle surmises, one reason we emphasize the differences between these moral theories and Confucian role ethics is because of the serious asymmetry that continues to skew comparisons between Confucian ethics and Western ethical theory. We do insist that the relatively recent encounter of Confucian role ethics with Western ethical theory cannot be taken as its defining moment. And although Angle does cite challenges in the secondary literature to our guiding premise that an interpretive context must be respected in our reading of these Confucian texts, he himself ultimately seems to take our side, concluding his own discussion of moral theory in the *Analects* with a cautionary note similar to our own. Speaking for himself, Angle (2014) avers there are many "hazards on the way to meaningful comparisons between ancient texts and modern theories" that arise when we forget that "the text has a complex social, conceptual, and historical context of its own" (252).

Our own project is certainly to remind readers of the Confucian canon to be cognizant of this general problem of interpretive context. But more specifically, as I have noted above, it is also clear to us that the notion of person in Confucian ethics resists some of our most familiar distinctions. For this reason, one prominent peril among these many hazards we believe might compromise responsible cultural comparisons is a failure to appreciate this alternative focus-field notion of person and its holographic understanding of the relationship between inner self and outer world.

Angle does allow that when Rosemont and I insist Confucian role ethics is a *sui generis* vision of the moral life, we "are not claiming that Confucian role ethics is incommensurable with Western moral theories."

We do attempt to articulate what we take to be the profound depth of the different cosmological assumptions that has occasioned the asymmetry in comparative philosophy—to begin with, the radically different conception of person that grounds Confucian role ethics. But this effort should not be taken to preclude any "productive, mutually-edifying dialogue" with Western ethical theories (Angle 2014, 245). In fact, in our published work Rosemont and I have been explicit on the need to have just such a conversation.[11] And beyond our own work, our graduate students as part of the next generation of comparative philosophers continue to write dissertations that make productive comparisons between Confucian role ethics, feminist care ethics, and Deweyan social ethics, as well as some of the other more mainstream moral theories.

The most substantial philosophical concern that Angle expresses about our position on Confucian role ethics is perhaps this: "The *Analects* clearly sees the need for critical evaluation of the ways that roles are inhabited by particular people. Does 'Confucian role ethics' provide adequate critical purchase for such an assessment? . . . If we need to be able to talk about good parents and bad, . . . the question then becomes in what terms we judge or articulate such goodness" (246–247).

It would seem that for Angle, if we are going to judge whether a person is living a particular role in a normatively justifiable way, the standard by which we are to evaluate whether the role is being lived well must precede and be external to the role itself. "Good" has to have some higher-order value than just "good parent"; one cannot establish that one is a good parent simply by asserting, "I am a good parent"—establishing the truth of that claim requires further justification. As an example, Angle cites A. T. Nuyen's version of Confucian role ethics as allowing that "the distinction between a good and bad occupier of a role is determined by how well a given individual fulfills the obligations associated with the given role"—obligations that as standards presumably exist independent of the role itself (Angle 2014, 248n42).[12]

Angle thinks that if we were to make a similar claim to be normatively committed to a general vision of interdependence and relationality as a preexisting standard, then we would end up with "virtuosity ethics" as opposed to "virtue ethics," where the quality of intimacy and mutuality would do the work of specific virtues—a position that might not in fact be role-dependent at all, and that could have a productive conversation with virtue ethics. But our claim is that in Confucian role ethics, all human relations are ultimately role-based, and that conduct that conduces to growth in these relations—to human flourishing—is the substance of morality. The centrality of *le* 樂— perhaps better understood in the early Confucian canon as "flourishing" rather than "happiness"—is often overlooked. Our argument is that a nonreductionistic flourishing of the role itself, with all of the complexity that attends it, is the proper standard of adjudication. The extent to which parents are to be deemed "good" parents is to be judged by the quality of their relationships with their always unique children in always unique situations. "Good with," "good for," "good in," "good to," "good at," and so on are prior to any derivative characterization. The moral artistry and the aesthetic achievement of making the most of a specific matrix of relationships—the role of being this parent, as a case in point—is in itself normative.

Said another way, Angle advocates for a separation between "virtues" and roles and then treats such virtues as higher-order standards that can be used to evaluate and justify roles. We on the other hand insist that virtuosity and roles are inseparable. Again it is the relations and their quality that are first-order, whereas abstracted "objects"— virtues or putative individuals—are second-order. The content of virtues, values, and principles is abstracted from the concrete conduct that constitutes lived roles, and then lived roles in turn in some degree come to be guided by such fluid abstractions. But importantly, as our roles change, the content of our moral categories change along with them. One important contribution that role ethics makes to the discourse is to alert us to the particularist, processual, provisional, and revisionist status of our moral vocabulary.

Indeed, we can use the term for "good" in classical Chinese— *hao* 好—as a heuristic for making the argument for both the assumed priority of relationships in expressing what is "good," and the evolving definition of what it means to be "good" in the roles we live. On the oracle bones and the bronzes, this graph initially depicts the specific relationship between a mother and her child 㛸, but over time its meaning is extended to describe productive roles more broadly, to the extent that it loses its original reference to mother and child. On the bronzes, for example, a brave and strong male is deemed a "stout fellow" (*haohan* 好漢) and a woman of striking appearance is deemed a "handsome woman" (*haonu* 好女). The content of the moral vocabulary—in this case, "good"—is not one thing; it evolves and is derived over time from the many changing roles and relations in the human narrative.

How then can we critically assess roles as they are lived? We certainly can stipulate general features of human flourishing as rules of thumb, but it is ultimately the growth in the specific role itself—my complex relationship with this specific student, for example—that is primary, and that gives the necessary specificity to what the content of such "flourishing" would be. We can no more provide a formula for the good teacher than we can for a work of art. We have all had good teachers, and we would not assume that some set of general characteristics defining the teacher-student relationship can do justice to the phenomenon. In fact, there are congeries of differences among such relationships. The role itself as lived between this teacher and this student has its own normative force that resists our generic reductions. Good teachers serve as exemplary models rather than as principles that can be articulated and followed, and as observed above, they are usually invoked anecdotally rather than by appeal to generic character traits. "I am her teacher" is itself a normative injunction referring us to concrete exemplars and our own past experience, and in determining what to do next, such an injunction is more helpful than any list of abstract virtues—justice, courage, prudence, and so forth. "Because she is my student" is a powerful justification for my actions.

Perhaps another way of responding to Angle's need for an independent standard would be to argue that these Confucian texts give primacy to the thick notion of an "achieved propriety in one's lived roles and relations" (*li* 禮). And while they regard the abstract rule of law and the application of punishments as necessary institutions, at the same time they construe appeal to law as a clear admission of communal failure. For example: "The Master said: 'Lead the people with administrative injunctions and keep them orderly with penal law, and they will avoid punishments but will be without a sense of shame. Lead them with moral virtuosity and keep them orderly through observing ritual propriety and they will develop a sense of shame, and moreover, will order themselves'" (*Analects* 2.3). It is the model of moral virtuosity in the role of the ruler and the proper functioning of roles and their commensurate sense of shame within ritually choreographed family and community relations that serve as a basis for critical assessment. A dynamic *li*-structured family and community is unique and concrete; abstract precepts are at best only secondary injunctions that might serve as guideposts.

Dewey and the Postulate of Immediate Empiricism: On Reinstating the Wholeness of Experience

I want to abjure the "Euthyphro problem," which insists that principles of adjudication must be prior to and separate from the object of our judgment. Something must be good in itself rather than deemed good as a summary of its relationships. For help in formulating an understanding of good that will do justice to the full complexity of the human experience, I appeal to John Dewey (1998), who, in asking what human experience is, and what it means, introduces what he calls his postulate of immediate empiricism: "Immediate empiricism postulates that things—anything, everything, in the ordinary or non-technical use of the term 'thing'—are what they are experienced as . . . If *any* experience, then a *determinate* experience; and this determinateness is the only, and is the adequate, principle of control, or 'objectivity.' . . . If you wish to find out what subjective, objective, physical, mental, cosmic, psychic, cause, substance, purpose, activity, evil, being, quality—any philosophic term, in short—means, go to experience and see what the thing is experienced *as*" (115, 116, 118).

I want to add "good" to "subjective," "objective," and the other terms on Dewey's list of philosophical categories that he insists can be adequately defined only by looking at how they are lived and what we experience them *as*. For Dewey this postulate is his further refinement of what his mentor, William James, had referred to as "radical empiricism": "To be radical, an empiricism must neither admit into its constructions any element that is not directly experienced, nor exclude from them any element that is directly experienced. For such a philosophy, the relations that connect experiences must themselves be experienced relations, and any kind of relation experienced must be accounted as 'real' as anything else in the system" (James 2000, 315).

A more recent advocate of a pragmatic approach to philosophy, Hilary Putnam, brings further clarity to this postulate of immediate empiricism by not only rejecting "view-from-nowhere" objectivism, but by further insisting that the subjective dimension of experience is always integral to what the world really is. Putnam (1990) insists: "Elements of what we call 'language' or 'mind' *penetrate so deeply into what we call 'reality' that the very project of representing ourselves as being 'mappers' of something 'language-independent' is fatally compromised from the start*. Like Relativism, but in a different way, Realism is an impossible attempt to view the world from Nowhere" (Putnam 1990, 28). Putnam will not admit of any understanding of the real world that cleaves it off from its human participation and that does not accept our experience of it as what it *really* is: "The heart of pragmatism, it seems to me—of James' and Dewey's pragmatism if not of Peirce's—was the supremacy of the agent point of view. If we find that we must take a certain point of view, use a certain 'conceptual system,' when engaged in a practical activity, in the widest sense of practical activity, then we must not simultaneously advance the claim that it is not really 'the way things are in themselves'" (Putnam 1987, 83).

In arguing for the reality of experience itself, these classical and neo-Pragmatists see the familiar equation between knowledge and reality that has grounded classical epistemology—"reality as the self-luminous vision of the Absolute" (Dewey 1998, 117)—as being a fundamental and persistent error. Simply put, experience is what it is, and it is all real.

Abjuring "the Perils of Abstraction"

Bernard Williams, in his search for "thick," "world-guided" ethical concepts, is famous for his reservations about the capacity of any moral theory to tell us what is right, what is wrong, and what we ought to do. In the preface to *Moral Luck*, for example, Williams announces: "There cannot be any very interesting, tidy or self-contained theory of what morality is, nor, despite the vigorous activities of some present practitioners, can there be an ethical theory, in the sense of a philosophical structure which, together with some degree of empirical fact, will yield a decision procedure for moral reasoning" (1981, ix–x). The implication is that experience itself will provide the basis for deliberate moral conduct.

And Alfred North Whitehead, who is often quoted as saying, "We think in generalities, but we live in detail," also worried about the cost of the persisting imbalance that has us relying upon the ostensive clarity of abstract theory at the expense of the more murky and tentative world of practice. In rehearsing the history of philosophy, Whitehead accuses Epicurus, Plato, and Aristotle of being "unaware of the perils of abstraction" that render knowledge closed and complete. According to Whitehead (1938), "the history of thought" that he associates with these great figures "is a tragic mixture of vibrant disclosure and of deadening closure. The sense of penetration is lost in the certainty of completed knowledge. This dogmatism is the antichrist of learning. In the full concrete connection of things, the characters of the things connected enter into the character of the connectivity which joins them . . . Every example of friendship exhibits the particular character of the two friends. Two other people are inconsistent in respect to that completely defined friendship" (58).

We should pay attention to the example Whitehead offers here to explain the prospective "sense of penetration" that is arrested and compromised by assumptions about the certainty of knowledge. For Whitehead, friendship is the creative advance in our lives that occurs when two, always unique persons are able to achieve and consolidate a continuing pattern of productive relations. Although the two persons in any continuing friendship are themselves nonsubstitutable, and, to use Whitehead's own language, anyone else would be "inconsistent" in the relation, for him it is the continuing quality of the process of friendship itself, including both unique friends *and their connectivity*, that is in fact concrete. And the two persons as putative "individuals," or evaluations of their relationship that appeal to fixed characteristics such as obligations, are simply abstractions from that lived reality.

Indeed, at a cosmological level for Whitehead, the very assumption that there are such things as discrete individuals is a prime and prominent example of what he calls the "Fallacy of Simple Location"— the familiar and yet fallacious assumption that isolating, decontextualizing, and analyzing things as simple particulars is the best way to understand the content of our experience. Whitehead rejects a world of "objects" as abstractions from our experience, and argues that the fundamental realities of both experience and nature itself are best understood as irreducibly extended and dynamic events. For Whitehead (1979), the notion of the discrete individual assumed in much of the liberal theorizing of the person is a specific and persistent example of the philosopher's *deformation professionelle,* and is a blatant case of what he has called elsewhere the fallacy of "misplaced concreteness." This second, closely related fallacy regards abstracted entities that are presumed to have a simple location as being "more real" than the field of their dynamic, extended relations with all of the untidy transitions and conjunctions that constitute the genuine content of the human experience (137).[13]

Charles Hartshorne (1950) elaborates upon this concern of Whitehead's, problematizing our commonsense understanding of our ostensive "inner" and "outer" domains by insisting on the mutual implication and interpenetration of persons in their relations with others (although our sense of "totality" will have to do the work of Whitehead's "God"): "As Whitehead has most clearly seen—individuals generally are not simply outside each other (the fallacy of 'simple location') but in each other, and God's inclusion of all things is merely the extreme or super-case of the social relativity or mutual immanence of individuals" (443).

And Sor-hoon Tan (2003), in her argument that the conduct of human beings is irreducibly social and organic, invokes John Dewey's "retrospective fallacy" as a challenge to the isolating reduplication of personal identity that occurs when we abstract persons from the connectivity of their narratives: "Those still preoccupied with *identity* often complain that Dewey's view is that of a 'self-in-action without a self.' They miss the point of Dewey's protest against traditional conceptions of the self. For Dewey, there could be no self outside of experience, outside of human doing and undergoing. The distinction between 'self' and action is 'after the fact.' Unity precedes distinctions in experience; to think otherwise is to commit the 'retrospective fallacy'—to mistake a distinction introduced into experience by later reflections as fully present in the original experience . . . Selfhood is an eventual function that emerges with complexly organized interactions, organic and social" (27).

Holographic "Focus" as the Functional
Equivalent of "Agency"

Indeed, this "narrative" understanding of persons that precludes a parsing of them as discrete, deracinated individuals provides us with the beginning of an answer to David Wong's question about the kind of agency we have ascribed to Confucian role ethics—what we have called a "focus-field" notion of agency. From Wong's description of the *Analects* as a shared narrative, it is clear that there is much in his understanding of early Confucianism that is consistent with our way of thinking about role ethics. And further, Wong seems to be wholly cognizant of the centrality of the aesthetic and aspirational ground of human flourishing and its justification within the Confucian vision of the moral life that I have appealed to in responding to Steve Angle above. Wong (2014) observes: "The Confucian notion of what it is like to live a fully good life has an aesthetic dimension that might look odd and unfamiliar to a contemporary Western audience . . . Such stylized action could be said to possess a moral beauty. The moral beauty lies in the gracefulness and spontaneity of what has become a natural respectfulness and considerateness" (177).

But Wong in his reading of Confucian ethics still seems to fall back on the primacy of discrete individuals over their relations with others. He frames his question to us thusly: "If I am the sum of my relationships, then who or what is the entity standing in each of these particular relationships?" For Wong, there must be two "entities" (albeit at first biological organisms rather than "persons") before there can be a relationship between them. Wong's own answer to this question, developed in his earlier work and retained in his most recent publications, is this: "We begin life embodied as biological organisms and become persons by entering into relationship with others of our kind" (192).

Our answer would be different. We would refrain from the retrospective fallacy by introducing a distinction that was not there in the original experience, and simply repeat the claim that we are the sum of and are constituted by our relationships themselves. I have never been a "me" without the "me" being this son, this brother, this teacher, this Canadian, and so on. We are our narratives. And there is no need to reduplicate this intense and habitual focus or center of relationships by positing an antecedent "substance" within which these relationships must inhere. William James (2000) challenges such "substance" thinking as our "inveterate trick" of turning names into "things": "The low thermometer to-day, for instance, is supposed to come from something called the 'climate.' Climate is really only the name for a certain group of days, but it is treated as if it lay *behind* the day, and in general we place the name, as if it were a being, behind the facts it is the name of. But the phenomenal properties of things . . . do not inhere in anything. They adhere, or cohere, rather, with each other, and the notion of a substance inaccessible to us, which we think accounts for such cohesion by supporting it, as cement might support pieces of a mosaic, must be abandoned. The fact of the bare cohesion itself is all the notion of the substance signifies. Behind that fact is nothing" (42).

For Confucian role ethics, behind the fact of the dynamic narrative of relations is nothing. As I will attempt to describe, we begin life as shallow, complex matrixes of what at first are largely physical and then become familial and communal relations. Through achieving focus and resolution in living these embodied roles and relations, gradually we evolve into always unique and somewhat coherent personal identities.

In order to be clear in formulating our own answer to Wong's question, we will need to go back to the distinction between contrasting doctrines of external and internal relations alluded to by Angus Graham. Substance ontology and its doctrine of external relations has become and continues to be our shared (but culturally bound) common sense. This ontology guarantees the primacy and the integrity of the discrete and independent entities Wong seems to assume when he allows that we as separate organisms "become persons by entering into relationship with others of our kind."

The Confucian "Intrasubjective" Person

A doctrine of internal relations begins from the primacy of the organic continuity that is constitutive of putative "things." Given the primacy of this vital relationality in the cosmology that gives context to Confucian role ethics, both embodied biological relations and social relations as they are captured in the cognate, aspectual terms *ti* 體 and *li* 禮— "lived body" and "embodied living"—are organically diffused as those dynamic, interactive, and interpenetrating patterns that make up the narratives of lives being lived.[14] Such patterns are initially so weak and tentative that we might be inclined to describe infants as "biological organisms," but this is to abstract them from their contexts. They are from the outset intrasubjective, nested in and informed by the field of familial and communal relations within which they evolve, and as these patterns are marked by continuing growth and depth in meaning, they enable infants to become increasingly distinctive as they learn to live well.

But let us be clear. There are no infants as "biological organisms" independent of the web of relationships that constitute them. Our claim is that an infant born into the world is not, either biologically or socially, a discrete or ready-made entity that, as an exclusive life form, has its own putative initial beginning. Instead, drawing nourishment from its physical, social, and cultural umbilical cords, the infant is born *in media res* as an intrasubjective narrative nested within narratives. Far from being discrete or isolated, the infant is the diffused yet focused presencing of a physical, social, and cultural matrix or field of radial relationships that extend to the furthest reaches of the cosmos.

Of course, just as we must be careful to distinguish a leg from walking as an activity in the world, we must not elide the activity of mind and the brain. The immediate family members who quite literally "mind" the infant communicate and impart their mature culture to this organism, and initially serve as the primary resource that an emerging "mindful" and "whole-hearted" child can draw upon in shaping a personal identity. If the phenomenon of infancy teaches us anything, it is certainly not the independence of our agency; on the contrary, by reflecting on our early years we come to understand that "mind" is a social phenomenon shared among us that emerges as embodied organisms communicate with each other to transform mere association into thriving families and communities. Infancy should teach us to appreciate our dependence on our relationships for our very survival, and ultimately for the evolving composing of our identities.

John Dewey's Challenge: An Intrasubjective Masterpiece

I began this essay by suggesting that Confucius's relational conception of person and his role ethics as an aestheticism might have something to contribute to Sandel's project of formulating an adequate conception of the intrasubjective person as an alternative to the deontological self that grounds much liberal thinking. Dewey sets a high bar with the kind of intrasubjective "individuality" he wants us to aspire to: Consonant with the benchmarks set by Sandel, Dewey requires nothing less than a unique and inexpugnable personal masterpiece from each of us that "is a manner distinctive sensitivity, selection, choice, response, and utilization of conditions" (1962, 167):

> Individuality is at first spontaneous and unshaped; it is a potentiality, a capacity of development . . . Since individuality is a distinctive way of feeling the impacts of the world and of showing a preferential bias in response to those impacts, it develops into shape and form only through interaction with actual conditions; it is no more complete in itself than is a painter's tube of paint without relation to a canvas. The work of art is the truly individual thing; and it is the result of the interaction of paint and canvas through the medium of the artist's distinctive vision and power . . . something original and creative; something formed in the very process of creation of other things. (1962, 168–169)

Notes

1. It should be noted that we need the term "role" in the English expression "Confucian role ethics," but it is redundant if we use the Chinese because "role" is already there in the language of "Confucian ethics" (儒學倫理學), as the term *lun* 倫 itself means "human roles and relations." Although *lunlixue* as a translation of "ethics" is a modern term, the binomial *lunli* dates back to Han Dynasty sources. That this same term *lun* also means "category" and "class" suggests that the construction of such discriminations as "categories" is a function of correlations and analogy rather than assumed essences.

2. To preclude such uncritical assumptions, Sandel suggests that we must be self-conscious about how we parse the notion of self or person, even when moving among the various philosophical positions as they are formulated within our own academy.

3. Verb is better than noun certainly. But perhaps the inclusive gerund as the verbal noun "person-ing" would be the better choice for Graham.

4. Revealed in the language itself, our human world (*shijie* 世界) is diachronic: *shi* 世 "worlding-as-intergenerational-temporal-succession" and synchronic: *jie* 界 "worlding-as-the-crossing-of-spatial-boundaries"; and our cosmos (*yuzhou* 宇宙) is *yu* 宇 "cosmos-as-it-extends" and *zhou* 宙 "cosmos-as-it-endures."

5. See, for example, *Analects* 15.29, 1.12; and *Zhongyong* 25 and 1.

6. See *Analects* 12.1: "Through self-discipline and observing ritual propriety one becomes consummate in one's conduct." 克己復 禮為仁. All translations are from Ames and Rosemont 1998.

7. "For Confucius, unless there are at least two human beings, there can be no human beings" (Fingarette 1983, 217).

8. *Analects* 7.1.

9. See Rosemont's contribution in this volume, Chapter 9.

10. Of course, *ren* does appear as early as the Shang Dynasty oracle bones and on the bronzes as well. Although its meaning remains obscure on the oracle bones, it clearly means love and kindness on the bronzes. Our point is that even though there are early yet infrequent occurrences of *ren*, this term accrues substantial philosophical import only with its development as a term of art in the *Analects*.

11. Early on and with consistency, Rosemont (1991b) anticipated this second step: "I do not wish to imply that the early Confucian writings are the be-all and end-all for finding answers to the multiplicity of questions I have posed . . . Some Western philosophical concepts will, and should remain with us, some others will have to be stretched, bent, and . . . or extended significantly in order to represent accurately non-Western concepts and concept clusters" (92, 94). And having first wanted to allow the vocabulary of Confucian role ethics to speak for itself, I have also been explicit on this further challenge: "The next stage in the effort to give full expression to role ethics as a new and compelling vision of the ethical life will require a sustained con-

versation between Confucian philosophy and existing Western ethical theories that is able to draw creatively upon these very different ways of thinking about the refinement and evaluation of human conduct" (Ames 2011, xvii).

12. One problem with an appeal to generic "obligations" that define roles is again that it focuses on individuals rather than on roles. Just as a role would be defined in terms of both trust and credibility simultaneously, so it would require an appropriate balance between privilege and obligation.

13. Whitehead (1979) observes: "This presupposition of individual independence is what I have elsewhere called, the 'fallacy of simple location' " (137).

14. See Ames 2011—in chapter 3 I use these two terms *ti* 體 and *li* 禮 as a heuristic for explaining the process of achieving personal identity in the early Confucian tradition.

References

Ames, Roger T. 2011. *Confucian Role Ethics: A Vocabulary*. Hong Kong: Chinese University Press, and Honolulu: University of Hawai'i Press.

Ames, Roger T., and Henry Rosemont, Jr. 1998. *The Analects of Confucius: A Philosophical Translation*. New York: Random House / Ballantine Books.

Angle, Steve. 2014. "The *Analects* and Moral Theory." In *Dao Companion to the Analects*, edited by Amy Olberding. Dordrecht: Springer.

Anscombe, G. E. M. 1958. "Modern Moral Philosophy." *Philosophy* 33: 1–19.

Aristotle. 1984. *The Complete Works of Aristotle: The Revised Oxford Translation*. Edited by Jonathan Barnes. Princeton, NJ: Princeton University Press.

Dewey, John. 1962. *Individualism Old and New*. New York: Capricorn Books.

———. 1998. *The Essential Dewey*. Volume 1. Edited by Larry Hickman and Thomas Alexander. Bloomington, IN: Indiana University Press.

Fingarette, Herbert. 1983. "The Music of Humanity in the Conversations of Confucius." *Journal of Chinese Philosophy* 10 (4): 331–356.

Graham, A. C. 1990. *Studies in Chinese Philosophy and Philosophical Literature*. Albany: SUNY Press.

———. 1991. "Replies." In *Chinese Texts and Philosophical Contexts: Essays Dedicated to Angus C. Graham*, edited by Henry Rosemont Jr., 267–323. La Salle, IL: Open Court.

Hartshorne, Charles. 1950. *A History of Philosophical Systems*. New York: Philosophical Library.

Hershock, Peter. 2006. *Buddhism in the Public Sphere: Reorienting Global Interdependence*. New York: Routledge.

James, William. 2000. *Pragmatism and Other Writings*. New York: Penguin.

Lai, Karyn. 2014. "*Ren* 仁: An Exemplary Life." In *Dao Companion to the Analects*, edited by Amy Olberding. Dordrecht: Springer.

MacIntyre, Alasdair. 1981. *After Virtue*. Notre Dame, IN: University of Notre Dame Press.

Nietzsche, Friedrich. 1966. *Beyond Good and Evil*. Translated by W. Kaufmann. New York: Vintage.

Putnam, Hilary. 1987. *The Many Faces of Realism*. La Salle, IL: Open Court.

———.1990. *Realism with a Human Face*. Cambridge, MA: Harvard University Press.

Rosemont, Henry Jr., ed. 1991a. *Chinese Texts and Philosophical Contexts: Essays Dedicated to Angus C. Graham*. La Salle, IL: Open Court.

———.1991b. "Rights-Bearing and Role-Bearing Persons." In *Rules, Rituals, and Responsibility: Essays Dedicated to Herbert Fingarette*, edited by Mary Bockover. La Salle, IL: Open Court.

———. 2015. *Against Individualism: A Confucian Rethinking of the Foundations of Morality, Politics, Family, and Religion*. Idaho Falls, ID: Lexington Books.

Rosemont, Henry Jr. and Roger T. Ames. 2016. *Confucian Role Ethics: A Vision for the Twenty-First Century?* Taipei: National Taiwan University Press and V&R Unipress.

Sandel, Michael. 1982. *Liberalism and the Limits of Justice*. Cambridge: Cambridge University Press.

Shun, Kwong-loi. 2009. "Studying Confucian and Comparative Ethics: Methodological Reflections." *Journal of Chinese Philosophy* 36 (3): 317–343.

Tan, Sor-hoon. 2003. *Confucian Democracy: A Deweyan Reconstruction*. Albany: SUNY Press.

Whitehead, Alfred North. 1938. *Modes of Thought*. New York: Free Press.

———. 1979. *Process and Reality: An Essay in Cosmology*. Corrected edition, edited by Donald Sherbourne. New York: Free Press.

Williams, Bernard. 1981. *Moral Luck: Philosophical Papers, 1973–1980*. New York: Cambridge University Press.

Wong, David B. 2004. "Relational and Autonomous Selves." *Journal of Chinese Philosophy* 34 (4): 419–432.

———. 2008. "If We Are Not by Ourselves, If We Are Not Strangers." In *Polishing the Chinese Mirror: Essays in Honor of Henry Rosemont, Jr.*, edited by Marthe Chandler and Ronnie Littlejohn. New York: Global Scholarly.

———. 2014. "Cultivating the Self in Concert with Others." In *Dao Companion to the Analects*, edited by Amy Olberding. Dordrecht: Springer.

How to Think about Morality
without Moral Agents

HENRY ROSEMONT JR.

In his contribution to this volume my friend and collaborator Roger Ames has ably placed the idea of an ethics of roles in the ancient Chinese metaphysical context from which it originally came. Herein I want to take the concept out of that Chinese context and place it squarely in our own, keeping the Confucian vision as much as possible and elaborating on it in the hope of demonstrating the contribution it might make in addressing many of the problems affecting our society.

To my mind few philosophers have faced and analyzed these problems as clearly as Michael Sandel has done (Sandel 1984, 2005, 2009, 2012). Our own laments regarding the sorry state of the United States are pretty much the same as his: erosion of moral values, commodification of virtually everything, decline in community engagement, loss of civility, distrust of government, and much more (Sandel 2012). He has broken with the dominant Western paradigm in moral and political philosophy to insist that the good must have priority over the right (Sandel 1984, 174–179.), with which we concur (as would Confucius). He similarly breaks with it when he insists that individuals are not altogether free, but encumbered by the mores of the community in which they were raised, which is at the heart of his critique of Rawls (Sandel 1984, 159). He does an excellent job of showing the implausibility of entrusting the creation of a just society to thoroughgoing amnesiacs: as he put it, "[My encumbrances] allow that to some I owe

more than justice requires or even permits, not by reason of agreements I have made but instead in virtue of those more or less enduring attachments and commitments that, taken together, *partly
define* the person I am . . . To imagine a person incapable of constitutive attachments . . . is not to conceive an ideally free and rational
agent, but to imagine a person wholly without character, without
moral depth" (2005, 167, italics added).

Unfortunately Sandel does not further define the self, the person,
beyond the attachments just described (Sandel 1984, 174). Had he done
so, he might have seen that apart from those attachments there is actually very little or nothing to define, as I have recently argued at length
(Rosemont 2015, 33–75) and as neuroscientists are telling us with increasing frequency as our knowledge of the brain grows. Yet for Roger
and me, foundational individualism of *any* kind is what justifies the
ideological mischief constantly in play in the capitalist market economy
and among a number of philosophers whom Sandel elsewhere rightly
criticizes, up to and including the libertarian concept of self-ownership
that can justify cannibalism by consenting adults (Sandel 2009, 74). As
a consequence, so long as foundational individualism remains the paradigm when thinking about our humanity, most of the current run of
commercial and other horrors Sandel describes in his recent work
(2012, 8–19) will not be eliminated—or at the least, he provides few
signposts for suggesting how we might do so, apart from claiming
that "reasoned argument" can be effective even in very difficult cases
(2005, 20).

Roger and I want to go farther than Sandel, and question not only
the unencumbered picture of the self, but the existence of any self at
all, which we believe is a fiction—one that is no longer merely benign
but has become oppressive—that is being used to justify gross inequalities of wealth and opportunity in the United States (Rosemont
2015, 57–76). And we want to proffer an alternative concept of
what it is to be a human being without using the standard language
of subjectivity / objectivity, choice, freedom, character traits, self-

consciousness, virtues, and similar terms employed in individualistic moral and political discourses (including Sandel's) and still be discussing moral and political issues.

How might we think about dealing with our fellows differently if we endeavor to picture them as fully interrelated role-bearing persons rather than individual selves? And what happens if, instead of concentrating on the loss of community and seeking ways to restore it, we advance the institution of the family as the best ground for generating the kind of person needed to appropriately address the problems we all agree must be addressed today?

These are the questions I speak to in this essay. Throughout, regarding Sandel, I will offer what is supposedly the sincerest form of flattery: imitation. I will attempt to do public philosophy as I see it, focus on contemporary problems, give many topical examples and not shrink from normativity—all of which he has done often, and well. Though I fear we disagree on a number of points, to my mind he is a model philosopher, and I am pleased to be in dialogue with him in this volume.

The Larger Issue

Every society must have a dominant ideology that includes an ordering of values, a view of what it is to be a human being, a morality, and a consequent rationale justifying the ways in which resources are produced and distributed in that society and in which people interact with one another. The societies may include a number of ideologies, but one will have pride of place in each if the economy is to run smoothly, the government is to govern, and the people at odds in their cultural setting. To take pride in belonging to a slave society, for example, its ideology must include the belief that some human beings are naturally inferior to other human beings and that belief must be widespread and deep. Or again, gross inequalities in the distribution of goods is *prima facie* an untoward state of affairs and must be rationalized, in some cases by viewing certain human beings as deserving by birthright (aristocracy, in medieval societies) or by merit (entrepreneurs in industrial capitalism). Given the inertial resistance to change in virtually every society, absent fundamental challenges to its dominant ideology it is doubtful that there will be any significant alterations in dysfunctional productive forces and / or social practices, no matter how badly they are needed.

The United States entered the postindustrial era several decades ago, with its citizens now living in a globalizing, high-technology, multiethnic, and consolidating society with many of its natural resources polluted or depleted, or nearly so, and sharing the planet with 7 billion other human beings, many of whom hate us or fear us (or both) some of whom have the capability to destroy us. But the dominant ideology of capitalism remains basically the same from when the United States had a small population, saw immigration on a large scale, was involved in extensive mining and logging, and there was agricultural expansion. This was true amid later mass production as well—which was supported by an abundance of unspoiled shorelines, clean air, and fresh water. In this environment, an ideology of "rugged individualism" appeared to fit in pretty well, focusing on self-reliance, independence, ingenuity, and above all, freedom to self-interestedly seek one's fortune.

To take only one small example, throughout the nineteenth and early twentieth centuries corporations were subsidized, and encouraged in many ways to become profitable because they were transforming resources into manufactures that people needed and wanted and they provided employment for a great many workers. But today corporations continue to be measured by and celebrated for maximizing profits. even though their actions are now significantly responsible for many of the current problems of our society; it is difficult to fault them for avoiding taxes, laying off workers whenever possible, outsourcing jobs to where labor is less costly, or polluting the environment when it is not illegal and is much cheaper than cleaning it up; hoarding wealth secretly overseas; and subverting democracy by using their money to persuade legislators to enact only those regulations that are in no one's interest but the corporations'. All of these activities are morally questionable at best, but very good for enhancing shareholder profits.

The celebration rather than condemnation of such activities at the corporate level applies no less at the individual level: seek wealth, maximize your self-interest, pay not a penny more in taxes than you absolutely have to, do not purchase solar panels until they are considerably cheaper than continuing with an air-fouling fossil fuel. If you're wealthy enough, it is okay give an obscene amount of money to help elect legislators who promise to leave you alone and lower your taxes. If corporations are supposed to compete, so are individuals—for schooling, jobs, partners, good housing, celebrity, and much more.

We can no longer afford to advance a capitalist ideology centered on competition and individualism, even of a less than rugged sort. It has become too dysfunctional (as well as morally and metaphysically dubious). Among many and growing shortcomings, grounding an ideology in competition by a society guarantees *by definition* that it must generate many losers as well as some winners, the number of losers growing over time as winners become fewer and more powerful. The richness of the resources of the earth—especially in the United States—has allowed us to ignore that simple logical fact for well over a century, believing instead that we can substantively reduce the number of losers simply by producing more, so that there is no need to speak of more equitable distributions of wealth. But many resources have been depleted, a number of our purple mountains are no longer majestic, and many of our plains bear little fruit. It is becoming much more expensive to exploit the remaining resources at an increased profit, and if that is the only way people can secure potable water, we may expect more and more people to die of thirst in the future (in some areas, the *near* future). Clearly—or so it seems to me, at least—as water grows more scarce, it must be collectively conserved and equi-tably shared. But if I see others only as competitors acting in their own self-interest, it is not rational for me to believe I am my brother's or sister's keeper, even though I will probably not be proud of acting on the rebarbative "Nice guys finish last."

Do we have other ideological options with which to confront today's realities?

Values and Value Orderings

Each person values many human qualities and behaviors (in addition to material things), sufficient in number and variety to form an incon-sistent set. We cannot consistently assert both "You can't teach an old dog new tricks" and "You're never too old to learn." But the incon-sistency holds only when asserting both statements at the same time with respect to the same situation. We do believe there are circumstances in which each of the statements would be altogether appropriate. If your grandfather has always believed Franklin Delano Roosevelt was the worst and most dangerous president the United States has ever had, and complains about it at every family gathering, then pointing out the salutary effects of the New Deal will almost certainly be a waste of time. On the other hand, if, upon his retirement he expresses an interest in learning to play the violin, it would likely behoove the family to chip in and buy one for him, and hire a violin teacher for him. This is no more than to say that neither adage quoted above about teaching the elderly should be taken as a universal principle, but that both are appropriate to invoke and act on at times. We tend to believe, in other words, that certain qualities and behaviors of others deserve praise (or blame) at different times in differing situations. Morality is nei-ther universal nor relative, but it is plural, determinatively so. It needs few, if any, universal principles, but much particularistic appropriateness.

This suggests that today's world calls for seeing human beings basically not as competitors but as cooperators; not isolated and autonomous but as interdependent and interrelated; not as self-reliant and alone, but as benefactor and beneficiary of others; not as free (to do as we choose), but as encumbered (to meet our responsibilities). And we must reorder our values accordingly. Thus, in a world with many people and shrinking resources, "May the best man win" should be replaced with "It isn't whether you win or lose, but how you play the game that counts." It is much less important now for children to learn the insight "Every man's home is his castle" than for them to come to feel and appreciate the truth of "No man is an island." Christian parents especially should devote less time teaching that "God helps them that help themselves" and more time expressing the injunction to "Love thy neighbor *as thyself.*"

I suspect that every one of my readers will acknowledge the "truth" of each of the quoted statements, even though they are inconsistent together. That is to say, virtually everyone will agree that cooperative values are not alien to us, despite the fact that we live in the "sweet land of liberty." This suggests fairly strongly that developing a new (or very old) ethical orientation will be less difficult if we stop thinking about it in terms of different peoples and cultures having to take on an entirely new set of values. It might be better (and more accurate) to think of different people in the same or different cultures having different orderings of values that virtually every human being holds, or may be presumed to hold, at some level. This orientation paves the conceptual way for dialogue inter-and intraculturally, not solely on the merits of the values but equally on the basis of which value ordering best reflects the physical demands of the society, and what place the other values can take therein. Otherwise we will end up with paralyzing endless debate eventuating in a mindless relativism—or "the one true morality" imposed by the group with the most machine guns.

There is more that is societally dysfunctional in the ideology undergirding American capitalism. That ideology is grounded in a moral

individualism that stresses freedom, choice, rationality, personal responsibility, autonomy, independence, competitiveness, self-interest,
self-reliance, and success, all of which we are led to believe are very
good things, full stop. In some respects, a few of which I will discuss
below, they are good things, but such an ideology does not simply
stress competitiveness—it gives high marks, or at least high tolerance,
to extravagance, encourages everyone to seek wealth, ranks independence and freedom as the highest goods, and allows people to fully
respect other people's rights simply by ignoring them: Of course you
have a right to speak, but not to have me listen (Sandel 2009, 268). Such
an ordering of values justifies capitalist economic, political, and legal
systems, but is no longer in keeping with the new American reality and
it requires ever greater amounts of governmental and corporate pro-
paganda to keep it going. It will be difficult to even think about how
best to reorder our values to conform to the world of 2018 unless we
also contemplate another vision of what it is to be a human being. Are
we really self-interested and competitive at heart? Are we really autonomous individual selves? How else might we view human beings
when reordering our value system?

Rights-Holding Individuals

In defense of the individualist position, if it can be said that we each
have an individual self, the concept of a bare self must be fleshed out
if it is to be morally and politically robust. That we are all social crea-
tures, strongly influenced by the others with whom we interact, has
always been acknowledged on all sides, but only very rarely has this
been taken to be of any real consequence at the moral and political (and
metaphysical) level. Sandel is an exception in this regard (1984, 173).
Nor, for most foundational individualists, can our social selves be of
compelling worth, because our concrete circumstances are for the most
part accidental, in that we have exercised no control over them—who

our parents are, the native language we speak, our citizenship, and so forth. Consequently, what must give human beings their primary worth, their dignity, integrity and value as individual *selves*, on this account—and what must command the respect of all—is human beings' ability to act purposively, to have a capacity for *self*-governance as well as *self*-awareness. That is, they must have *autonomy*. And of course, in order to be autonomous, human beings must be *free*, and *rational*, not merely governed by instinct or passion.

This morally, politically, and metaphysically fleshed-out concept of the self as a free, rational, autonomous individual has clearly been the foundation for virtually all modern and contemporary Western moral and political theories, from Hobbes, Locke, and Kant through Marx, Bentham, and Mill to Rawls and their champions and critics, continuing to this day, and including Michael Sandel.[1] We cannot speak of duties or obligations if we do not have the *freedom* to meet them. We cannot command respect if it is merely instinct that impels us to our duties (it seldom makes sense to say that we have an obligation to make love or duty to urinate). We must have been able to choose otherwise than to do our duty; else we could not be *autonomous*.

If everyone has the highly valued qualities of freedom, rationality, and autonomy associated with the concept of the individual self, and it is just these qualities that we must respect at all times, then, aside from minor details, their sexual orientation, age, ethnicity, religion, skin color, and so on should not play any significant role in our decisions about how to interact with them morally and politically. It is not simply that these qualities are contingent for each of us; details aside, they are irrelevant, too. On this account it seems incumbent upon us to seek principles for our morals and politics that are applicable to all peoples at all times, or else the hope of a world at peace, devoid of group conflicts, racism, sexism, homophobia, and ethnocentrism, supposedly could never be realized.

This is an impressive vision, and the values ordered in it have much to recommend them; who does not want to champion freedom and autonomy? This individualist account is, however, flawed in a number of ways. First, it is a highly abstract reading of our humanity, with little purchase on our everyday lives. More importantly, it is just these qualities of individuals that supposedly demand we accord everyone dignity and respect. But the dignity and respect demanded for all individual selves is grounded in the vision of those selves being unencumbered. So if we accept Sandel's claim—made in virtually all of his work—that individual selves are encumbered by the values and preferences reflective of the society in which they were raised, we need a new ground for insisting that all human beings deserve dignity and respect. What might that be? The question takes on an additional bite when the society that has encumbered certain people is one that is perceived as a threat to our own. If, like far too many Americans, I have a distrust of all things Russian, why should I accord Vladimir Putin dignity and respect?

We have been living with this ideology of the unencumbered individual under the umbrella of capitalism for two centuries, and even though the benefits have improved the lives of tens of millions of people during that time, capitalism has also been responsible for no small number of horrors too; far too many to list, including slavery, slaughters of Native Americans, colonization, sweatshops, Bhopal, and, militarily, the large-scale killings at Dresden and Hiroshima to My Lai and Falluja. The benefits of capitalism have not come cheaply—and these horrors also provide the Russian people with ample reasons for disliking and distrusting us, and thus being unwilling to accord our U.S. encumbered selves dignity and respect.

Michael Sandel has not said how his selves might be no less worthy of being accorded dignity and respect than their unencumbered brethren. Perhaps he can explain this, or some other philosopher can; but until someone makes a strong case for such, I hope Roger and I may be forgiven for rejecting both options. For us the problem is not with the encumberedness of the individual self or the lack of it, but more basically with the concept of the individual self. As John Stuart Mill (2000) said,

"When society requires to be rebuilt, there is no use in attempting to rebuild it on the old plan" (57)—to which we now turn.

Role-Bearing Persons

A key element of the overall capitalist ideology today that hinders the search for a new value-ordering for morality is the belief that the only alternative to being a free, autonomous individual is to become part of a faceless collective, communist or fascist. But these correctly discredited positions do not exhaust the possible answers to the question of what it is to be a human being. The answer I want to take up now is that of the role-bearing person, which Roger and I originally derived from our readings and translation of the Confucian *Analects* (Ames and Rosemont 1998). Roger has encapsulated the Master's (Confucius's) overall vision splendidly:

> For Confucius and for generations of Chinese that have followed after him, the basic unit of humanity is *this* particular person in *this* particular family rather than either the solitary, discrete individual or the equally abstract and generic notion of family. In fact, in reading Confucius, there is no reference to some core human *being* as the site of who we *really* are and that remains once the particular layers of family and community relations are peeled away . . . The goal of living, then, is to achieve harmony and enjoyment for oneself and for others through behaving in an optimally appropriate way in those roles and relationships that make us uniquely who we are. (Ames 2011, 122, italics in the original)

So we have universal (abstract) individuals on the one hand, and particularistic (concrete) persons on the other. By emphasizing our sociality, Confucians simultaneously emphasize our relationality: an abstract individual I am not, but rather, as Ames emphasizes, a *particular* son, husband, father, grandfather, teacher, student, colleague, neighbor, friend, and more. In all of these roles I am defined in large measure by the others with whom I interact, highly specific persons related to me in one way or another; they also are not abstract autonomous individuals. Moreover, we do not "play" these roles, as we tend to speak dismissively of them, but instead *live* our roles, and when all of those roles have been specified, and their interrelationships made manifest, then we have, for Confucius, been thoroughly individuated, but with nothing left over with which to piece together an autonomous individual self. Being thus the aggregate sum of the roles I live, it must follow that as I grow older my roles will change, and consequently I become quite literally a different person. Marriage changed me, as did becoming a father, and later, grandfather. I interacted differently with my daughters when they were children than when they were teenagers, and differently again now that they are adult mothers themselves. Divorce or becoming a widower would change me yet again. In all of this, not only do I change, but others with whom I relate perceive me in changed ways as well. And of course they, too, are always changing as we change each other. Now that they have children of their own, my daughters (and my wife) now see me as "grandpa" no less than "dad." All the more so is this true when old and cherished friends and relatives die, making me yet again different, and diminished.

But describing our interpersonal behavior from this perspective goes strongly against the grain of the *essential* self that we have been enculturated to think and feel we *really* are, or "have," something that remains constant and unchanging throughout the vicissitudes of our lives. On the Confucian account, seeking that essential self must be like chasing a will-o'-the-wisp, for we are *constituted* by the roles we live in the midst of others. Who we "really are" is a function of who we are with, when, and under what circumstances. And the same may be said of them; each of us has a unique but always changing identity. If you remain skeptical of the Confucian account on this score and believe you do indeed have an *essential* self that makes you uniquely yourself, try describing it without reference to any other human beings and the relationships you have to them (Rosemont 2015, 40–56).

This early Confucian view of the human being is very different from the notion of an abstract autonomous individual—the rational, free, and almost surely self-interested locus of moral analysis and political theory current in Western philosophical, legal, and political thinking today. But it is, I hope, not seen as remote from ourselves. In order to *be* a friend, neighbor, or lover, for example, I must *have* a friend, neighbor, or lover. It is very difficult to feel or even imagine the bonds of friendship or love when contemplating abstract individuals, but easy when I'm with my wife, children, and friends. On the Confucian view, other persons are not accidental or contingent to my goal of following the path of being as fully human as possible; they are fundamental to it. My life can have meaning only as I contribute to the meaningfulness of the lives of others, and they to mine. Indeed, they confer personhood on me, and do so continuously; to the extent that I live the role of a teacher, students are *necessary* for my life, not incidental to it. In this regard it should also be noted that while Confucianism should be seen as fundamentally religious, there are no solitary monks, nuns, anchorites, anchoresses, or hermits to be found in the tradition. The way is made in the walking of it, but one never walks alone (Rosemont 2002, 82–90).

Our first, and always most fundamental role, a role that defines us in significant measure throughout our lives, is as children; *xiao,* which Ames and I translated as "family reverence" (Rosemont and Ames, 2009), rather than "filial piety," is one of the highest excellences of integrated thought and feeling to be nurtured in Confucianism. We owe unswerving loyalty to our parents, and our manifold obligations to them do not cease at their death. As Confucius said in the *Analects:* "While [the parents] are alive, serve them according to the observances of ritual propriety; when they are dead, bury them and sacrifice to them according to the observances of ritual propriety" (2.5).[2] Confucian moral epistemology is thus easily described: it all begins at home, in the role of son or daughter with which every human being begins their life. We learn loyalty and obedience by deferring to our mother and father, but it is easier to understand the Confucian vision, I believe, if you do not see deference (positive) as subservience (negative), and that learning early on to defer to parents is best done not by having them insist on it by scolding or worse, but from having watched *them* defer to *their* parents, your grandparents. For Confucians, attitudes of deference—no less than, say, generosity, loyalty, compassion, or responsibility—are a basic ingredient of personal development, and developing patterns of deferential behavior are as important for maximizing the quality of our role interactions as any other behavioral patterns. You should not, therefore, simply see yourself as deferring to parents, but rather as deferring to deferrers. The point is an important one. Deference to parents and grandparents should come fairly easily to children whose parents and grandparents interact with them appropriately. You are helpless before them, yet they care for you unstintingly and affectionately; being deferential should be a natural response. (Most of the time, anyway.) Subservience is very different: here you must bow down to the powerful no matter how unworthy of respect or affection they might be.

If your parents are subservient in dealing with your grandparents, that is strong encouragement for you to be subservient as well. You defer as your parents defer—and their parents before them. And you should come to see actions of loyalty and obedience on their part as simultaneously expressions of gratitude to parents for all that they have done for their children, and so on across the generations. At times the loyalty and family reverence—and hence gratitude—will be best expressed not by obedience, but remonstrance, when the parents or others have gone astray. Confucius saw such actions are being obligatory at times. When asked once how best to serve the ruler, he said, "Let there be no duplicity when taking a stand against him" (14.22). Even stronger: "Failing to act on what is seen as appropriate is cowardice" (2.24).

From our initial role as sons and daughters—and as siblings, play-mates, and pupils—we mature to become parents ourselves, and become as well spouses or lovers, neighbors, workmates, colleagues, friends. All of these are reciprocal relationships, which begin at birth. In terms of their applicability to the contemporary world, these recip-rocal relations are best described as holding between benefactors and beneficiaries. When young, we are largely beneficiaries of our parents. As our benefactors they give us love, care, sustenance, security, educa-tion, and more. We are to reciprocate with obedience, love, loyalty, and attentiveness to parental concerns. The roles are thus clearly hierar-chical, but not elitist. In the latter, the positions seldom change: the elite and the masses remain the elite and the masses; patrons tend to remain patrons and clients, clients; admirals never take orders from ordinary seamen, and royalty never bow to commoners.

But although certainly both traditional and hierarchical, Confucian roles, beginning with the family, are fluid. First, the reciprocal nature of the roles goes in both directions in all interactions. While our par-ents are giving us love, care, and attention as benefactors, we are also giving them loyalty, attentiveness, love, and obedience in return. Even though they are basically beneficiaries, children can give not inconse-quential gifts, as all parents of inattentive and disobedient offspring know only too well. Children are also both a locus and a focus for par-ents to express their capacity to love and to nurture. In all of this lies true reciprocity; I am not at all describing tit for tat, but loving, inte-grated interactions.

Third, as we grow up, each of us moves from being benefactor to being beneficiary, and back again, with both the same and different people depending on the others with whom we are engaged, when, and under what conditions. I am son to my mother, father to my daughter. When young I was largely beneficiary of my parents; when they be-came old and infirm, I became benefactor and the same holds with my children. I have worked to be a good teacher, but I have also learned much from my students. I have probably changed some of them; I know they have changed me. We are benefactors of our friends when they need our help, beneficiaries when we need theirs. Taken together the manifold roles we live define us as unique persons, undergoing changes throughout our lives, and the ways we instantiate these relations in associative living are the means whereby we achieve dignity, satisfaction, and meaning in life, and give concrete expression to our creative impulses.

Role interactions are thus mutually reinforcing when performed appropriately. The ideal Confucian society is basically family and communally oriented, with customs, traditions, and rituals serving as the binding force of and between our many relationships and the responsibilities attendant on them. To understand this point fully we must construe the term *li*, translated as "ritual propriety," not only for its redolence with religion, nor as only referring to ceremonies marking life's milestones like births, weddings, bat mitzvahs, and funerals, but equally as referring to the simple customs and courtesies given and received in greetings, sharing food, caring for the sick, leave-takings, and much more: to be fully social, Confucians must at all times be polite and mannerly in their interactions with others. And these interactions should be performed with both grace and joy. We are all taught to say "Thank you"—a small ritual—when we receive a gift or a kindness from someone. From the Confucian perspective, however, to say "Thank you" is also to *give* a gift, a small kindness, signaling to the other that they have made a difference, however slight, perhaps, in your life.

As the young see their parents remonstrate with their parents at appropriate times, they will learn that lesson, too. Both court and (especially) family remonstrance became subdued over time in imperial China as obedience came to be more and more expected and rewarded. It is the stereotype we have of Chinese society since time immemorial, and has contributed much to many Westerners dismissing Confucianism as a reactionary sexist, elitist, and agonizingly formal set of behavioral prescriptions. But with the current example, as with most others, there is no reason a felt and reasoned balance between deferential and remonstrative behaviors could not be inculcated and maintained in fully human fashion, blending contemporary sensibilities with the original Confucian vision.

Gratitude is an essential component of family reverence, and can be effective in fostering a proper sense of deference, obedience, and loyalty along with remonstrance. Cultivating the feeling of gratitude (usually with the aid of rituals) is an important component of personal cultivation. Deference motivated by a feeling of gratitude will not descend to servility. Gratitude is not to be construed in terms of merely the obligation to repay a debt. If we are role-bearing persons raised intergenerationally in a loving home, we should come to realize fairly early in life that what our parents did for us was for *our* sake, not their own, and they did a great deal of it. And we should also come to realize how we are thus linked to them, and through them to our grandparents, and to their parents in the lineages. And these realizations should give rise to a sense of joy when we have the opportunity to care for them.

We cannot, however, simply "go through the motions" of following custom, tradition, and ritual in our interactions, nor should we fulfill our obligations mainly because we have been made to feel obliged to fulfill them, else we will not continue to develop our humanity. Instead must we make them our own, and modify them as needed. Remember that for Confucius, many of our responsibilities are not, cannot be, chosen. But he would insist, I believe, that if the term "freedom" is to be used in ethics, it must be as an achievement term in our value ordering, not a stative one, such that we can begin to think of becoming truly free only when we *want* to meet our responsibilities, when we want to help others (be benefactors), and enjoy being helped by others (as beneficiaries). This point is not at all common in individualistic moral theories, so an illustration may be useful to bring it home clearly.

When younger, your grandmother did you a particular kindness one day, and you decided to reciprocate by drawing a picture for her, so you get out your colors and do so. You know from many past interactions with her that your grandmother will enjoy the picture immensely, and thus you enjoy doing the drawing all the more. And of course she does fuss lovingly over the finished product. All well and good. The next morning, however, as your friends are calling you out to play, your grandmother tells you her arthritis is hurting a lot, will you please give her a neck and shoulder massage? Now as a good Confucian youngster, you will give her the massage, full stop. But you may well feel a tad resentful, or at least put upon or frustrated. Continued self-cultivation in the context of a loving family with proper role models should, however, lead you to the point of deriving *more* pleasure from relieving your grandmother's aches and pains than playing with your friends, after which you will become more fully human by beginning to *prefer* doing so. As I read him, then, for Confucius it is through the family and familial roles that we all serve our apprenticeships for full membership in the human race. It is where we learn to love, and to be loved, to trust and be trustworthy; to be obedient, loyal, and grateful as beneficiary, and nourishing, caring, and encouraging as benefactor; to discern when our role behavior requires gentleness and when firmness; when to accept others as they are, and when to encourage change. Above all, it is in the family that we first come to take pleasure in pleasing the others with whom we are interacting, and come to appreciate fully what joy others bring to us. The sheer physicality and the closeness of some of our interactions in an all-encompassing atmosphere of familial trust contribute much to the inculcation and growth of these feelings.

When we have siblings and experience the feelings attendant on loving sibling relations (even during occasional less-than-loving interactions), being our brother's and sister's keepers should come more easily to us. When we come to fully appreciate how our grandmothers enjoy our backrubs, and we have come to enjoy administering them, we will be more inclined to insist on governmental policies that are both contributory to everyone having full health care, and geared toward having both younger and elderly people in a household at the same time.

It may seem odd or paradoxical at first to exhort people to have a certain attitude or emotion—feeling—in meeting the responsibilities of their roles.[3] But having just those feelings will often be important—indeed, necessary—in a number of familial interactions in order to learn to meet ongoing responsibilities appropriately and consistently. Resentment at having to give your grandmother a backrub should not last long, for after all you really do love her a lot, and she thus becomes an emotional training ground, if you will, for acquiring the feeling of enjoying relieving the pain of others you know less well. Besides being a dear grandmother she is a splendid teacher. For Confucius, we are certainly responsible for our human qualities, and to lack feelings for one's parents or grandparents would be less than fully human. Moreover, it is important to note that in the language of the Confucian persuasion it would not be correct to say that we learn to *choose* these actions after due deliberation of the options. You simply *do* these things—emulating appropriate role models—and you do them better as you do them more often. You cannot be formally taught to "read" the moods and attitudes of the people with whom you relate, an ability that is important for the interactions to be maximally appropriate. But the more you simply "read" the other, the better you become as a reader. Similarly, you cannot rationally *decide* to take delight when you contribute to the flourishing of another in an interaction; after a while it should just come to you, and more naturally with time.

I suspect that many readers here would say I am describing the impossible, but William James—a Confucian at the core even if he didn't know it—would disagree: "Where would any of us be were there no one willing to know us as we really are or ready to repay us for our insight by making recognizant return? We ought, all of us, realize each other in this intense, pathetic and important way. If you say that this is absurd, and that we cannot be in love with everyone at once, I merely point out to you that, as a matter of fact, certain persons do exist with an enormous capacity for friendship and for taking delight in other peoples' lives, and that such persons know more of truth than if their hearts were not so big" (James 2007, 52).

Most of your interrelations will be with people you know. You are not to do what is *right* with them, for that suggests an objective, external standard applicable to all; rather must you do what is maximally *appropriate for this person*, and that can only be determined by the unique features of the specific person with whom you are engaged, as well as the time and circumstances of the engagement. Role ethics learned in the home is thus to be seen as acquiring and enhancing dispositions to behave spontaneously with an increasingly cultivated and creative sense of appropriateness that grows as you live your roles beyond the family and local community as well as within them.

With these lessons learned and interpersonal skills acquired, we will be suitably prepared to go beyond our home to school, to the neighboring community, and beyond it. Friendship is the basic role for entrance to the world outside the family, and it is one of the most important relations for role-bearing persons, as the early Confucians emphasize; indeed, the opening section of the *Analects* asks: "To have friends come from afar; is this not pleasant?" (1.1). When young we have first playmates, then schoolmates. Many in both categories will remain such; a few of them will become our friends, and the role of friend requires the same emotional responses as familial ones: love, trust, nurturance, loyalty, and the joy of contributing to the friend's flourishing. Most friends will be more or less our peers. A few may belong to the generation preceding or following ours.

Even here, however, the concepts of benefactor and beneficiary are applicable to the description and analysis of friendship roles almost all of the time, and thus this role, too, can be thought to be hierarchical, although not oppressive; interactions among absolutely equal role-bearing persons would surely be an oddity. When I dine at my friend's house, he is obviously the benefactor; when he dines at my house,

I am. My neighbor is benefactor when she brings a can of gas to me at my stranded car by the roadside; I am benefactor when I watch her children when her babysitter is ill.

All of this is obvious, but what may be less immediately apparent is that in these descriptions of everyday human interaction, the principle of reciprocity involved is not "repaying the favor" (or "debt"), nor is it "payback," or "Now I owe you one," or anything similar that smacks of the social-*cum*-economic contract we have left to autonomous individual selves to draw up and execute in the market society. Role-bearing persons engage in these activities because that is what friends (and on occasion, neighbors) do in their interactions with their fellow human beings. Reciprocity is thus to be seen *within* interactions no less than between them: the beneficiary role exhibiting a set of behaviors appropriate to that position—gratitude, obedience, attentiveness, and so on—and different from those of the benefactor, wherein care, sensitivity, courage, and such are exhibited.

In the extreme case, we can see the difference between "payback" and Confucian senses of reciprocity with great clarity: some of the responsibilities we have are to others no longer living, so there can be no "You owe me one." Grief is another feeling we must cultivate, and funerary rituals and memorial gatherings are the means whereby we continue to interact with our predecessors, and bond more closely with our peers, and descendants.

These attitudes and behaviors, again, we must continue to develop as we begin to spend more time outside our home. It can be hard work, but that is what Confucian personal cultivation is all about, as a spiritual no less than ethical practice. It take effort to develop an appropriate sense of being appreciative without being fawning; dissenting while remaining polite and proper; thankful without becoming servile. At the same time we must continue to get better as benefactors by assisting without being domineering, giving of ourselves mightily without complaint, accepting thanks for our efforts graciously without seeking undue recognition; and more.

My account here might seem altruistic, but only to those for whom the image of the social contract remains foregrounded. Altruism denotes selfless behavior, but that behavior requires a self to negate, which Confucian role-bearing persons do not have. On the contrary, it is just through such interactive behaviors as I am now describing that role-bearers *mutually* achieve a more fulfilling personhood, beginning in the family, but then extending beyond it—to share the scarce water equitably, and to conserve the environment jointly.

The Family

Even for those who wish to retain the concept of the autonomous individual self, I believe it is of signal importance to bring the family center stage in thinking about forming and reforming institutions to address the Herculean economic, social, political, and environmental tasks we face today. Surely a great many families can be characterized as sexist, oppressive, or just generally dysfunctional. These are the families that make the news. Many more families, however, are functioning quite well, fairly happily interacting with one another. Such happy interactions are reflected in countless advertisements in the media every day, suggesting their widespread appeal. Moreover, families are not going to disappear as an institution no matter what some people might wish, because there don't appear to be any alternatives: barring a nuclear holocaust or the coming of Huxley's *Brave New World*, children will continue to be born and require much human nurturing for many years if they are even to survive, let alone flourish. This point bears repetition: there are *no alternatives* to the family system in any society for rearing the young right now, consequently there can be no question of *whether* to keep the institution. Instead we should be looking for ways to reform it to enhance its ability to both enrich its members and create better societies.

The phrase "family values," of course, justifiably scares a great many thoughtful people today because the phrase has regularly been employed in the service of arch-conservative social and political orientations, reinforcing patriarchy, sexism, and homophobia, orientations usually grounded in a particular interpretation of a religious creed that defies reasonable belief. I have a great deal of sympathy for readers, especially women readers, who will be inclined to scorn my arguments on the grounds that I have taken as the cure what has in fact been the disease from which they and their grandmothers—and minorities, gays and lesbians, and so on—have long suffered. But what other cures for abusive husbands and lovers, campus sexual assaulters, gay-bashing thugs, and other similarly dehumanized individuals are on offer from moral or political theories grounded in foundational individualism? Punishment for the convicted seldom brings about attitudinal change, either in the perpetrators or in the larger society, and has deterrent value only at the margins, if at all. And of course it is pretty much worthless except for the most vengeance-seeking of the victims.[4] Certainly there can be no guarantee that some role-bearers will not behave badly. But at the same time, if we can learn from infancy onward to *enjoy* contributing to the well-being of others, we will very probably be more concerned with rehabilitation than revenge, more restorative and less retributive when seeking justice.

From a Confucian perspective the family is dynamic, not static. My wife and I undergo significant changes in our role relations with her mother and each other when the mother still lives alone, when she moves in with us and becomes a caregiver and babysitter, and when she later becomes infirm and needs our care. We behave differently in our roles toward our children when they are in second grade than when they are in high school, and of course they do, too. A death in the family can significantly alter the family dynamic, as does another entrant into it. Families must always be seen temporally and in flux while working for continuity, constancy, creativity, and growth.

A second, altogether fundamental component of the Confucian family, already hinted at, is intergenerationality. It is not just mom, pop, and the kids, but grandma and grandpa too, and perhaps others; whatever else it is, it is multigenerational, serving ethical, aesthetic, and spiritual functions in addition to economic and social ones. This intergenerationality is the key to understanding the Confucian account of what it is to be a human being, and what makes it *sui generis* ethically, politically, and spiritually. When asked what he would most like to do, Confucius responded: "I would like to bring peace and contentment to the aged, share relationships of trust and confidence with friends, and love and protect the young" (*Analects* 5.26).

Full human flourishing can be achieved within a variety of extended familial configurations. Hence, this section should be read as suggestive and not at all definitive of the options possible for different people. What is essential is intergenerationality itself, with attendant benefactor / beneficiary roles. Beyond this bare Confucian foundation I am otherwise assuming authentic democratic procedures for any and all families throughout this discussion—where "authentic" means everyone should have a say in all matters that directly affect them—both within the family nexus (to cooperatively ascertain the specifics of the roles) and at the societal level (to cooperatively ascertain the specific relations of families to each other, and to the state). Some people have already begun to form reconfigured families in this way (AARP 2014) and appear to be thriving.

Further, these two elements of traditions / rituals and democracy can be combined by having a number of family decisions voted upon by its members. What to do for Grandpa on his seventy-fifth birthday? Where should we go on vacation this year? What movie do we want to see this weekend? What shall we have for Sunday dinner? Initiating a ritual of voting on such issues strengthens family ties, especially if a period of lobbying and speechmaking precedes the voting. Letting the children be taken as seriously as the adults in these matters should enhance measurably their desire to discharge their role responsibilities as citizens by voting as they mature. Their education will be furthered by observing their elders taking the voting seriously, and also by perhaps having a two-ballot system: What do you most want to do on this matter? What do you think the family as a whole would most want to do?

Families can be constituted in a multiplicity of ways. Children might be biological, adopted, or arranged for in other ways. Parents will usually be heterosexual and monogamous, but could be in an "open" marriage or "wedlease." There should be at least two parents, but here could be more than that, and they might be gendered the same, or differently. The elderly might be the parents' parents, or a neighbor widowed early, or an older sibling of a parent, or another oldster well known to the couple. After those involved decide to commit to one another, they should devote lengthy discussions to everything from the division of labor as between breadwinner(s) and primary caregiver, to which parents or other elders the younger parents will most be able to commit, and how many children to have in their midst. In all of these discussions the young couple's parents and grandparents might profitably be involved.

The basis of the discussions, however, is not the self-interest of social contract theory negotiated by autonomous individuals, but people wishing to assume the new roles—of parent, caregiver, spouse, and so on—in order to contribute to the flourishing of related others in new ways and to thereby, and with help, more fully flourish themselves, realizing their humanity across time, which is difficult for autonomous individuals to do.

Another defining feature of the Confucian family is ancestor veneration (not "worship"). It occupied a more prominent place in classical China than we would think appropriate today, but there is much to be said for knowing who our forebears were, and remembering them on occasion. This idea should not seem foreign to anyone who has visited a cemetery or columbarium to pay respects to a deceased relative or friend, or who has gone far out of their way to fulfill a deathbed promise. Veneration can serve important psychological functions as well as being effective family glue. It contributes to our sense of who we are, and is of religious significance.

Relatedly, families are strengthened by having rituals and traditions to follow, which need not be confined to major events like weddings, Ramadan, or funerals. The rituals and traditions need not be overly elaborate, either. In the Nordic countries, for example, traditional weddings are all but extinct along with the attendant pomp and circumstance, but family ties are stronger than ever as other rituals and traditions develop, and the elaborate welfare states these countries have become are strongly family-centered. Modest but meaningful family traditions and rituals can also include what is done every year on mom's birthday, the particular rules we follow when dining together, using the same mispronounced words our children once used long after they have ceased doing so ("pasketti," "brekstiff"), the games we play together, or a hundred other possible activities that are more warmly shared now because they've been shared before. And of course rituals and traditions can be created at any time: "instant tradition" is probably better seen as an intergenerational bonding heuristic grounded in mutual affection than as an oxymoron.

The overall point here should be clear: we can all easily identify with these and similar simple activities. What Confucius helps us do is see their profound human significance, and the contribution they make to continuing to link us to each other, to the past, and to the future throughout the stages of our lives (Rosemont 2015, 149–159).

Remember that I am here contrasting two strong images of what it is to be a human being: autonomous individual self and role-bearing person. Early Confucians were not profession-oriented, or would-be capitalists, nor did they believe that seeking fame and glory are worthwhile activities. "Exemplary persons help the needy," Confucius said. "They do not make the rich richer" (*Analects* 8.6). Instead, these family activities I have been describing are engaged in cooperatively for their own sake, in order to jointly flourish, and thus for each of us to come as close to fully realizing our humanity as possible. These interactions are not undertaken merely as preparation for entering the world of work, or as an ideal working-out of a set of related social contracts, or for any other purely instrumental reason. For the early Confucians, they were ends in themselves. It is the full realization of our humanity through the performance of our roles harmoniously with our fellows that was the Confucian aim in life, and to do so with ever more poise, grace, and beauty, achieving disciplined spontaneity and consequent beauty in our human interactions. To realize this aim requires cooperation and increasing fellow-feeling, not competition, and has its genesis in developing our roles in the family, extending outward therefrom as we mature.

There are many more reasons why the family should be a major object of moral, political, social, and religious analyses and evaluation today, other than simply the family's being central to the fostering of cooperative rather than competitive views of their fellows in society. A great deal of the corruption seemingly endemic in China can be traced to family ties, and hence calls for lessening those ties are becoming increasingly common both inside the country and beyond. But in my opinion even the most moral, intelligent, and competent Chinese government that can be imagined will not be able to provide adequate social and economic services for one and a half billion people. Other institutions must come into play to provide needed services: social security, health care, education, transportation, and so forth. Purged of its potential corrupting and oppressive elements—and I do not wish to downplay those either—the institution of the extended family is a viable candidate for the provision of many of these services. It is both more humane and less expensive to subsidize families who keep their elders at home than to pay for the incarceration of elders in impersonal institutions. There is no reason every child cannot have excellent day care followed by a truly public education, no reason the sick should not be able to obtain needed care both at home and in hospital. China is by no means alone in having to worry about this issue. The United

States, and in fact most of the countries in the world today, are confronted with large, varied, and aging populations, dwindling natural resources, and the effects of climate change.

It is somewhat paradoxical that while the Confucian insistence on the interdependence of role-bearing persons were put forth almost 2,500 years ago, contemporary developments in technology and medicine have made us more, not less, dependent on others. And consequently moral and political thought grounded in the notion of free, rational, autonomous individuals is becoming more counterproductive for addressing our present circumstances as we prepare for the future, both personally and with respect to the state's provision of social services

According to the Kass Commission on Bioethics, the defining characteristic of our time seems to be that "we are both younger longer and older longer" (Brooks 2005). The former is due to economic pressures, the latter to advances in medicine and technology. We are spending more years when we are young and old being cared for by others, and much of the time in between caring for others ("from diapers to diapers"). This is not a minor matter. According to a recent *Washington Post* poll, fully one-third of the eighteen-to thirty-four age cohort today are living with their parents (Bahrampour 2016). And it has been estimated that it would cost the government *480 billion dollars a year* to provide institutional care for the elderly who are currently being cared for by roughly 40 million unpaid family caregivers in their homes (AARP 2016, 30).

But capitalist ideological pressures that can result in many people being unwilling to take on the role of family caregiver today, even when other circumstances would permit. More than a few social scientists are inclined to see the two options "capitalist individualist" and "communist / fascist collectivist" as exhausting the possibilities of who we are, or could become. Two decades ago, for example, a political scientist developed a very short test that "has since become the standard measurement of authoritarianism" in America. The first question reads: "Please tell me which one you believe is more important for a child to learn: independence or respect for elders" (Taub 2016). Can authoritarians make good volunteer caregivers? We can also ask, "Independence from what?" And why should we not be able to foster creativity in our children while yet inculcating respect for elders? Or again: Won't that respect come pretty automatically when grandmother is living in the same home? And most basic of all for individualists supposedly raised in an anti-authoritarian house: Why would you *want* to be independent of your parents when they are old and infirm?

The family-fostered ideology of role-bearing persons is much more in keeping with our present situation and problems than individualist-oriented ideologies. Both visions may be wrong as accounts of our basic humanity, and the question may thus come down to which ideology it is more appropriate for us to embrace. I hope that at a minimum I have shown that our presuppositions about human beings as individual selves—semi-encumbered or otherwise—is not *de rurum natura*, but is rather the basic ingredient in our ideology, an ideology that became dominant during the Enlightenment and has meshed very well with the rise and development of capitalism ever since. And unfortunately, it has the quality of being a self-fulfilling prophecy, exacerbating the problem.

I surely cannot *prove* that seeing ourselves and others with whom we interact as fellow role-bearing children, parents, neighbors, colleagues, friends, and citizens will be capable of resolving all the issues that Michael Sandel and I agree are rending the U.S. social fabric today. But personally and philosophically, I do not see any hope that rights-holding, self-interested, autonomous individuals—unencumbered or otherwise—confronting one another competitively will do any better; more probably, they will do much worse.

Notes

1. See, for example, Sandel 1984, 171.
2. All quotations from the *Analects* are from Ames and Rosemont 1998. The numbers in parentheses are to specific passages.
3. Without considering roles, Nivison (1980) first discussed the importance of motivation in the thought of Mencius, and the discussion was followed by several other comparative philosophers in the *Journal of Chinese Philosophy* and *Philosophy East and West* in the early 1990s.
4. It might also be well to note in this regard that most things that are targeted by repressive legislation and boycotts based on "family values" don't threaten family structures at all. The American Family Association's website, for example, calls for a boycott of Target stores for permitting transgendered customers to choose what restroom they will use. What the threat to families is here, I have no idea. But I don't believe the AFA has ever advocated boycotting Walmart or any of the other countless corporations that want to keep wages at near-starvation levels and resist unionization—whereas not giving breadwinners an opportunity to win a full loaf of bread is threatening, indeed, to the welfare of their families.

References

American Association of Retired Persons (AARP). 2014. "The New American Family." *AARP Bulletin*, June / July 2014.

———. 2016. "Caregiving in America: The Invisible 40 Million Heroes That Devote Their Lives to Loved Ones." *AARP Bulletin*, May, 30; first printed in the November 2015 issue at 6.

Ames, Roger T. 2011. *Confucian Role Ethics: A Vocabulary*. Hong Kong: Chinese University Press.

Ames, Roger T., and Henry Rosemont Jr. 1998. *The Analects of Confucius: A Philosophical Translation*. New York: Random House / Ballantine Books.

Bahrampour, Tara. 2016. "Young People Now More Likely to Live with Parents than Partners." *Washington Post*, May 24, accessed at https://www.washingtonpost.com/local/social-issues/young-people-more-likely-to-live-with-parents-now-than-any-time-in-modern-history/2016/05/24/9ad6f564-2117-11e6-9e7f-57890b612299_story.html.

Brooks, David. 2005. "Longer Lives Reveal the Ties That Bind Us." *New York Times*, Op-ed page, October 2005.

James, William. 2007. *On Some of Life's Ideals*. New York: Maugham Press.

Mill, John Stuart. 2000. *Dissertations and Discussions*. Boston: Adamant Media.

Nivison, David S. 1980. "Mencius and Motivation." *Journal of the American Academy of Religion, Thematic Issue S,* supplement to 47 (3) (September): 417–432.

Rawls, John. 1971. *A Theory of Justice*. Cambridge, MA: Harvard University Press. Revised editions published in 1975 and 1999.

Rosemont, Henry, Jr. 2002. *Rationality and Religious Experience*. Chicago: Open Court.

———. 2015. *Against Individualism: A Confucian Rethinking of the Foundations of Morality, Politics, Family, and Religion*. Lanham, MD: Lexington Books.

Rosemont, Henry, Jr., and Roger T. Ames. 2009. *The Chinese Classic of Family Reverence*. Honolulu: University of Hawai'i Press.

Sandel, Michael J., ed. 1984. *Liberalism and Its Critics*. New York: NYU Press.

———. 2005. *Public Philosophy: Essays on Morality in Politics*. Cambridge, MA: Harvard University Press.

———. 2009. *Justice: What's the Right Thing to Do?* New York: Farrar, Straus and Giroux.

———. 2012. *What Money Can't Buy: The Moral Limits of Markets*. New York: Farrar, Straus and Giroux.

Taub, Manda. 2016. "The Rise of American Authoritarianism." Accessed at www.vox.com/2016/3/1/11127424/trump-authoritarianism.

10

A Sandelian Response to
Confucian Role Ethics

PAUL J. D'AMBROSIO

People enlarge the Dao [Way], the Dao does not enlarge people.

—Confucius

Honing in on a subtle yet substantial distinction, Henry Rosemont has summarized how his and Roger Ames's understanding of the role-based person in Confucianism differs from Michael Sandel's situated self as "the onion or peach question" (Rosemont 2016). Confucian role ethics takes the view that the person is *entirely* constituted by their roles and relationships. There is no peach-like "pit" either existing prior to or enshrouded by social connections. A person is instead like an onion, made up entirely of the layers of their social roles and relationships. Rosemont and Ames thus employ the language of "living" roles rather than playing them (Rosemont 1991), and "human becomings" rather than "human beings" (Ames 2008). Michael Sandel has been accused of holding a similar view, even though he refutes such a position as early as *Liberalism and the Limits of Justice* (1982).[1] The self is not, Sandel argues, entirely a conglomeration of roles, attributes, or social environments—although it is partly composed of these factors. Sandel's position is an intermediary between the wholly role-based person and the isolated atomic individual "unencumbered" by concrete existence (as found, for example, in Rawls 1971). Residing somewhere between these extremes, Sandel (2005) finds social encumbrances to be "enduring attachments and commitments that, taken together, partly define the person I am" (167). There is something more to the person, Sandel believes, than one's "constitute aims and attachments" (167). He promotes a conception of "a self that is situated, but reflectively situated" (Sandel 2016b). Accordingly, Rosemont and Ames endeavor to ask what exactly is gained by presupposing a subject or self outside of the roles and relationships that constitute a person. As Rosemont (2016) frankly puts it: "Tell me who you are without referring to your roles or relationships."

One response has been articulated by Sandel's long-time friend and colleague Tu Weiming 杜維明. Tu's own reply to Ames and Rosemont's Confucian role ethics comes, in part, from a concern about the accuracy of ascribing to the Confucian tradition a view of the person as simply an aggregate of roles. The *Lunyu*'s 論語 (or *Analects*) famously says, "The commander of a great army can be captured, but the will of an ordinary person can never be taken away" (*Analects* 9.26).[2] Invoking that saying, Tu argues that in Confucian conceptions of the person there is a more robust core self, what he calls a "critical spirit," than Confucian role ethics admits (Tu Weiming 2016). When the self is reduced to social roles, we lose sight of the agency of this critical spirit. Rosemont and Ames maintain that agency exists, but argue that Confucian role ethics forces us to rethink some of our foundational assumptions about it.

Truly, there are many ways that we can account for the manifestation of critical reflection. But in comparing Confucian role ethics to Sandel's encumbered self, there is more at stake than the metaphysical or ontological status of the person. Beyond this, these two perspectives highlight different aspects of moral reasoning that are complementary and, moreover, uniquely equipped to establish a bridge between traditions that does not rely on eisegetical interpretations.

This short essay consists of three main parts. First I will respond to the "onion or peach" question from a Sandelian position, sharpening some of the challenges Rosemont and Ames have raised in this volume.

Next I will present an alternative view of the "onion or peach" question, based on the distinction between the ontological assumptions made in Sandel's philosophy and Confucian role ethics. Lastly I will show how Confucian role ethics and Sandel hold complementary moral views. My goal is not to unite these theories but to explore their differences, consider the ways they overlap, and highlight how they inform one another.

Narrowing the "Onion or Peach" Question

In his *Against Individualism* (2015) Henry Rosemont claims that in Confucianism, or at least in his reading of it, people are "more distinctively individuated and individuating human others than rights-holding individual selves" (104–105).[3] This individuating function is a product of understanding the person as an assemblage of particular roles and individual relationships. As opposed to individualistic conceptions of "rights-holding individual selves," Confucian role ethics develops a more nuanced vision of the person that takes into consideration a wide variety of concrete factors. The focus remains, however, on "individuating" roles and relationships, which deemphasizes the importance of broader associations—especially when compared to Michael Sandel's philosophy.

According to Michael Sandel the communities we inhabit, ranging from our neighborhood to our nation, are largely responsible for informing who we are and how we see others. In his book *Justice: What's the Right Thing to Do?*, in the section titled "The Claims of Community," Sandel writes, "Unless we think of ourselves as encumbered selves, open to the moral claims we have not willed, it is difficult to make sense of these [community-based] aspects of our moral and political experience" (220). Like Rosemont and Ames, Sandel is resisting the image of the person as an abstract individual subject. Our positions in society, and our society itself, lay claims on us that are not merely accidental: "If you think that the self is given prior to, and in-dependent of its ends and roles, then the only obligations that con-strain me, the only moral ties I owe, are the ones I choose through acts of will or acts of consent; individual consent for a social contract" (Sandel 2016b). Throughout his works Sandel argues that not only who we are as persons but also our very morals and reasoning are mapped out according to social considerations, such as loyalty, respon-sibility, and solidarity. But Sandel's alternative is not the "radically situated self"—which is more or less identical to the conception of the person given in Rosemont and Ames's Confucian role ethics. Sandel worries about "incoherences associated with a radically situ-ated self, indefinitely conditioned by its surroundings and constantly subject to transformation by experience" (1982, 100).

Accordingly, the "onion or peach" question is an excellent model for sharpening distinctions. Sandel's self is enshrouded by encum-brances, which make the person who they are. After all, a peach is not a peach-pit; without the meat it becomes substantially different. In Confucian role ethics the human broadens with new roles and rela-tionships, adding layers. But there is no core to the onion. There is nothing left over once all the layers are peeled away. The absence or presence of a core or "pit" is precisely the difference between these two conceptions of the person. And for Sandel the lack of a core self implies the lack of critical reflection. Sandel thus agrees with the meta-phor and knowingly sides with the peach.

The challenge Sandel raises for Confucian role ethics turns around Rosemont's provocative injunction "Tell me who you are without re-ferring to your roles or relationships" (Rosemont 2016). Sandel (2016b) argues:

> There is a certain similarity with some aspects of [Ames and Rose-mont's] account, which spoke of narrative, of a self in the world, of "human-becomings." But there can be no becoming, there can be no narrative, if we are radically situated selves. There is no scope for

competing narratives, there can be no scope for reflection, and there is no space for what [Tu] Weiming was calling the "critical spirit." The critical spirit comes not from legislating or willing, I would say, but from reflecting critically—using moral imagination to offer narratives of how we become, how we are situated as selves in the world. What selves? What world? Everything depends on that narrative. The alterative as I would see it is a reflectively situated self. Here there is maybe a disagreement with Roger [Ames] because this conception would not see the self just as the aggregate of roles. I would resist the aggregative idea of identity. That is the view of identity my critics have [used to attack me as a communitarian]. They assume that the only alternative to the unencumbered self is the aggregative, radically situated self.

The difference in views can, at least in part, be understood in terms of the separate discourses Rosemont and Ames and Sandel are involved in. Confucian role ethics is an attempt to liberate Chinese philosophy from yet another phase of Westernization. Before the publication of Alasdair MacIntyre's *After Virtue* (1981), contemporary scholarship on Confucianism had largely run with mainstream deontological views, and was taken as another version of Kantian ethics. With the rise in popularity of virtue ethics (due in large part to the publication of MacIntyre's work) scholars began to question Confucian categorical imperatives and gradually settled, unsurprisingly, on a strong affinity between Confucian ethics and Aristotelian notions of virtue. Rosemont and Ames seek to loosen Western philosophy's stifling grip on Confucianism, and hope to give it a seat beside, rather than behind, Kant and Aristotle. Sandel's project does not face similar comparative challenges.

In offering an alternative to John Rawls's theory of justice (Rawls 1971), Sandel embraces much of MacIntyre's vocabulary and many of his arguments. In particular, Sandel attacks Rawls's foundational conception of the "veil of ignorance." Behind Rawls's veil everyone is "unencumbered," which means that they have no concrete character-istics and are not part of a narrative. Sandel finds two crucial errors here: Rawls's position mistakenly prioritizes the right over the good, and it is impossible, and morally undesirable, to detach ourselves from our narratives or "encumberedness." But Sandel does not completely reduce the person to narratives or encumbrances; he only stresses the importance of the claims they make on the self and on moral reasoning, as integral *parts* of a larger whole.

Within their respective discourses, the philosophies of Confucian role ethics and Sandel both standout as radically innovative. And in-sofar as they reject abstract notions of individualism they form a united front. But each faces distinct problems, which play a role in how they work out differing conceptions of the person. Nevertheless, there might be room for an intermediary view between the role-ethics onion and Sandelian peach. Because they work with different traditions, the rela-tionship between the ontological claims each makes is complex, and should be understood in terms of their unique backgrounds. Moreover, even if no intermediate position between the onion and peach is pos-sible, there are still a number challenges Sandel's perspective poses to Confucian role ethics that should be considered in order to fully ap-preciate the distinction between these positions.

Can Onions Grow Cores?

According to classical Confucianism, a human is not born as a full "person" (*ren* 人)—this word is defined morally, and development of the person requires cultivation. "Becoming established" (*li* 立) as a person occurs through living family relationships and social roles. When one carries out these interactions appropriately, one also engages in what Rosemont and Ames might call "moral personing," and be-comes a full person. The emphasis here is on cultivation, which refers to the development of the human through practice. There is no "self" to begin with, only a primary social context, which gradually enlarges as the human interacts with others. This is an essentially process-based ontology that engages, as Roger Ames and David Hall strongly argue, terms of becoming rather than being (Ames and Hall 2003).

Sandel does not work with the same ontological assumptions. Compared with what Rosemont, Ames, and Hall describe in the Chinese tradition, Sandel's approach rests on assumptions of "being" rather than "becoming." Accordingly, the "onion or peach" distinction can be manifest in another way. It is possible that something like a core self—at least something similar to what Sandel argues is required for the critical reflection—could be "grown" in the person. Responding from a Sandelian position, but preserving the process-based ontology Rosemont and Ames posit, there are at least two challenges that can be raised.

First, recognizing the starting point, or "roots," from which a person is cultivated as the major locus of the debate between Confucian role ethics and Sandel, we can ask: To what extent is there a substantial starting point for cultivation? What is it that is being cultivated? We can also direct questions at the Confucian notions of human tendencies or nature (*ren xing* 人性) or Mencius's "four sprouts" (*siduan* 四端), asking, Might human tendencies or the four sprouts include something like a 'reflective subject'?[4]

Second, we may venture to inquire about the nature of the person as an aggregate of roles and relationships, or onion. We can ask, Is it possible to arrive (through cultivation) at some substantial core, as some readings of Mencius suggest? Can the process view produce anything like the self Tu Weiming and Sandel find necessary for a reflective subject? Indeed, in a process philosophy we do not have to assume a "self" as a starting point to account for its existence later on.

Rosemont and Ames would likely respond that these questions rest on an unnecessary belief that we need a "self" in order to be reflective. But these issues ought to be further explored. The exact requirements of this self, and the ontological distinction employed by Rosemont and

Ames and Sandel account for their most basic differences. And even if these issues cannot resolve the conflict between Confucian role ethic's onion and Sandel's peach, they will help define exactly what is at stake here. These questions are especially important because Confucian role ethics and Sandel's justice are close companions in the sphere of moral philosophy (even despite their differing conceptions of the person, and regardless of whether any intermediary position can be worked out). Both approaches prioritize concrete aspects of the person, situated-ness, and community in moral considerations, and they complement one another in their varying degrees of focus on the family, roles, (individuating) relationships, and communities.

Roles, Relationships, and Communities

Sandel's moral philosophy argues against what he calls "moral individualism" (2009, 212), which is perhaps best exemplified by the philosophies of Immanuel Kant and John Rawls. Kant's autonomous will and Rawls's veil of ignorance give similar visions of the self and moral imagination.[5] For both thinkers these ideas are divorced to the fullest extent possible from concrete, contingent characteristics. The person becomes an "unencumbered self" (Rawls's term) who reasons according to rational laws divorced from their consequences (Kant's categorical imperative). Sandel's alternative rests on an overarching theme, which has remained consistent throughout his philosophy, and is well summarized in a single statement: "We need to think through some hard questions about collective responsibility and the claims of community" (Sandel 2009, 210). His various works on liberalism (1982), public philosophy (2005), genetic enhancements (2007), justice (2009), and markets (2012) have all sought to fill out "moral individualism" with conceptions of the person and moral reasoning that include a more robust sense of our inescapable ties to personal aims and communities. These links include considerations of loyalty, responsibility, and solidarity, and are not accidental or trivial claims. They are located in our very sense of self and figure prominently in the way we (should) think about moral problems.

Rosemont and Ames battle similar dragons. They put forth Confucian role ethics as an alternative paradigm to "moral individualism." Borrowing heavily from the Chinese tradition, Rosemont and Ames emphasize the importance of family relationships and social roles for theorizing the "person" and thinking about morality.[6] One begins becoming a person through interactions with family members. This process later translates into wider social spheres, and ultimately ends up being a driving model for the political community as a whole.[7]

In terms of rejecting abstract judgment and taking seriously the concrete elements of the self, others, and the situation, Sandel's reflectively situated self has a lot in common with Confucian role ethics. But the Confucian role ethicist might ask Sandel, "What about your most immediate community—the family? How do you account for these important ties, which are foundational in shaping no only who we become, but our moral landscape?" Likewise, Sandel may want to ask Rosemont and Ames about broader communal constraints—for example, constraints associated with being not only a professor at a specific university and also a member of the campus community or an academic in general.

Sandel does not have a lot to say about the family as a specific community. The family undoubtedly is the person's closest and most influential community, at least in one's younger years, but Sandel spends comparatively little time discussing its importance.[8] He does speak, for example, of viewing ourselves "as members of this family or community or nation of people, as bearers of this history, as sons or daughters of that revolution, as citizens of this republic" (1982, 179), but the emphasis here is on being part of something particular, *this* . . . or *that* . . . The family itself is not given special priority. Similarly, the virtues of loyalty, responsibility, and solidarity are generally regarded as associated with broad communities, such as the town one lives in, one's place of study or employment, the religious groups one is involved in, or the nation of which one is a citizen. And in the discussion of virtues, little attention is given to the way one treats family members as a special type of association. For instance, Sandel does not stress versions of family reverence / filial piety (*xiao* 孝), sibling bonds (*ti* 悌), or the special love a parent has for a child (*ci* 慈). If put in collaboration with the emphasis, in Confucian role ethics, on the primacy of family ties, individuated (and individuating) relationships, and social roles, Sandel's moral philosophy could include a more comprehensive view of how we develop our moral sensibilities as "*sons* or *daughters* of these parents, as *bearers* of these family traditions, the *husband* or *wife* of that person, *parents* of these children" (Sandel 1982, 179).

In describing Confucian role ethics, Ames and Rosemont have also provided an explanation of how persons can become moral members of their communities. By interacting appropriately with family members, the person learns ethical habits that spread to other areas. "Simply put, when family reverence is functioning effectively within the home, all is well within the community, the polity, and indeed, the cosmos" (Rosemont and Ames 2009, 22–23). However, their focus remains on the tighter family sphere, especially when compared with Sandel. In their presentation of role ethics, there is a tendency to reduce all ethical issues and civic concerns to family-related bonds. "Family feeling is the ground for morality in Confucian role ethics—it is where we develop our moral sensibilities" (58). Additionally, one's roles are paramount, which means that one is less likely to see oneself as, for example, a *member* of a campus community—instead, one is a *teacher*, a *student*, a *security guard*, part of the *maintenance crew*, or *administrative staff*, which can reduce their responsibilities to the community at large and to each other, to the confines of one particular role. This view can also foster hierarchies and role-specific duties, which in turn, can diminish our awareness of the more general obligations we have toward one another or the wider community. Sandel's concentration on the larger community can open this type of role-specific conception to expand its view of what we owe to others beyond our particular roles and established relationships, even extending moral obligations to include responsibilities toward others and objects with which we have less-defined or even no relationships.[9]

In the alternative conceptions of the person offered by Confucian role ethics and Sandel, there are similarities and also fundamental disagreements. The trajectories they take in theorizing about the person run parallel, loosely overlapping in many places. Collaboration between the two approaches could maximize these intersecting points, and would provide a more globalized philosophical argument against the strong current of "moral individualism."

I have not attempted to resolve the differences between Rosemont and Ames's Confucian role ethics conception of the person and Sandel's radically situated self. The differences cannot easily be resolved. The ontological or metaphysical disagreement about the nature of the person or self can neither be explained away nor worked out. Unless one side modifies their position, the two are simply at odds. Nevertheless, they have similar orientations in their critiques of individualism, and therein promote dialogue between Eastern and Western philosophical traditions.

If we look instead for a collaborative approach, which Sandel (2016b) has suggested might be a productive alternative to comparison, then a much more substantial, productive, and even practical union can be synthesized. As Ames makes clear, theorizing about the person is a good place to start ethical discussions. And as the commentary to the *Book of Changes* [*Yi Jing* 易經] reads, "The same endpoint can be reached from different beginnings" (*Yi Jing, Xi Ci Xia* 2.5).

For Rosemont and Ames, recognizing the importance of roles and relationships in constituting the person will contribute to more healthy, flourishing, and ethical interactions. We achieve this, at least in part, through developing new ways to think and talk about persons and ethics. Ames (2011) emphasizes that role ethics provides a "vocabulary." Rosemont (2015), in his chapter "Doing Ethics in a Global Context," similarly stresses the important effects that thinking of ourselves as role-bearing persons rather than as individual agents has on value-orderings (21–28). In other words, in explicating their view that the person is constituted entirely of roles and relationships, Rosemont and Ames are also promoting new terminology for discussing ethics.

Sandel's own refutation of libertarian individualism also promotes using new language. Sandel speaks about the importance of communities and underscores the importance of human emotion in moral reasoning.[10] Yet he directly opposes the "vocabulary" of role ethics. In response to Ames, Sandel says, "Instead of the language of aggregation [pure "role and relationship" language] I think we need to work out this intermediate conceptual language of narrative and of reflection" (2016b). But this is also, from the perspective of collaboration rather than comparison, a good starting point.

There is significant overlap between the view that we should learn to think about morality without invoking to moral agents and the view that moral reasoning requires reference to a reflectively situated self. Moreover, the two views share a complementary semantics. Confucian role ethics emphasizes the individual roles and relationships a person has (or is), whereas Sandel notes the importance of the communities the person inhabits. Developing these vocabularies alongside one another, or searching for an "intermediate conceptual language," which may include narrative and reflection, will challenge mainstream ideas about agency and the self. Shifts in vocabulary might not overcome the two perspectives' ontological and metaphysical differences, but whether they remain separate or become synthesized, Confucian role ethics and Sandel's philosophy offer robust challenges to individualism. They thus encourage collaboration between, and offer new ways to think about, Chinese and Western philosophical traditions.

Notes

Some sections of this chapter are modified versions of similar arguments from my article "*Against Individualism* and Comparing the Philosophies of Rosemont and Sandel" (D'Ambrosio 2016a). All translations from the Chinese are my own unless otherwise noted.

1. Sandel (1982) writes, for example, of the "incoherences associated with a radically situated self, indefinitely conditioned by its surroundings and constantly subject to transformation by experience" (100).

2. Chapter and section numbers for classic Chinese texts, such as the *Analects*, are from the online versions at the Chinese Text Project website (www.ctext.org).

3. Rosemont (2015) admits that some may have problems with his reading of Confucianism. "But even if we [Rosemont and Roger Ames] are both interpretively mistaken in attributing an ethics of roles to the early Confucians, it would not alter my basic position about the importance of challenging individualism and advancing an ethics of roles, for I could simply retitle this work 'Role Ethics: A Different Approach to Moral Philosophy Based on a Creative Misreading of Early Confucian Writings'" (9).

4. Confucius famously answers the question "What is humaneness (*ren* 仁)?" differently each time he is asked in the *Analects*. The general interpretation reads the Master as offering specific answers based on the individual disciple's personality or situation. But couldn't this degree of individuation exist, at least to some extent, already in infancy or early childhood?

5. Sandel (2005) summarizes Rawls's development on Kant as a movement "from transcendental subject to unencumbered self" (161).

6. For details, see Chapters 8 and 9, this volume.

7. For more details on the political aspects of Confucian thought, see especially Chapters 2 and 5 in this volume.

8. Sandel (1982) does note, for example, that the family is an example of a social institution where the "values and aims of the participants coincide closely enough that the circumstances of justice prevail to a relatively small degree" (31).

9. These problems can also be dealt with using resources from the Chinese tradition, as I have discussed elsewhere (D'Ambrosio 2016a). However, Sandel's philosophy is decidedly more focused on the community writ large, and thereby helpful for providing a more balanced approach.

10. For a more detailed account of the similarities between the Confucian account of emotions and Sandel's, see D'Ambrosio 2016b.

References

Ames, Roger. 2008. "What Ever Happened to 'Wisdom'? Confucian Philosophy of Process and 'Human Becomings.'" *Asia Major*, 3rd series, 21 (1): 45–68.

————. 2011. *Confucian Role Ethics: A Vocabulary*. Honolulu: University of Hawai'i Press.

Ames, Roger, and David Hall. 2003. *Daodejing: "Making This Life Significant"; A Philosophical Translation*. New York: Ballantine Books.

D'Ambrosio, Paul. 2016a. "*Against Individualism* and Comparing the Philosophies of Rosemont and Sandel." *Comparative and Continental Philosophy* 8 (July): 224–235.

————. 2016b. "Approaches to Global Ethics: Michael Sandel's Justice and Li Zehou's Harmony." *Philosophy East and West* 66 (3): 720–738.

Lee, Haiyan. 2014. *The Stranger and the Chinese Moral Imagination*. Stanford, CA: Stanford University Press.

MacIntyre, Alasdair. 1981. *After Virtue*. Notre Dame, IN: Notre Dame University Press.

Moeller, Hans-Georg, and Paul J. D'Ambrosio. 2017. *Genuine Pretending: On the Philosophy of the* Zhuangzi. New York: Columbia University Press.

Rawls, John. 1971. *A Theory of Justice*. Cambridge, MA: Harvard University Press.

Rosemont, Henry. 1991. "Rights-Bearing Individuals and Role-Bearing Persons." In *Rules, Rituals and Responsibility: Essays Dedicated to Herbert Fingarette*, edited by Mary Bockover. Chicago: Open Court.

————. 2015. *Against Individualism: A Confucian Rethinking of the Foundation of Morality, Politics, Family, and Religion*. Lanham, MD: Lexington Books.

————. 2016. Personal communication, August 16.

Rosemont, Henry, and Roger Ames. 2009. *The Chinese Classic of Family Reverence: A Philosophical Translation*. Honolulu: University of Hawai'i Press.

Sandel, Michael. 1982. *Liberalism and the Limits of Justice*. Cambridge: Cambridge University Press.

————. 2005. *Public Philosophy: Essays on Morality in Politics*. Cambridge, MA: Harvard University Press.

————. 2007. *The Case against Perfection*. Cambridge, MA: Belknap Press of Harvard University Press.

————. 2009. *Justice: What's the Right Thing To Do?* New York: Farrar, Straus and Giroux.

————. 2012. *What Money Can't Buy: The Moral Limits of Markets*. New York: Farrar, Straus and Giroux.

————. 2016a. "Closing Remarks." Paper presented at the International Conference on Michael Sandel and Chinese Philosophy, East China Normal University, Shanghai, March 10.

————. 2016b. Response to papers presented by Roger Ames and Paul D'Ambrosio at the International Conference on Michael Sandel and Chinese Philosophy, East China Normal University, Shanghai, March 8.

Tu Weiming. 2016. "Self from the Perspective of Spiritual Humanism." Paper presented at the International Conference on Michael Sandel and Chinese Philosophy, East China Normal University, Shanghai, March 8.

V
Reply by Michael Sandel

11

Learning from Chinese Philosophy

MICHAEL J. SANDEL

During my first visit to China, in 2007, I brought along three short texts, which I invited students at Tsinghua University and Peking University to discuss: an excerpt from John Stuart Mill's *On Liberty*, a passage from the *Analects* (13:18), and a passage from *Mencius* (7A:35).

The excerpt from Mill argued that people should be free to choose their life plans for themselves. Society may prevent people from harming others, but may not interfere with people's choices for their own good, or for the sake of improving their moral character: "The only part of the conduct of any one, for which he is amenable to society, is that which concerns others. In the part which merely concerns himself, his independence is, of right, absolute. Over himself, over his own body and mind, the individual is sovereign" (Mill 1859, 13).

The passages from the Chinese classics recounted two conversations. In the first, the Duke of She tells Confucius, "In my village, there is an upright man. When his father stole a sheep, he [the son] bore witness against him." Confucius is not impressed: "The upright men in my community are different from this. Fathers conceal the misconduct of their sons and sons conceal the misconduct of their fathers. Uprightness is to be found in such mutual concealment" (*Analects* 13.18).

The second passage describes an exchange between Mencius and one of his disciples about a hypothetical moral dilemma. Suppose the father of the emperor committed a murder and was apprehended by the police chief. Should the emperor allow the police to enforce the law against his father or intervene to protect him? Mencius replies that the emperor should not use his power as ruler to prevent the police from enforcing the law. How then could the emperor fulfill his filial duty to his father, the disciple wondered? Mencius replied that the emperor could renounce the throne, secretly carry his father on his back to the edge of the sea, and live there with him happily, never giving a thought to the power he had relinquished (*Mencius* 7A:35).

On one level, these texts—Mill on the one hand, and the two Chinese stories on the other—could be seen as exemplifying the differences between Western and Chinese philosophy. Mill celebrates individuality and liberty, while Confucius and Mencius affirm the moral priority of family and filial piety. For Mill, the cultivation of virtue is a private, not a public, concern; for the Chinese sages, the boundary between private and public morality is less clear. Mill insists on "one very simple principle," namely, that society must never interfere with liberty except to prevent harm to others; Confucius and Mencius, by contrast, do not enunciate abstract principles, but convey their moral teaching through stories and particular cases.

Although there is some truth in this stylized contrast between Western and Chinese philosophy, my aim in putting these texts to the students was not to compare the two traditions. Not being a Confucian scholar, I was in any case not qualified to tell them how Chinese philosophy, taken as a whole, differs from Western philosophy. What is more important, I do not believe that wholesale comparisons of this kind are the most interesting or illuminating way of bringing philosophical traditions into contact with one another.

My aim was less grandiose: I was interested in hearing how these students would respond to the texts I put before them. Would they be attracted to Mill's liberalism, or critical of it? Would they agree or disagree with the strong family ethic of Confucius and Mencius? Not surprisingly, opinions differed. And some of the disagreements drew us into competing interpretations of the texts themselves.

The discussion of Mill's *On Liberty* (which was, I discovered, well known to most of the students) was lively but academic, reminiscent of many such discussions with my Harvard students. Is it possible, some asked, to distinguish between self-regarding and other-regarding actions, or do even our seemingly private choices have implications for the quality and character of public life?

The discussion of the Chinese classics was more heated, even passionate. Some students thought it was wrong to put family loyalty above justice or the duty to tell the truth. How could it be right to conceal wrongdoing, or to enable a criminal—even one's father—to evade the law? Stealing a sheep is one thing. But is it admirable to help a family member flee conviction for murder?

Others defended the Confucian teachings by questioning whether the stories actually posed a conflict between justice and loyalty; perhaps what counts as a just act, some argued, depends on the relationship of the parties. Others raised the possibility that the filial piety involved in these cases consists not only in protecting one's father from punishment for his misdeeds, but also in remonstrating with him to reform his ways. And perhaps such moral suasion is best done quietly, within the family, out of public view.

Over the past decade I've had the privilege of engaging with Chinese students on many occasions, sometimes in China, sometimes in global discussions using video-linked classrooms and television studios.[1] I have found that many of the liveliest philosophical arguments arise within, rather than between, traditions. Encounters across cultures often prompt those debates by challenging us to see our settled assumptions in a new light.

Justice, Harmony, and Community

To encounter a philosophical tradition is not only to grasp its key concepts but also to glimpse its internal disagreements about how to interpret those concepts. Sometimes comparison across cultures can shed light on the disagreements within them. Consider the standard contrast between Western and Chinese philosophy: Western philosophical tradition is individualistic, placing emphasis on liberty, autonomy, and freedom of choice; Chinese philosophy is communitarian, placing emphasis on family, harmony, and filial piety. The standard contrast is not false, but it conceals a wealth of complexities.

Some of these complexities are displayed in the essays in this volume. I have learned a great deal from these essays, not only about points of contact between my own work and the Confucian tradition but also about some of the competing interpretations at play in contemporary Chinese philosophy. I have also experienced the philosophical vertigo that comes from having one's views challenged from unaccustomed directions.

Several of the essays in this volume draw upon Chinese philosophy to recast the familiar debate between liberals and communitarians. At the center of the debate is how to think about justice: Should a just society try to be neutral toward particular conceptions of virtue and the good life, or should it affirm a conception of the good and seek to cultivate certain virtues among its citizens? And a related question: Should we think about justice without reference to our attachments to family, friends, neighbors, and compatriots, or should our understanding of justice reflect such loyalties and allegiances?

Those of us who hold the second set of these views—tying justice to virtue, the good life, and the attachments that situate us in the world—are associated with the communitarian critique of liberalism. Within Anglo-American political philosophy, the terms of this debate are by now familiar to the point of exhaustion: Communitarians argue that it is not possible to define justice without drawing, implicitly or explicitly, on substantive conceptions of the good life; moreover, the liberal's claim to offer a framework of rights that is neutral toward the moral and spiritual convictions its citizens espouse gives rise to resentment among those whose moral convictions are neglected or excluded. Liberals reply that people in pluralist societies disagree about the meaning of virtue and the good life; basing law on contested moral and spiritual conceptions therefore opens the way to coercion and intolerance, to imposing on everyone the values of the majority, or of those in power.

One aspect of this debate concerns competing conceptions of the self, and of community. I have argued that conceiving of ourselves as "unencumbered selves," defined prior to and independent of our roles and relationships, leads to an impoverished conception of community. Many liberals object that conceiving of persons as claimed by moral ties antecedent to choice is at odds with freedom.

Having become accustomed to the objection that the conception of community I defend is too morally demanding, or "too thick" in the philosophers' vernacular, I find it intriguing to encounter the challenge that my conception of community is "too thin." Chenyang Li, a scholar of Confucian philosophy who teaches in Singapore, begins by identifying certain affinities between my conception of community and the Confucian conception: "Confucians would unhesitatingly endorse Sandel's conception of community as a primary value. In the Confucian view, personal identity is partly constituted by social relationships and is integral to the very fabric of community." He then describes a key difference: "Confucians can endorse many of Sandel's critiques of liberalism. From a Confucian perspective, however, Sandel's version of communitarianism is too thin for a robust communitarian society. Confucians maintain a thick notion of community and take it to be vital to human flourishing."

What makes my account too thin, according to Chenyang Li, is that it takes insufficient account of harmony, a concept at "the very center of the Confucian notion of community." Harmony is so central a virtue of social life that, on the Confucian account, it is higher than justice. "In the Confucian view, practicing the virtues of *li* ["ritual propriety"] and *ren* [benevolence, or a "caring disposition toward human beings"] establishes positive human relationships. These virtues enable people to develop a strong sense of community. In such communities, the highest virtue is harmonious relationship rather than justice."

What to make of the claim that harmony, not justice, is the first virtue of social institutions? Thinking about this question brings to mind a much-criticized passage in my first book, *Liberalism and the Limits of Justice*. In challenging John Rawls's claim that "justice is the first virtue of social institutions," I argued that, for some social institutions, notably the family, virtues other than justice may be primary. To the extent that family members relate to one another on the basis of love, generosity, and mutual affection, I suggested, questions of justice may not loom large (Sandel 1982, 32–35). Of course, no family, however harmonious, is without conflict. My point was simply that the primacy of justice depends on the attitudes and dispositions a good family, or a good community, seeks to cultivate.

Some criticized this argument as implying an idealized vision of family harmony that ignores traditional gender hierarchies and the oppression of women (Friedman 1989, 275–290). It is certainly true that such oppression exists and is unjust; it would be a mistake to claim that justice does not apply to the family. But this does not resolve the question of how to rank justice and harmony as virtues of family life, or of social life generally. The answer to that question depends on how these virtues are understood.

Until encountering the Chinese tradition, it had not occurred to me to consider harmony as the primary virtue of social life. Notwithstanding my critique of the unencumbered self and my argument for a deeper conception of community than the social contract tradition affords, I have always defended a pluralist conception of the common good, in which citizens argue publicly and openly about moral and even spiritual questions. Such arguments are typically more clamorous than harmonious.

I have always been wary of Jean-Jacques Rousseau's notion of a general will that is unitary and undifferentiated. When the general will prevails, Rousseau tells us, there is silence in the assembly. The reason for the silence is not that dissent has been stifled; it is that each individual's will has come to coincide with the general will, so there is nothing left to debate. Like Rousseau, and like the Confucian tradition as I understand it, I conceive civic life as a formative project, concerned with cultivating the character of citizens. But I do not think such cultivation should seek to dissolve the distinctive goods our different lives express. The persistence of clamor, dissonance, and disagreement does not necessarily show that selfishness has triumphed over the common good. They can be signs of a healthy pluralism, reflecting ongoing debate about the meaning of the common good.

Is such pluralism consistent with a harmonious society? Chenyang Li sheds some light on this question by distinguishing two conceptions of harmony. One is harmony as conformity, in which disharmony is overcome through domination and the suppression of dissent. He rejects this a recurring misconception that "has given Confucian harmony a bad name." As an alternative, he articulates a conception of harmony as a project of individual and collective self-cultivation that enables each person to realize his or her potential in ways that, at the same time, promote the common good: "In harmonious communities, each individual not only forms and discovers his or her identity, but also contributes to the identity and the good of other members; in harmonizing with others, each person benefits from the contributions of fellow community members . . . The Confucian conception of community is a social harmony that is to be realized by its members through mutual transformation for the common good." Chenyang Li offers a practical example: In Singapore, whose population consists of ethnic Chinese, Malays, Indians, and others, a recent attempt to promote social harmony involves a proposal to rotate the presidency, an elected but ceremonial post, among the various ethnic communities. While some might complain that the rotation system would deprive certain aspiring candidates of the right to seek office in a given year, this right should give way to considerations of harmony. Having all groups represented would create a strong sense of citizenship and Singaporean national identity. "Such a move would be justified," Chenyang Li writes, "on the ground of the Confucian philosophy of harmony."

Tongdong Bai, who teaches Chinese philosophy at Fudan University in Shanghai, offers a somewhat different Confucian account of community. He argues that my conception of community is not too thin but too thick—too morally demanding for what he calls a "society of strangers." He agrees that we are claimed by certain loyalties and obligations that arise, not from acts of will, but rather from our identities as members of families and nations. And he agrees that such loyalties can have sufficient moral weight to compete even with the duty to apprehend a murderer. Tongdong Bai cites a story I tell in *Justice*, about a well-known Massachusetts public official who refused to help the government find his brother, a notorious mob leader and murderer who had fled and was hiding from authorities (Sandel 2009, 237–239). He points out that this story finds a striking parallel in the Mencius scenario, in which the father of the emperor has committed murder: Should the emperor intervene to protect his father, or allow the police to arrest and prosecute him? Mencius suggests that the emperor could renounce his throne and flee with his father to live in hiding.

Although he agrees that family loyalties, as well as loyalties to wider communities, can sometimes outweigh universal moral duties, Tongdong Bai identifies two respects in which Confucian philosophy, as he interprets it, departs from my account of moral and civic virtue. First, only "the few" can go far in cultivating sufficient virtue to participate effectively in politics. Confucians therefore "reject the strong republicanism in communitarianism" and favor a meritocratic regime, in which the learned and virtuous few govern on behalf of the rest. A hybrid regime, with a lower house representing the people and an upper house with members selected according to merit, would be one way of combining meritocratic rule with some degree of public participation. But according to Tongdong Bai, Confucians would insist that, "in a large society of strangers, which is the default condition for most contemporary nations, the masses can never be lifted up to a level of competence that can make their political participation meaningful, even in terms of selecting their own representatives."

The idea of a hybrid regime combining democratic and meritocratic elements is of course not unique to Confucian thought. Aristotle favored a mixed regime, in which the highest offices would go to those who excelled in political judgment and civic virtue. In the early American republic, the indirect election of the president (by the electoral college) and of the U.S. Senate (by state legislatures) was intended to give the people a voice while at the same time placing the highest political offices in the hands of people like George Washington and Thomas Jefferson.

Allowing a meritocratic element in governance is not necessarily at odds with civic republican ideals. But for Tongdong Bai, it implies certain limits on the republican project of cultivating the moral and civic virtue of all citizens. If the contemporary nation is less a community than "a society of strangers," then the family is not a good analogy after all for the moral bonds and allegiances that political communities should cultivate among their members. Tongdong Bai concludes that the republican project is too morally ambitious for pluralist societies. In a surprising twist, he endorses Rawls's notion of "political liberalism," which would avoid public deliberation about comprehensive moral ideals and instead seek a framework of rights based on an overlapping consensus of values. For reasons I have offered elsewhere, this seems to me too constrained a view of moral education and political community.[2] To what extent it finds support in Confucian teaching, I am not qualified to judge. But it clearly differs from the more thoroughgoing conception of community presented by Chenyang Li.

Aristotle, Confucius, and Moral Education

In a rich and complex essay, Yong Huang, a philosopher at the Chinese University of Hong Kong, shifts the focus from "justice as a virtue," which concerns the importance of justice relative to other virtues (such as harmony, for example), to "justice according to virtues," a certain account of distributive justice. He rightly notes my sympathy for this account, which is indebted to Aristotle. According to Aristotle, the just way of distributing a good depends on what the good is for; the best flutes should go to the best flute players, because that is what fine musical instruments are for—to be played well. A just distribution allocates goods to those who deserve them in the sense that they possess the relevant virtues, merits, or excellences.

The moral intuition lying behind this Aristotelian idea can be seen if we imagine a fine Stradivarius violin up for auction, with two bidders: the world's greatest violinist and a wealthy collector who wants to display the violin on his living room mantle. If the collector succeeds in outbidding the violinist, we would consider that the auction, even if conducted fairly, produced an unfortunate result. It would be more fitting—more just, in Aristotle's sense—for the Stradivarius to go the great violinist. This is not only because his or her playing would bring more pleasure to more people than would the collector's private display. It is also because a fine violin is not a mere ornament of wealth. It is meant to be played, not displayed. The purpose, or potential, of a Stradivarius violin is most fully realized when a great violinist brings forth its resonant sound.

This way of reasoning is teleological in the sense that it involves reasoning about the *telos*, or purpose, of a violin. But such reasoning is not, as some may think, a metaphysical inquiry into the essence of an inanimate object; it is an inquiry into the meaning and purpose of a social practice—in this case, musical performance. This feature of teleological reasoning brings out its close connection to questions of honor and recognition. One of the reasons we have concert halls, symphony orchestras, music critics, and the like is to honor and recognize excellent music, to cultivate its appreciation, and to inspire gifted young musicians to emulate great violinists.

For Aristotle, then, justice is both teleological and honorific. To decide how to distribute Stradivarius violins, we need to think through the *telos*, or purpose, of musical performance and the virtues it honors and cultivates (Sandel 2009, 186–189).

Aristotle applies the same line of reasoning to the distribution of offices and honors in a political community. The highest offices and honors should not be allocated solely on the basis of wealth, he argues, or solely on the basis of majoritarianism. The reason: Political community, properly understood, is not merely for the sake of protecting property or giving the majority its way. Instead, the purpose of political community is to cultivate the character of citizens and to promote the good life. Therefore, the highest offices and honors should go to those best suited to this role, those who excel in civic virtue.

One reason people such as Pericles should hold the highest offices is that they will enact wise policies. But a further reason is honorific: According public recognition to people who excel in civic virtue holds them up to citizens as exemplary, thus serving the educative role of the good city.

Yong Huang finds an affinity between what he describes as my neo-Aristotelian account of "justice according to virtues" and the Confucian approach. Unlike theories, such as Rawls', that detach justice from virtue and moral desert, a Confucian conception of justice aims at cultivating the virtue of citizens: "Confucians agree with Aristotelians that an important function of the government is to make its people virtuous."

But Yong Huang sees an important difference in the means by which Aristotelians and Confucians believe political leaders can cultivate virtue. For Aristotle, he argues, political leaders promote virtue by enacting laws, whereas for Confucius, they promote virtue by personal example, and by rules of propriety. The notion that "people can be made virtuous by legislating and applying punitive laws is totally alien to Confucius," writes Yong Huang. He quotes Confucius: "If you lead common people with political measures and keep them in order with punitive laws, they will stay out of trouble but will have no sense of shame; if you lead them with virtue and keep them in order with propriety, they will have a sense of shame and not make trouble" (*Analects* 2.3)."

Yong Huang's contrast may be overdrawn to this extent: The idea that law can shape moral norms or cultivate virtue does not necessarily depend on the punitive aspect of law. Consider laws establishing public schools. Requiring parents to send their children to be educated together with children from a wide range of social and economic backgrounds may cultivate in students (and also in their parents) habits of solidarity, mutual respect, and common purpose that are otherwise difficult to achieve. If a system of public education succeeds in promoting these virtues, it would be thanks to the legislation (and its implementation by teachers and school administrators). But it would implausible to claim that the students acquired these virtues under the threat of punishment.

Law can exert a formative influence on the character of citizens without being punitive. This is not to suggest that we should rely on the criminal law as the primary means of moral education. Punishing thieves is not the best way to teach people that stealing is wrong. Aristotle emphasizes that moral education proceeds less by precept and principle than by habit and emulation. We learn to be virtuous by observing virtuous behavior and practicing it. On this, Aristotelians and Confucians seem to agree.

Yong Huang's rejection of law as an instrument of moral education does, however, highlight an important difference in the way the two traditions conceive of the role of politics in cultivating virtue. "For Confucius it is not the laws made by government but the exemplary virtues that people who hold political offices display in their acts that can make people virtuous." Public officials teach virtue by the force of their personal example, as moral exemplars. The contrast can perhaps be described as follows: For Aristotelians, public life contributes to moral education indirectly, through the mediation of formative practices and institutions (such as public schools); for Confucians, it does so directly, through the example of political leaders. "The more those in higher positions revere their parents, the more those in lower positions will practice filial piety; . . . the more charitable those in higher positions are, the more generous those in lower positions will become; . . . the more those in higher positions dislike greed, the more those in lower positions will feel it shameful to compete for benefit," and so on (*Kongzi Jiayu* 3, 20).

But the contrast between mediated (Aristotelian) and unmediated (Confucian) moral tutelage may itself need qualification. If I understand correctly Yong Huang's account of the Confucian view, the moral education promulgated by virtuous political leaders is not altogether unmediated, but finds expression in rules of propriety (rites) that, though not laws, guide behavior by mobilizing shame. As he explains: "Rules of propriety are different from punitive laws. When such rules are violated, people will not be punished but will be looked down upon and feel ashamed."

So there seems to be an interplay between the virtues as exemplified by leaders and their embodiment in rules of propriety (rites). Perhaps virtuous leaders display in their behavior what the rules of propriety (rites) require; and perhaps those rites are shaped over time and given concrete meaning in the light of the exemplary behavior of virtuous leaders. This would explain what otherwise might seem puzzling: If moral education were thought to depend only on observing and emulating the conduct of political leaders, it would be hard to see how an entire population could observe such behavior closely enough and interpret it clearly enough to live by its example. Embodying virtuous behavior in rules of propriety (rites) backed by social (and internal) sanctions of shame would seem a more effective mechanism for the promulgation of moral teaching than emulation on its own.

If this interpretation of the Confucian view is plausible, then, notwithstanding their disagreements on the role of law, the Aristotelian and Confucian accounts of moral education have much in common. There nonetheless remains an important difference: For Aristotle, those who deserve the highest offices and honors are those who excel in civic virtue, leaders who care for the common good and who are capable of deliberating well about how to bring it about. Ideally, they serve as exemplars for citizens generally, who most fully realize their nature by sharing in self-government and deliberating with their fellow citizens about justice and injustice, and about the meaning of the good life.

For Confucius, what makes a person worthy of being a political leader is not civic virtue as such but moral virtue more generally. Referring to Aristotle's emphasis on civic virtue, Yong Huang asks: "But is it really necessary for every citizen to have such virtues, given that only a small number of people are needed to make laws in any given society at any given time?" By contrast, the Confucian model insists that "the virtues that political leaders ought to have and that they aim to make common people possess are moral virtues, virtues that everyone, whether a political leader or a common person, in order to be a healthy or nondeficient human being, must possess."

Civic Virtue or Moral Virtue?

The distinction between civic virtue and moral virtue also figures in the essays by Zhu Huiling and Chen Lai. From different perspectives, these two scholars raise questions about my emphasis on civic virtue rather than moral virtue. Zhu Huiling, a gifted young Chinese philosopher who has studied contemporary Western political theory, worries that my version of civic republicanism does not adequately address the danger that a government might, in the name of promoting virtue, impose a coercive, oppressive conception of morality. Chen Lai, a distinguished senior scholar of Confucian philosophy, observes that my version of republicanism is "not thick enough." He suggests that, by focusing on the virtues necessary for self-government, my republicanism neglects the cultivation of personal moral perfection.

Zhu Huiling rightly emphasizes the civic republican rather than the communitarian aspects of my political theory. She points out that I reject the moral majoritarian view that justice and rights should be defined by whatever values happen to prevail in a given community, and that I also reject the Rousseauian view that the common good is unitary and uncontestable. Instead, the republican conception I defend conceives of freedom as the activity of sharing in self-government, and deliberating with fellow citizens about the meaning of the good life.

Zhu Huiling worries that I have not adequately addressed questions that any attempt to revive republican virtue must face: How can we deliberate about the common good in a pluralistic society, in which people disagree about the meaning of virtue and the good life? How can we guarantee that such deliberation does not devolve into coercion and oppression, with the majority imposing its values on the entire society? And if civic republicanism encourages virtues such as loyalty and solidarity, how can it avoid the risk that loyalty to the state or political community may undermine respect for rights?

These important challenges, though familiar in the liberal–republican debates of Anglo-American political theory, may have a special resonance in the context of China. Zhu Huiling raises another, related challenge: If I reject the sharp distinction, characteristic of liberal political theory, between public and private morality, then why insist that public officials should cultivate civic virtue rather than moral virtue? Why cultivate good citizens rather than good persons?

As several of the essays in this volume make clear, the Confucian tradition holds that political leaders should aim at cultivating good persons; from the standpoint of making people virtuous, the civic virtues emphasized by Aristotle and republican political thought appear as secondary, even peripheral. Zhu Huiling is right that I cannot answer this challenge by replying that civic virtue is public whereas moral virtue is private, and that self-government is only about public goods. I would instead have to articulate more fully than I have done so far the way in which some moral virtues are also civic virtues, and vice versa. Liberals might agree, at least with regard to a limited set of virtues. Toleration and respect for the rights of others, they might argue, are not only political virtues but also personal virtues, a mark of good character.

But I would not limit moral and civic education to the cultivation of toleration and mutual respect. If the boundary between public and private morality is more porous than liberals suggest, so too is the difference between forming good citizens and cultivating good persons. Thomas Jefferson argued against large-scale factories on the grounds that they would create a dependent class of property-less workers who lacked the independence of judgment and mind that good citizenship requires. He also thought such independence (which he associated with yeoman farmers and artisans) was a desirable quality of character, an aspect of the good life.

Here is a contemporary example: the single-minded pursuit of consumerism is inimical to civic virtue, as it distracts citizens from concern for the common good. But consumerism and materialism are attitudes that should also be discouraged, or at least kept within bounds, on the grounds that they are undesirable qualities of character; those in the grip of materialist preoccupations typically lead shallow lives. Or consider the view, increasingly prevalent in meritocratic societies, that the rich, by virtue of their presumed talent and hard work, deserve their success and that the poor (assumed to be less industrious) deserve their misfortune. This attitude is corrosive of civic virtue, as it undermines community, solidarity, and a sense of mutual obligation among citizens. But it is also morally unattractive. It promotes hubris among the successful, who underestimate their indebtedness to others, overestimate their own virtue, and look down upon those less fortunate than themselves. Unlike some liberals, I would not relegate questions of character to private life, or insist that government be neutral toward competing conceptions of the good life.

In a thoughtful and illuminating commentary on my book *Democracy's Discontent: America in Search of a Public Philosophy*, Chen Lai identifies some similarities between my republicanism and Confucianism, but also a key difference. "As a Confucian," he writes, "I agree with Sandel's criticism of the moral neutrality of liberalism, as well as his advocacy of republicanism's concern for the community. The Confucian position undoubtedly has an affinity with republicanism's promotion of virtues." He is struck by the American founders' concern with character formation and a similar concern among Confucians: "John Adams wrote, 'It is the part of a great politician to make the character of his people.' . . . This understanding is shared, as least in form, by the Confucian tradition, from the early Confucian text *The Great Learning* (*Da Xue*) to Liang Qichao's (1873–1929) *New Citizen* essays (*Xin Min Shuo*)."

But what virtues should government inculcate? It is here that Chen Lai sees an important difference between civic republicans and Confucians: "We can also ask how republicanism views qualities of character and virtues that are not based on a conception of self-government." In his view, government should concern itself not only with forming good citizens but also with forming good persons. "The virtue of the good person, or the virtue of the Confucian moral exemplar (*junzi*), is higher and broader in scope than that of the good citizen."

Chen Lai recognizes that, unlike some liberals, I do not insist on a sharp separation between public and private morality. Instead I hold the view, indebted to Aristotle and congenial to Confucians, that politics should aim at forming character and cultivating the good life. But Chen Lai observes that the republican virtues I emphasize in *Democracy's Discontent* "are limited in that they cannot be broadly involved with personal moral perfection. Confucian theories of virtue are comparatively thicker. From the Confucian perspective, the virtue promoted by republicanism is not thick enough."

Chen Lai sets out the "thicker" set of virtues that he believes "personal life in contemporary China" requires. One group includes virtues associated with benevolence (*ren'ai*), filialness (*xiaoshun*), and harmoniousness (*hemu*); a second includes self-improvement (*ziqiang*), uprightness (*zhengzhi*), and sense of shame (*lianchi*); a third includes virtues of patriotism (*aiguo*) and law abidingness (*shoufa*).

The first two groups of virtues are about personal moral perfection. "In ancient Confucianism these are considered the virtues of the moral exemplar (*junzi*)." The third group of virtues is categorized as "public virtue" and governs the appropriate attitude of individuals toward the political community. As Chen Lai explains, these are the virtues, both public and private, that, according to the Confucian tradition, government should promote. "Chinese culture has always seen the government as representative of the community and bearing responsibility for the civil education and moral edification of the people."

Chen Lai rejects the tendency of contemporary political philosophy to assert the independence of politics from substantive moral judgments, calling it "dangerous." "This changes politics into simply an electoral game where each person gets a vote, and leaves politics without commitment to society, order, ethics, or morality. The result is an absence of morality in social political life. Without the support of a traditional moral force, politics may throw society into moral confusion" and be "left without political legitimacy."

Part of what prompted me to write *Democracy's Discontent* (1996) was a sense that American public discourse was becoming increasingly empty and technocratic, unable to address large moral questions. The attempt to detach politics from moral argument coincided with a growing dominance of markets in social and civic life, leaving citizens feeling disempowered and dislocated. I worried not only about the hollowness of liberal public discourse, but also about what might fill the moral vacuum. I feared that, absent a morally more robust public discourse, American politics would fall victim to those who would "shore up borders, harden the distinction between insiders and outsiders, and promise a politics to 'take back our culture and take back our country,' to 'restore our sovereignty' with a vengeance" (Sandel 1996, 350).

Two decades later, that fear has come true. America and the world must now contend with the moral and political consequences. Although *Democracy's Discontent* was about America's search for a public philosophy, other nations, including China, also face the challenge of seeking moral meaning and social cohesion, a challenge all the more daunting at a time when market values and market thinking exert unprecedented pressures and temptations.

Both Zhu Huiling and Chen Lai offer observations about the public role of philosophy in contemporary China. Zhu Huiling attributes the interest in my work in China to "an emptiness and discontent in public philosophy here. With the rapid development of our burgeoning market economy, the Chinese need political theory and moral discourse in order to deal with the many problems that market-based reasoning brings with it." Chen Lai observes that the Chinese government is seeking a public philosophy rooted in the Confucian tradition. "The Chinese government is pushing for the preservation of traditional Chinese values and promotion of traditional Chinese virtues . . . [which] manifest[s] the self-consciousness of a civilization." The virtues being advocated "are not limited to civic virtue and political participation, but rather are more comprehensively oriented toward Confucian virtues and seek to carry out creative development of the practice of these virtues in times of change."

My own impression, as a sympathetic observer, is that after a period of astounding economic growth, China is now in search of a public philosophy beyond GDP, seeking sources of meaning and happiness that market relations cannot provide. As in so much else, China's success or failure in this quest will matter greatly for its own future and for the rest of the world.

Gender, Pluralism, and *Yin-Yang*

In her contribution to this volume, Robin Wang asks whether voices within the Chinese philosophical tradition offer resources for pluralism and moral disagreement—not as unfortunate facts of life but as intrinsically valuable features of social existence. She offers a rich and suggestive account of two such voices: One she finds in the traditional Chinese account of gender differences; the other she locates in the Daoist celebration of human diversity represented by Zhuangzi (369–289 BC).

Wang, who has taught philosophy in China and, more recently, in the United States, wants to activate aspects of traditional Chinese thought that cherish rather than resist the multiplicity of human experience. She suggests that the *yin-yang* cosmology of Chinese philosophy offers a way of understanding gender relations that is less dualistic than Western conceptions of gender, and less given to male dominance. Gender in traditional China was "constructed on notions of interdependence and complementarity that are modeled *yin* and *yang*, earth and heaven, inner and outer."

"As a result of the *yin-yang* matrix," Wang writes, "in early Chinese thought there was little exclusion of women or separation between men and women." There was, to be sure, a differentiation of roles, as described in the *Book of Songs* (*nangeng nüzhi*): "The men are ploughing and planting while the women are weaving and spinning." But Wang argues that this gendered division of labor exhibits "a relationship of complementariness rather than subordination." The complementarity is not contingent but a cosmic necessity. "Women's work is a necessary and imperative part of human life," and women "represent a cosmic *yin* force next to men as a cosmic *yang* force."

The importance of women's contribution to the common good is affirmed in the ancient text *Lienu Zhuan (Categorized Biographies of Women)* by the scholar Liu Xiang (77 B.C.) The *Lienu Zhuan* consists of 125 biographies of women from early Chinese civilization to the Han Dynasty who confront moral dilemmas and exemplify various virtues, often involving self-sacrifice. Wang finds in these stories a sturdier basis for the moral agency of women than is conveyed in Western fairy tales such as Snow White, Sleeping Beauty, and Cinderella, whose heroines are "devoid of any moral agency until their princes come to awaken them." She attributes the moral agency of Chinese women to its basis in communal honor and recognition. "The women in *Lienu Zhuan* attain self-respect because they are honored and esteemed by others, and their identity as moral agents is bound to the community they inhabit." She sees a parallel between this "feminist conception of self-respect" and my emphasis on encumbered selves, whose moral agency is bound up with forms of solidarity and membership.

According to Wang, Liu Xiang's ancient text has shaped the understanding of women's lives throughout Chinese history, and created an enduring tradition of *lienu* (exemplary women). It also supports the belief that "the permutations of *yin*, identified with female power, and *yang*, identified with male power, produce all things and events." She hears echoes of this vision of women's cosmic potency in Mao Zedong's famous statement that "women hold up half the sky."

The complementarity of men and women's roles, intimated in *yin-yang* cosmology and expressed in everyday life, provides one source in the Chinese tradition for affirming human diversity. But is there support for the notion that moral disagreement is worthy of celebrating? Wang observes that I emphasize the need for pluralist societies to engage in robust moral argument, but that I do not adequately explain why moral disagreement is necessary for a just society. This need may seem self-evident in the West, she suggests, but is less obvious in the context of China, where in modern times moral disagreements "seem to be difficult and discouraged." To answer this question, she turns to the Daoist tradition, and the thinker Zhuangzi.

Wang begins by explicating the Daoist account of the generation (*sheng*) of the world and its myriad things. She then explains Zhuangzi's account of knowledge. According to Zhuangzi, we seek to know the myriad things of the world from our various unique perspectives. No one such perspective is privileged over others. Coming to a fuller understanding requires that we become aware of the factors that condition our judgments. It also requires that we recognize and appreciate perspectives other than our own. Wang explains: "A Dao-based (*daoshu*) vision of life relinquishes personal, one-sided perspectives and appreciates, even celebrates, different ways of look at reality . . . Seeing things from the perspective of the Dao . . . requires both the ability to appreciate diversified views and the ability to see bigger and more panoramic patterns of the world."

According to a summary of Zhuangzi's view by Livia Kohn (cited by Wang), the "True Person" (*zhenren*) observes by "looking at things from his unique perspective and understanding what his particular viewpoint is; he witnesses, watching the flow of reality from a detached position; he examines, detecting relations between things and seeing hidden strands of connections; and he comprehends, opening himself to the full clarity and brightness of totalizing knowledge."

There is much that is powerful and attractive in this view, which seems similar in some respects to Spinoza's. For Wang, Zhuangzi's position has the merit of affirming, not merely tolerating, moral disagreement: "Zhuangzi recognizes the inherent values and intrinsic functions of diversity, and he articulates the need for us to be open to alternative perspectives that will shake our common fixed conceptual categories and values . . . Allowing for multiple perspectives elevates the human mind and allows it to reach for higher horizons (and this is *daoshu*)."

Daoism, Hubris, and Restraint

Paul J. D'Ambrosio, an American scholar of Chinese philosophy who teaches in Shanghai, draws on another aspect of Daoist thought to explore ideas I raise in my book *The Case against Perfection: Ethics in the Age of Genetic Engineering* (2007). In that book I argue that biotechnology should be used for medical purposes—curing disease or repairing injury—but not for genetic enhancement. We should not try to bioengineer our children (or ourselves) to be taller, stronger, or smarter, nor should we use genetic technologies to choose the sex or the sexual orientation of our children. I worry that the drive for genetic enhancement represents "a kind of hyper-agency, a Promethean aspiration to remake nature, including human nature, to serve our purposes and satisfy our desires." This drive to mastery fails to appreciate "the gifted character of human powers and achievements" (26–27).

Seeking to pick and choose the genetic traits of one's children regards them as if they were consumer goods. But this attitude is at odds with the norm of unconditional love. "To appreciate children as gifts is to accept them as they come, not as objects of our design, or products of our will, or instruments of our ambition. Parental love is not contingent on the talents and attributes the child happens to have." This is why parenthood teaches what the theologian William F. May calls "an openness to the unbidden" (Sandel 2007, 26–27).

As D'Ambrosio points out, some scholars of Confucian philosophy have debated whether my case against genetic enhancement, and the "ethic of giftedness" it invokes, is consistent with Confucianism. Ruiping Fan has argued that if genetically enhancing the IQ or athletic prowess of a child does not harm her ability to lead "a family-based, ritual-following, virtuous way of life," Confucians should not object (Ruiping Fan 2010, 68). Joseph Chan (2010) disagrees, suggesting that this "construal of the Confucian perspective on genetic engineering is too narrow." He argues that Confucian family is "embedded in a larger social and cosmic context in which Heaven and Earth, nature and humans, and the social and political order are interdependent and interrelated" (83). Confucians therefore have a stake in the questions I raise about "the moral status of nature, and about the proper stance of human beings toward the given world."[3] If genetic technology empowered human beings "to determine or change their own nature as well as those of the myriad things as they please," Chan writes, this would be something for Confucians to worry about rather than welcome, "for the triadic balance among Heaven, Earth, and humans would be fundamentally upset" (84).

D'Ambrosio suggests that Daoist thought offers another source of support, or at least philosophical sympathy, for my argument against genetic enhancement. He points to three concepts in Daoism: the rejection of "mechanical thinking," or "mechanical heart-mind" (*ji xin*); the ideal of "knowing what is enough," or "mastering satisfaction" (*zhi zu*); and the description of the "*zhen*uine person," or "sage" (*zhen ren*) in the *Zhuangzi*.

The Daoist rejection of the mechanical heart-mind is a rejection of purely instrumental rationality. D'Ambrosio compares it to Heidegger's critique of the calculative thinking he saw embodied in the modern orientation to technology. The *Zhuangzi* warns against the tendency of people who become infatuated with machines to think in purely calculating terms, a tendency familiar today among engineers, economists, and utilitarians. The *Zhuangzi* illustrates the mechanical heart-mind with a story about an encounter between an old Daoist gardener and Zigong, a disciple of Confucius. The gardener, laboring to carry a pail of water to his garden, is approached by Zigong, who recommends a device that would enable him to transport more water, enough to water a hundred plots in a single day. The gardener scoffs at the advice, saying he has enough water for his purpose, and has no need to grow more crops. He does not aspire to go into agribusiness, and in any case, mechanical things like the water pump only lead to a mechanical heart-mind.

The story also illustrates the theme of "knowing satisfaction" (*zhi zu*), or "mastering satisfaction," a concept that appears in the *Laozi* as well as the *Zhuangzi*. Those who master satisfaction do so not by devising new means to fulfill their ever-expanding appetites—that would be the technological approach—but by learning to rein in their appetites and desires.

The gardener's scornful refusal of the water pump may seem a severe response to an innocent suggestion. But it does shed light on the complex relation between technology and the way we conceive our activities and purposes. We sometimes view technology simply as a value-neutral means to pursue our ends more efficiently. If a newly invented water pump or irrigation device can lessen the toil of watering the garden, it gives me a choice: I can complete the same modest task with less effort, or I can expend the same effort and, thanks to the device, grow more crops and sell them in the market. The technology does not determine my choice, but simply expands my options and, therefore, my freedom.

But the Daoist gardener glimpses that something more is at stake—something about the attitudes we take toward the activities in which we are engaged. Technology can change our relation to our purposes and ends. The invention of irrigation systems changes the meaning of traditional gardening, casting it now as a backward, inefficient mode of farming that creates only enough crops for subsistence rather than a surplus to be sold for profit. This redescription of the activity may not force Daoist gardeners to abandon their vocation and go into agribusiness. But it does exert a certain pressure. Zigong's advice about the water pump carried with it an implicit attitude toward the activity of gardening—that it is mainly for the sake of crop production, and that more crops are always better than fewer. This attitude exemplifies instrumental rationality, or the mechanical heart-mind. It also assumes and encourages the proliferation of wants and desires, an attitude at odds with the Daoist ideal of "mastering satisfaction."

As D'Ambrosio suggests, these Daoist sensibilities are in line with my worries about using biotechnology to create designer babies and genetically enhanced children. In both gardening and parenting, the recourse to technology may change the meaning of the activity by promoting instrumental, calculating norms. Ambitious parents already spare no effort to help their children succeed, filling their every waking hour with tutoring, exam prep sessions, music lessons, athletic conditioning, and so on. Even these low-tech, high-pressure parenting techniques can exert a damaging toll, eroding parents' ability to accept children as gifts to be cherished rather than products to be improved. Equipping anxious, affluent parents with genetic technologies to give their kids a competitive edge over their unenhanced peers would entrench these corrosive attitudes more deeply.

I do not suggest that appreciating children as gifts requires parents to be passive in the face of illness or disease. Healing a sick or injured child, even with the help of advanced biomedical technologies, does not override the child's natural capacities but permits them to flourish. Although medical treatment intervenes in nature, it does so for the sake of health, and so does not represent a boundless bid for mastery and dominion. This is because medicine is governed, or at least guided, by the norm of restoring and preserving the natural human functions that constitute health.[4]

I do not know whether Daoists would agree. If even a water pump (or for that matter, a garden hose) intimates the depredations of the mechanical heart-mind, then it is possible that coronary bypass surgery would prompt similar qualms. Or perhaps the question is not whether medical intervention is permissible, but whether the surgeon wields her scalpel in alignment with nature, so to speak. Perhaps there is a difference between medical treatments that "follows natural patterns" and interventions that are a bid for mastery, an assault upon the given.

I was struck, in this connection, by the story (in the *Zhuangzi*) of Cook Ding deftly wielding his knife as he carves an ox. So deft is his cutting, so aligned with the natural patterns and spaces of the ox, that the blade of his knife has not dulled over the past nineteen years. If a skilled butcher can carve an ox while nonetheless displaying respect for nature, it would seem possible that a skilled surgeon can repair a heart, or a brain, in a similar spirit. "Approaching the world from this standpoint," D'Ambrosio writes, not only expresses "respect for the world as mysterious in some sense, but also naturally resists the temptation to master it . . . Daoism thus offers a more concrete account of what an ethics of giftedness might look like, and in a way that makes no appeal to the divine."

A third Daoist concept D'Ambrosio brings to bear on my critique of genetic engineering is the ability of the sage (*zhen ren*) of the *Zhuangzi* "to maintain a critical distance from social norms and roles while performing them." In an artful pun, D'Ambrosio describes this exemplary figure, who displays spontaneity and imperturbability, as a "*zhen*uine person." "In direct response to the Confucian sage or exemplar, who seeks to develop and cultivate his 'self' through social roles and personal relationships, the *zhen*uine person is cautious about getting carried away by social influences."

Learning to maintain a critical distance from the social roles one inhabits can be a valuable corrective to hubris, the tendency of the successful to assume that their success is their own doing and that they therefore deserve the rewards that society lavishes upon them. A lively sense of the contingency of our talents and gifts is conducive to humility. Part of what worries me about the drive for genetic enhancement is that, by eroding the role of contingency and chance, it may harden the conviction of the successful that they are wholly self-made and self-sufficient, rather than indebted for their good fortune. This would be corrosive of humility and a sense of responsibility for those less fortunate than themselves.

The *Zhuangzi*'s emphasis on not taking too much pride in one's career is a corrective to this way of thinking. Having certain talents or capacities, D'Ambrosio observes, "may allow one to work successfully at one job or another . . . [People] should not, however, get carried away by thinking that they are especially great, or especially terrible, because of their role, status, or position." The Daoist sage "engages in society while maintaining a critical distance from norms, roles, and other various social expectations."

D'Ambrosio identifies an intriguing connection between this Daoist sensibility and my argument for restraining the project of mastery and dominion I associate with genetic enhancement. But he rightly suggests that I do not share "the broader implications of Daoism's quietistic tendencies." Part of my objection to seeking biotechnological fixes to social problems is that it distracts us from reflecting critically on existing arrangements and asking how we might bring about a more just society.[5]

Confucian Conceptions of the Person

How to conceive our social roles—and how lightly or deeply to bear them—raises deep questions about what it means to be a person. These questions are at the heart of the essays by Roger Ames and Henry Rosemont Jr., two of the most distinguished North American scholars of Confucianism. In addition to their many writings, they have together produced a translation of *The Analects of Confucius* and made a compelling case for philosophers in the West to understand Confucian thought in its own terms, rather than bending it to fit Western philosophical categories.

Ames and Rosemont are highly critical of the "concept of the self as a free, rational, autonomous individual" familiar in Western philosophy. They view this conception as philosophically flawed and responsible for what Rosemont calls "the ideological mischief constantly in play in the capitalist market economy." They identify in the Confucian tradition an alternative conception of the person that they find morally attractive and true to human life as we actually live it. They believe this conception deserves "a seat at the table in this continuing quest for an adequate alternative to . . . foundational individualism" (Ames).

How to characterize the Confucian alternative to the individualistic ethic of Western philosophy is the subject of controversy among Confucian scholars. Many describe Confucian ethics as a version of virtue ethics, similar to Aristotle's, according to which the good life consists in cultivating certain attitudes, virtues, and qualities of character. Ames and Rosemont describe Confucian ethics instead as a role ethic, according to which we become humane, not by living up to a set of virtues independently conceived, but by living in accordance with the roles and relationships that define us, beginning with the family. Persons become humane, Ames explains, "by cultivating those thick, intrinsic relations that constitute our initial conditions and that locate the trajectory of our life narrative . . . within family, community, and cosmos." Resolving the debate between these interpretations of Confucian ethics, Ames observes, depends on examining the conceptions of the person upon which they rest.

Here they find a point of contact between my work and the Confucian tradition. I too have been critical of the notion of freely choosing, individual selves, defined prior to and independent of their aims and attachments. I have argued that this conception of the person, the "unencumbered self," figures in liberal moral and political philosophy from Immanuel Kant to John Rawls, and leads it astray. This conception of the self supports the idea that a just society must be a neutral framework of rights within which individuals can choose their ends for themselves. If the self is given prior to its ends, then the right must be prior to the good. If we are freely choosing, independent selves, then respecting our freedom requires a framework of rights that is neutral among ends, not a political community that affirms a particular conception of the good life or seeks to cultivate the virtue of its citizens.

Ames and Rosemont accept my critique of the unencumbered self, and agree with my claim that justice and rights cannot be defined without reference to conceptions of the good life. But they do not think my critique goes far enough. "Roger and I want to go farther than Sandel," writes Rosemont, "and question not only the unencumbered picture of the self, but the existence of any self at all." In place of the self we should adopt a picture of "fully interrelated role-bearing persons." He quotes Ames's summary of their position: "In reading Confucius, there is no reference to some core human being as the site of who we really are and that remains once the particular layers of family and community relations are peeled away . . . The goal of living, then, is to achieve harmony and enjoyment for oneself and for others through behaving in an optimally appropriate way in those roles and relationships that make us uniquely who we are."[6]

Once all of our roles have been specified and their interrelationships made manifest, Rosemont adds, there is "nothing left over" to call a self. He does not shrink from the implication that this picture of personhood offers no account of the continuity or unity of personal identity over the course of a life. "Being thus the aggregate sum of the roles I live, it must follow that as I grow older my roles will change, and consequently I become quite literally a different person." He acknowledges that this account "goes strongly against the grain of the *essential* self that we have been acculturated to think and feel we *really* are, or 'have,' something that remains constant and unchanging throughout the vicissitudes of our lives. On the Confucian account, seeking that essential self must be like chasing a will-o'-the-wisp, for we are *constituted* by the roles we live in the midst of others."

Whether role ethics offers a truer reading of Confucian texts than virtue ethics is not for me to say. But Ames and Rosemont are not only offering a textual interpretation; they are also arguing that the role-bearing view offers the best way of understanding ethics and personhood. Are they right? How plausible is a conception of morality that rejects altogether the existence of a self in favor of a role-bearing person wholly constituted by its roles and relationships? As Ames and Rosemont observe, my view has much in common with Confucian ways of thinking but nonetheless differs from theirs. With them, I reject the notion that morality issues from the choices of autonomous, individual selves. But I do not agree that we can "think about morality without moral agents."

Let me see if I can explain why: I do not think that the continuity of our identities over a lifetime is given by an "essential" self at the core of our being whose contours are fixed once and for all, untouched by the vicissitudes of life. And yet neither do I think that a person is only "the aggregate sum" of his roles and circumstances. What the purely aggregative picture misses, it seems to me, is the role of narrative and reflection (including critical reflection). Not only social roles and relationships, but also interpretations of those roles and relationships, are constitutive of personhood. But narration and interpretation presuppose narrators and interpreters—storytelling selves who seek to make sense of their circumstances, to evaluate and assess the aims and attachments that would claim them. And this interpretive activity, this making of sense, constitutes moral agency.

In his essay attempting to mediate between the Ames-Rosemont conception of the person and mine, Paul D'Ambrosio discusses an analogy introduced by Rosemont in his book *Against Individualism* (2015). Those who believe in an essential, enduring self think of persons as if they were peaches with a pit. Although the skin and the fruit may change, the pit persists. On such a conception of personal identity, it makes sense to ask, "Who is the (real) person who is playing these various social roles?" But those who believe that social roles and relationships are constitutive of identity think of personhood as an onion; peel away the roles—son or daughter, husband or wife, parent, grandparent, friend, teacher, neighbor, and so on—and nothing remains. Rosemont offers the onion analogy to illustrate the anti-essentialist, role-bearing conception of the person.

I am uneasy with both vegetarian options. I do not accept the essentialist implication of the peach pit; if our identities are partly constituted by our aims and attachments, then it is a mistake to think they cannot be transformed by changing life circumstances. But neither do I accept the analogy of the onion. Or at least I would want to know more about who is peeling the various layers, and why. This matters, because our identities are shaped by our self-interpretations. Changes in our roles and relationships do not simply happen to us; they typically reflect, and contribute to, revisions in the narratives by which we seek to make sense of our lives.

More than three decades ago, before I had the benefit of my encounter with Chinese philosophy, I tried to articulate this narrative conception of the self. At the time my target was the unencumbered self of Kantian and Rawlsian liberalism. Now, looking East, I see how my account resonates with the Confucian tradition in some respects, even as it differs in others:

> To imagine a person incapable of constitutive attachments such as these is not to conceive an ideally free and rational agent, but to imagine a person wholly without character, without moral depth. For to have character is to know that I move in a history I neither

summon nor command, which carries consequences nonetheless for my choices and conduct. It draws me closer to some and more distant from others; it makes some aims more appropriate, others less so. As a self-interpreting being, I am able to reflect on my history and in this sense to distance myself from it, but the distance is always precarious and provisional, the point of reflection never finally secured outside the history itself. A person with character thus knows that he is implicated in various ways even as he reflects, and feels the moral weight of what he knows. (Sandel 1982, 179)

Dialogue across Cultures

Engaging with responses to my work by scholars of Chinese philosophy is for me a learning opportunity on several levels. It requires me to consider challenges to my views from unfamiliar directions, it brings to light some of the competing perspectives at play within Chinese philosophy, and it prompts me to wonder how dialogue across cultural and philosophical traditions can best proceed.

I can imagine two ways of approaching such dialogue. One is to compare, at a high level of generality, traditions of thought, and to identify similarities and differences between them. This approach depends on scholars who have mastered both traditions, and who report back, so to speak, on what they have found. Conceived in this way, comparative philosophy can provide an important challenge to self-enclosed traditions of thought. Scholars who bring Confucian and Daoist philosophical traditions into contact with Western thought offer a much-needed antidote to the parochialism that afflicts much Western (and in particular, Anglo-American) philosophy and political theory. They also provide a corrective to the caricatured accounts of Eastern thought that appear even in some of the greatest works of Western philosophy, such as Hegel, for example.

This highly generalized approach to comparative philosophy can contribute to a broadening of intellectual horizons. But it can inadvertently obstruct rather than promote mutual learning across cultures. The project of identifying similarities and differences between traditions of thought requires scholars to characterize, in wholesale fashion, Chinese thought on the one hand and Western thought on the other. This generalizing impulse is in some respects antiphilosophical. It risks stripping traditions rich with nuance, internal tensions, and interpretive disputes of the very disagreements that make philosophy interesting.

If not by wholesale comparison, how might philosophy across cultures proceed? One possibility would be to begin more concretely, by taking interpretive disputes or moral dilemmas as a starting point for shared reflection, argument, and deliberation. In the cross-cultural dialogues I have engaged in with students from China and the West, I have not invited the participants to speak on behalf of their respective philosophical traditions, or to be self-conscious about the cultural provenance of their views. Instead, I have asked them to reply to simple, concrete questions. For example: Is it wrong for a shop owner to raise the price of bottled water in the aftermath of a natural disaster, when demand is high and supplies are scarce? What do they think of the young man who sold one of his kidneys so he could buy an iPhone? Should a high public official whose father has committed a crime intervene with the police to protect him from prosecution?

As the debates proceed, and as the participants find themselves arguing about competing conceptions of justice, obligation, and the common good, it is sometimes possible to glimpse patterns of response that reflect cultural differences. But identifying such differences is not the point of the exercise. The point is rather to invite the participants to reflect critically on hard philosophical questions, and to reason together with those who disagree with them. Often, the disagreements within national groups and philosophical traditions are as passionate and interesting as the differences between them.

A similarly concrete, dialogic approach to learning across cultures might also be feasible among philosophers. Rather than begin with the ethical dilemmas that draw students and members of the public to philosophy, scholars of Chinese and Western philosophy might come together over a period of time to study, interpret, and debate the central texts of their respective traditions. Such a project would doubtless shed light on broad comparative questions, but its primary aim would be to deploy plural perspectives to illuminate and interrogate key texts—the *Analects*, *Mencius*, and *Zhuangzi*, for example, and perhaps the works of Aristotle, Spinoza, and Kant. (This list is only suggestive; others might nominate different texts.)

This text-based form of dialogue across philosophical traditions might be described as a "collaborative hermeneutics." Of course, for any given text, some of the collaborators will be more knowledgeable than others; and yet even experienced scholars of this or that text might learn something unexpected as colleagues steeped in one philosophical tradition bring their questions and outlooks to bear on another.

A final thought: Any project of mutual learning between Chinese and Western philosophy should begin by acknowledging a certain asymmetry. My friend and former Harvard colleague Tu Weiming once observed that China is a learning civilization, whereas the West is a teaching civilization. He did not mean this as a compliment to the West. I think he was suggesting that societies that see themselves as delivering instruction to the rest of the world fall into a certain hubris. Their teaching devolves into preaching. Beyond generating resentment, a civilization bent on teaching and preaching loses its capacity to encounter the world, to listen and to learn from it. I am grateful to my interlocutors in this volume for their generosity of spirit and for the gift of their critical engagement.

Notes

1. For some examples, see http://news.harvard.edu/gazette/story/2012/12/a-class-open-to-the-world/, https://www.youtube.com/watch?v=-W1-vN9Ucx0, and https://www.youtube.com/watch?v=6bqelXSRRMI.
2. See "A Response to Rawls' Political Liberalism," in Sandel 1998, 184–218.
3. Sandel 2009, 9, quoted in Chan 2010, 83.

4. See Sandel 2007, 46–47.
5. See Sandel 2007, 97.
6. Ames 2011, 122, quoted in Rosemont 2015 at 94.

References

Ames, Roger T. 2011. *Confucian Role Ethics: A Vocabulary.* Hong Kong: Chinese University Press.

Chan, Joseph. 2010. "Concerns beyond the Family." *American Journal of Bioethics* 10 (April): 83.

Friedman, Marilyn. 1989. "Feminism and Modern Friendship: Dislocating the Community." *Ethics* 99 (2): 275–290.

Mill, John Stuart. (1859) 1989. *On Liberty.* Edited by Stefan Collini. Cambridge: Cambridge University Press.

Rosemont, Henry, Jr. 2015. *Against Individualism: A Confucian Rethinking of the Foundation of Morality, Politics, Family, and Religion.* Lanham, MD: Lexington Books.

Ruiping Fan. 2010. "A Confucian Reflection on Genetic Enhancement." *American Journal of Bioethics* 10 (April).

Sandel, Michael. 1982. *Liberalism and the Limits of Justice.* Cambridge: Cambridge University Press.

———. 1996. *Democracy's Discontent: America in Search of a Public Philosophy.* Cambridge, MA: Harvard University Press.

———. 1998. *Liberalism and the Limits of Justice,* 2nd edition. Cambridge: Cambridge University Press.

———. 2007. *The Case against Perfection.* Cambridge, MA: Belknap Press of Harvard University Press.

———. 2009. *Justice: What's the Right Thing to Do?* New York: Farrar, Straus and Giroux.

Contributors

Michael J. Sandel teaches political philosophy at Harvard University. His writings—on justice, ethics, democracy, and markets—have been translated into twenty-seven languages. He has lectured widely in universities and public venues in Beijing, Shanghai, Xian, Guangzhou, Xiamen, Shenzhen, and Hong Kong. Six of Sandel's books have been published in mainland China: *Justice: What's the Right Thing to Do?*; *What Money Can't Buy: The Moral Limits of Markets; The Case against Perfection: Ethics in the Age of Genetic Engineering; Democracy's Discontent; Public Philosophy: Essays on Morality in Politics;* and *Liberalism and the Limits of Justice.*

Paul J. D'Ambrosio teaches Chinese philosophy at East China Normal University in Shanghai, China, where he also serves as the program coordinator for ECNU's English-language MA and PhD programs and dean of the intercultural center. He has published numerous articles on Confucianism, Daoism, Neo-Daoism, and contemporary comparative philosophy, and has translated several books from modern Chinese into English. He is the author of *Genuine Pretending: On the Philosophy of the* Zhuangzi, with Hans-Georg Moeller (Columbia University Press, 2017), and recently completed another manuscript, 中国古代哲学中的虚伪, 撒谎和假装 (*Hypocrisy, Lying, and Pretense in Early Chinese Philosophy*).

Roger T. Ames is Humanities Chair Professor of Philosophy at Peking University and a Berggruen Fellow. Ames has authored several interpretive studies on Chinese philosophy and culture, the most recent being *Confucian Role Ethics: A Vocabulary*. He has often worked in collaboration with other scholars to produce explicitly philosophical translations of classical texts. These have included Confucius's

Analects, the *Daodejing,* and the *Classic of Family Reverence.* He is presently advocating Confucian role ethics as an attempt to take this philosophical tradition on its own terms.

Tongdong Bai is a full professor and the Dongfang Chair Professor at the School of Philosophy at Fudan University in China, and is a Berggruen Fellow (2016–2017) at Harvard's Edmond J. Safra Center for Ethics. His research interests include Chinese philosophy and political philosophy. He has published two books on these subjects: *A New Mission of an Old State: The Comparative and Contemporary Relevance of Classical Confucian Political Philosophy* (in Chinese, Peking University Press, 2009), and *China: The Political Philosophy of the Middle Kingdom* (in English, Zed Books, 2012). He is now working on a significantly revised and expanded, English version of the first book. He is also the director of an English-based MA and visiting program in Chinese philosophy at Fudan University.

Yong Huang holds a PhD in philosophy from Fudan University, and a ThD in religious studies from Harvard University. Professor Huang teaches in the department of philosophy at the Chinese University of Hong Kong. He is the author of several books and more than a hundred journal articles and book chapters in Chinese and English. In 2005 he received the Chambliss Research Award, which recognized both the number and quality of his scholarly publications. Professor Huang is currently completing another manuscript, *Ethics of Difference: Learning from the Daoist Zhuangzi.*

Chen Lai is a professor in the philosophy department at Tsinghua University and dean of Academy of Chinese Learning (Guoxue 國學) at Tsinghua University. Professor Chen has made important contributions to research in Confucian philosophy, especially *Song-Ming Ru* (Confucian) thought. His most famous writings include: *Zhu Xi Zhexue Yanjiu* (Research in the Philosophy of Zhu Xi) (1988); *Zhu Zi Shu Xin*

Biannian Kaozheng (A Chronological Record of Zhu Xi's Books and Letters: Textual Investigation and Verification) (1989); *You Wu Zhi Jing: Wang Yangming Zhexue de Jingshen* (Here and Beyond: The Spirit of Wang Yangming's Philosophy) (1991); and *Song-Ming Lixue* (Song-Ming Lixue) (1992); as well as numerous essays and articles. Professor Chen is an honorary professor at eleven universities and is a member of the editorial boards of sixteen academic journals.

Chenyang Li is a professor of philosophy and the founding director of the Philosophy Program at Nanyang Technological University, Singapore. He is author of *The Confucian Philosophy of Harmony* (2014); *The Tao Encounters the West: Explorations in Comparative Philosophy* (1999); *Confucianism in a Pluralist World* (in Chinese, 2005); and more than one hundred journal articles and book chapters. He is also editor of, among others, *The Sage and the Second Sex* (2000); *The East Asian Challenge for Democracy: Political Meritocracy in Comparative Perspective* (with Daniel Bell, 2013); *Moral Cultivation and Confucian Character: Engaging Joel J. Kupperman* (with Peimin Ni, 2014); and *Chinese Metaphysics and Its Problems* (with Franklin Perkins, 2015). He was the founding president of the Association of Chinese Philosophers in North America (1995–1997), Senior Visiting Fellow at the City University of Hong Kong (2005–2006), an ACE fellow (2008–2009), and an inaugural Berggruen Fellow at the Center for Advanced Study in the Behavioral Sciences at Stanford University (2015–2016). Currently he serves as president of the International Society for Chinese Philosophy and on the editorial / academic boards of over two dozen scholarly publications and organizations.

Evan Osnos is a staff writer at *The New Yorker* and a fellow at the Brookings Institution. Based in Washington, DC, he writes about foreign affairs and politics. He is the author of *Age of Ambition: Chasing Fortune, Truth, and Faith in the New China*, which won the 2014 National Book award. He lived for eight years in Beijing, where he was the China Correspondent for *The New Yorker* from 2008 to 2013. Prior to that, he worked as the Beijing bureau chief of the *Chicago Tribune*, where he contributed to a series that won the 2008 Pulitzer Prize for investigative reporting.

Henry Rosemont Jr. is George B. & Willma Reeves Distinguished Professor of the Liberal Arts at St. Mary's College of Maryland, and since 2002 been Visiting Scholar of Religious Studies at Brown University. He also spent three years in China as Fulbright Senior Lecturer at Fudan University in Shanghai. His books include *A Chinese Mirror; Rationality and Religious Experience; Is There a Universal Grammar of Religion?* (with Huston Smith); and *A Reader's Companion to the Confucian Analects.* He has edited and / or translated ten other books, including *Leibniz: Writings on China* (with Daniel Cook); and, with Roger Ames, *The Analects of Confucius: A Philosophical Translation.*

Robin R. Wang is a 2016–2017 Berggruen Fellow at the Center for Advanced Study in the Behavioral Sciences at Stanford University and professor of philosophy at Loyola Marymount University. She is the current president of the Society for Asian and Comparative Philosophy (2016–2018) and is the author of *Yinyang: The Way of Heaven and Earth in Chinese Thought and Culture* (Cambridge University Press, 2012) and the editor of *Chinese Philosophy in an Era of Globalization* (SUNY Press, 2004) and *Images of Women in Chinese Thought and Culture: Writings from the Pre-Qin Period to the Song Dynasty* (Hackett, 2003). She has published articles in academic journeys and has done fieldwork on contemporary female Daoists around China. She has regularly given presentations in North America, Europe, and Asia and has been a consultant for media, law firms, museums, K–12 educators, and health-care professionals. She was a credited cultural consultant for the movie *Karate Kid*, 2010.

Zhu Huiling is an associate professor of philosophy at Capital Normal University in Beijing. She holds a PhD in philosophy from Tsinghua University, and was a visiting scholar at Harvard University (2009–2010). She teaches political philosophy and ethics. She has published many papers and translated several texts on political philosophy from English into Chinese, including many of Michael Sandel's books, such as *Justice: What's the Right Thing to Do?* and *Public Philosophy*. She has also translated Thomas Scanlon's *Moral Dimensions* and Martha Nussbaum's *Frontiers of Justice* into Chinese.

Acknowledgments

We would like to express our gratitude to Tong Shijun, Yang Guorong, Yang Haiyan, Yu Zhenhua, and the entire Philosophy Department and Institute of Modern Chinese Thought and Culture at East China Normal University for hosting the international conference "Michael Sandel and Chinese Philosophy" in March 2016, an event that inspired this volume. Without the help of Zhang Pengqian, Liu Xiangmei, and many other faculty and students at ECNU it would not have been possible to have such a successful event. In addition to those who contributed to this volume, participants included Tu Weiming, Yang Guorong, Karl-Heinz Pohl, Junren Wan, Jimmy Zhu, and Josef Gregory. We also extend thanks to the more than 100 professors and graduate students who participated in this conference, and to Seth Crownover for his help finalizing this volume.

We are deeply grateful to Ian Malcolm, editor extraordinaire at Harvard University Press, who supported this book from its inception and provided his characteristically astute but gentle guidance along the way.

Michael Sandel would like to express his appreciation to students and faculty at the following universities and academic institutions who welcomed him, over the past decade, to give lectures on his work and engage students in discussion of philosophical issues: Tsinghua University, Peking University, Renmin University of China, Chinese Academy of Social Sciences, University of International Business and Economics, China University of Politics and Law, Fudan University, Shanghai Jiao Tong University, East China Normal University, Sun Yat-sen University, Shaanxi Normal University, Xiamen University, University of Hong Kong, Chinese University of Hong Kong, and National Taiwan University. He would also like to thank the following organizations and institutions for hosting lectures and discussions open to members of the public: Shanghai Forum, Beijing Forum, Shanghai Centre Theatre, Shenzhen Bookstore Mall, Kaifeng Foundation, Genesis Beijing, and China CITIC Press.

The participants in these events, in universities and public settings, enriched his encounter with China beyond measure.

Michael J. Sandel
Paul J. D'Ambrosio

Index